959.704    Led

68.5401

# FIGHTING EVIL

*The Ordinary Man who
went to War Against ISIS*

## Macer Gifford

SEVEN DIALS

First published in 2020 by Seven Dials,
an imprint of The Orion Publishing Group Ltd
Carmelite House, 50 Victoria Embankment,
London EC4Y 0DZ

An Hachette UK company

1 3 5 7 9 10 8 6 4 2

A CIP catalogue record for this book is
available from the British Library.

ISBN (Paperback): 978 1 409 195702
ISBN (eBook): 978 1 409 195719

Typeset by Born Group
Printed and bound in Great Britain by Clays Ltd, Elcograf S.p.A.

www.orionbooks.co.uk

This book is dedicated to my family.
My anger took me to war, your love brought me home.

# Statement by the
# Syrian Democratic Forces

Since the emergence of ISIS in 2014, it became a global threat to security and stability, but its greatest impact has occurred on the indigenous peoples of the Middle East, where it has threatened the existence of various ethnic societies including Arabs, Kurds, Syriacs and Armenians, also the religious groups, whether Christians, Yezidis and even Muslims as well.

To counter this threat, the local military groups in Syria have risen and defended the peoples living in the region, and have become the world's frontline of defence in the face of this epidemic.

Due to the slow response of the Western world to confront this danger, we found solidarity from international fighters, who on their own accord joined the military forces in the region – the People's Protection Units – YPG and the Syriac Military Council, where a new relationship between the different people of the world was created, alongside the Syrian Democratic Forces, which eventually led to the defeat of ISIS.

This book presents a picture of the heroic deeds of hundreds of international fighters, and through it we extend our thanks and a token of appreciation for all that they have done in order to defend our peoples and the world.

—Kino Gabriel, Official
Spokesperson of the Syrian Democratic Forces

# Foreword
## By Andy McNab CBE DCM MM

There have always been young men and women prepared to fight for what they believe is right. Long ago, perhaps, it was purely about defending your homeland and your family, and any fight for national security usually started on your own doorstep, when there was an immediate and obvious danger. Over time, our awareness of conflicts further afield has grown, so when we have a choice whether to fight or not, idealism has become an increasingly powerful force.

It is not a new phenomenon. You can see evidence of great callings throughout history. Those men of eighteenth-century Britain who would not sign up to fight in the American War of Independence (because they had some sympathy with the colonies) nevertheless flocked to the colours when the French and Spanish saw an opportunity and laid siege to Gibraltar. Fast forward to the mid-thirties, and idealism was key for those who joined the International Brigades fighting against fascism in the Spanish Civil War – people like George Orwell and the future union leader Jack Jones.

Those who are prepared to fight usually have a sense that it is their time, that what they are doing is right and that when they have done what they need to do they will return to their ordinary lives. But any involvement in conflict is likely to have a profound effect and can often change the course of a life. Ted Heath, who went on to be our prime minister, was deeply affected by the rise of fascism he witnessed as a young man in Nuremberg before the Second World War, and was inspired by the idealists of the International Brigades he met in Barcelona. More recently, there were plenty from the West who, without fanfare, went to fight for the Bosnians or the Croats in the Bosnian War. They too felt the need to stand up against injustice.

For most people, however, it is an alien concept. We have been fortunate to have had seventy years of peace in this country. We live in a liberal democracy and we are uncomfortable with the idea that there are some among us who actually want to fight. I don't mean in bars, but going abroad to fight for a cause that they really don't need to get involved with. Such people are too often seen as knuckle-draggers and troublemakers, too thick to do anything else . . . unless, of course, we one day need their fighting skills to protect us. As Kipling wrote in his poem 'Tommy', 'For it's Tommy this, an' Tommy that, an' "Chuck 'im out, the brute!" / But it's "Saviour of 'is country" when the guns begin to shoot'.

So it's refreshing for me to see that a clearly intelligent, public-school-educated young man, as Macer is, made a conscious decision to fight for something he believed in, as men and women have done for generations before him. It is not as if he was thrown into it because he had no choice, through conscription or unemployment. The rest of us might be aware of things happening in the world that we think are wrong, but it is sometimes hard for us to understand the complex politics and to assimilate all the facts, and it is even further removed from our thinking to want to put ourselves in harm's way to do something about it. If it doesn't affect the prices in Tesco or stop us taking the kids to school, why should we worry? And the idea of taking up arms really doesn't occur to us. You could argue that the people like Macer who are drawn to fight have more moral courage than the rest of us, not just to recognise that something is not right but to say, 'Do you know what? I'm going to do something about it.' Because, ultimately, if people like them don't make a stand, whatever it is they have felt the need to fight for, or against, will affect us all in the end.

Of course, once you get involved in a conflict it becomes less about ideals and more about survival, and anyone who has ever seen action will recognise the story that Macer tells: the constant 'hurry up and wait', the days on end of boredom and the intense moments of terror. Any infantryman will identify with that existence. Infantry life has always been the same, standing around trying not to be cold, wet or hungry. Or killed. Mundane things take on huge importance – like getting water, food and ammunition. It's bad enough in a large, institutionalised military force but it's surely far worse in a militia, though the hardships and the adversity of taking on the so-called Islamic State as part of a much smaller force were perhaps part of the romantic attraction for Macer. It's not just about the ritual of eating and drinking but often about whether you actually get *anything* to eat or drink at all.

Military service brings together some strange bedfellows, especially if you are conscripted, or come together from different parts of the world for different reasons, but on the battlefield you're all in it together, which is what forges bonds of brotherhood. When it's boring, yes, you do long for action, but it's that age-old thing about being careful what you wish for, because when the bullets are flying it's hell. For those of us who have seen action, it's uncomfortable to admit that we find it exciting, but you've got the uniform and the weaponry, and you've done the training, and then all of a sudden you're actually doing it and it *is* exciting. Then, when it gets too hairy, you think, 'F★★★ this!' but when it's over and you've survived, bravado takes over and you're all, 'Yeah, it was all right', because you don't want to be the one who admits he was scared. And then it happens again, and it's 'F★★★ this!' again. Afterwards, when you've survived, there is an undeniable feeling of exhilaration. You think, 'I've done it. Somebody was actually shooting at me and I was shooting back!' There is a feeling of completion. And then, of course, it all happens again and you're not so sure!

The trouble is that, as Macer says, people do get used to it. It was the same in the First World War when, after a while, people couldn't be bothered to bend down walking along the trench lines and, guess what, they got shot. You really don't want to be working closely with someone who has reached the point where they think, 'So what? F★★★ it!' We talk about 'the gift of fear', and it is a really good thing. People often say they weren't scared in battle, but yes they were and, do you know what? It's all right. Fear can keep you alive, just as much as idealism can get you killed. Macer's honest portrayal of both makes his story a fascinating personal insight into a conflict that will take its own important place in history.

"Bad men need nothing more to compass their ends,
than that good men should look on and do nothing."

*John Stuart Mill*

# Prologue

I stood in the wrecked bathroom and stared into the sliver of broken mirror, trying to recognise the gaunt, unfamiliar face that stared back at me. I couldn't help but wonder what the hell he was doing there. I was still looking into those dark-ringed eyes and that weathered face when I heard a cry from outside – the agonised, animal-like howl of a man grievously injured. I instantly spun on my heels, grabbed my body armour, rifle and medical bag from the balcony, and ran down the stairs. By the time I had negotiated my way through the barricade of furniture and reached the ground floor, the Syriacs were already dragging the wounded Kurd into the courtyard, out of the immediate range of ISIS snipers. He looked about thirty, but was probably younger, and in his eyes burned a fierce look that was more than shock: it was a determination to survive this outrage inflicted upon him. I could see beneath his blood-soaked shirt the jagged hole of an exit wound on his back, about the size of a two-pence piece. It gave me a gaping view inside his body, but the exposed flesh and shoulder ligament were barely bleeding. It was not a good sign. I turned the groaning fighter over. 'Where's the entry wound? Where's the fucking entry wound?' I yelled. I tore off the wounded man's shirt, searching anywhere on his torso that might correspond with the exit wound on his back. It felt like an eternity before I noticed the tiny black spot in the 'V' of his throat beneath his Adam's apple, like a small, pea-sized scab. Now what? It was too small to bandage. I turned the man over, packed the exit wound with gauze and wrapped a bandage around him to hold it in place. 'Think!' I urged myself, frantic to know what to do about the entry wound. Seconds were rushing by. Was he getting air into his chest? I decided to cut a chest seal in half and used that to plug the hole in his throat. His breathing seemed to stabilise, but he was fading in and out of consciousness as a result of major blood loss. I shouted at the Christians up on the balcony to radio for an ambulance to be ready at the defensive lines of the Kurdish militia, the YPG, behind us. The only thing that would save this man's life was to get him out of here as soon as possible. When he awoke, his eyes locked on to me with a ferocious stare, like he was fighting for his life. I was desperate to help him win his battle. I'm a pretty big guy, and reason-ably fit, though a couple of weeks on the front line with a poor diet soon leaves you out of shape. I managed to pick him up and start running in the direction of the YPG lines. My strength came from pure adrenaline mixed with frustration and determination. A giant palm tree − felled by an air strike that had destroyed a neighbouring block of flats a few weeks before − blocked my path. Even before I reached it, my lungs were burning. The heat of the day was like an oven, and every time I opened my mouth to gulp in air I could feel precious moisture being sucked from my body. I tried to get more oxygen but my swelling chest was constricted by my body armour, which gripped me like a vice. Sweat was pouring off me, getting in my eyes like the flies buzzing around my head with impunity because I had no hands free to swat them. My thighs felt like they were on fire and my back, too, was screaming in protest at this unexpected exertion. After 150 metres of fast walking under the weight of the injured man, sticking as closely as possible to the buildings which fringed the street, I began to flag. Some of the Christians were running with me and, without needing to be asked, they grabbed the man's shoulders and legs and together we half-ran, half-stumbled to where the ambulance would be waiting near the YPG positions. There were five of us now, but we were clumsy and bumping our casualty on the ground as we each tried to hold on to a limb while still running – and I knew we had to be more organised. I spotted a carpet buried under rubble in an abandoned building and yanked at it with all my might to free it from the bricks and concrete. 'Put him on the carpet!' I yelled. With one of us on each corner we made much better progress, but by now the Kurd fighter was deathly pale and, as we ran, he was regularly blacking out. A couple of times I thought we had lost him and then he would suddenly come to with a loud gasp for breath and lock eyes with me once more. For a few seconds, he would hold me with a look of pure defiance, and then his eyes would roll back into his head and he would collapse into a faint again. 'Keep running!' I urged the exhausted Syriacs. The heat was suffocating. As we got within a couple of hundred metres of where the ambulance was meant to be, I rushed ahead. The armoured vehicle arrived at the rendezvous point just as I ran up, panting, exhausted, and I threw open the back door and told them exactly what the casualty's wounds were. 'He needs fluids, urgently,' I gasped. I turned to run back to help carry the makeshift stretcher but the Syriacs had been joined by others who were helping. Together we managed to hoist the casualty into the back of the vehicle. I waited for another convulsive gasp for air and that defiant glare, but none came. We slammed the back door and the ambulance sped off.

I was utterly shattered, drenched in sweat and desperate for a drink. As we walked to a nearby Syriac Military Council (MFS) position, I spotted an unopened bottle of water on the ground and took a large swig, then immediately spat it out. The bottle had been sat in the sun and the contents were scalding hot, but I was grateful even for that moisture in my parched mouth. At the Syriac lines, I stopped to try to recover my energy, head bowed, hands on hips, still gulping for air. As I did so, there was a garbled burst of messages over the radios and I knew before my comrades translated for me exactly what it was about. 'He's dead,' one of them told me. I felt drained; so incredibly tired and so powerless. If I had the energy I would have screamed, but my throat was too dry for any sound to come out.

Deflated and downbeat, we grabbed some food, before the fall of night would allow us to return to our post. As we began to reassemble, I snatched a wistful glance at the star-filled sky. In London, the clouds and the light pollution hide the full beauty of the night sky. Here in Raqqa, the Syrian sky looked incredible. The inky blackness, seemingly dusted with a billion sparkling diamonds, was in stark contrast to the ugliness and suffering around me. As I stood in hell and looked up at the heavens, I could make out a few of the constellations that were familiar to me in the UK. The Plough, Orion's Belt . . . I wondered how many of my friends at home would be looking up at the same stars that evening and what they would be doing.

The whispers of my Syriac comrades around me faded out of my consciousness, and I was transported for a second to a city pub and the happy chatter among friends over a Friday-night beer after work. Had I really left behind my loving family for the risk of spilling my blood in the dust of this devastated country? How would my family feel it if was me who took a sniper's bullet tonight, a tiny black entry wound ending my life? It didn't bear thinking about, but I couldn't help myself. I'd seen too much death already not to know that the chances of becoming a statistic were frighteningly high. It wasn't even as if I was a soldier. I was a foreign exchange broker from London who had sacrificed a good job, a flat and my girlfriend to be here. Driven only by the conviction that I had to fight against the atrocities of ISIS, I'd confidently got myself to the front line of the bloodiest conflict of the twenty-first century. Exposure here meant risking everything; margins were between life and death, and they were wafer thin. This war wasn't over by a long way, but Raqqa was where I had wanted to be since I had first become aware of the horrors unfolding in this part of the world, and now that the defeat of ISIS was within our grasp, my part in the fight against evil was reaching a climax.

# The Dream Job

I had arrived early for my hard-earned appointment in the City of London and made my way to the somewhat intimidating edifice that housed one of Britain's biggest banks. Now I was waiting nervously for my interview. As I glanced at my watch, I was aware that my hands were clammy. Damn! I so wanted to offer a warm, dry, firm handshake to whoever came down to fetch me.

One of the lift doors opened and a smartly suited figure stepped out. 'It's Harry, isn't it? I'm Nick, one of the senior brokers here,' he said, offering his hand. We swapped pleasantries and he ushered me towards the lifts. I felt a lurch in my stomach as we shot upwards and I watched the lobby area shrink beneath us. We walked from the lift to another reception, where, written in giant plastic letters, were the words 'Foreign Exchange'. Through another set of doors was the trading room, which teemed with shirt-sleeved workers busy at desks arrayed with multiple computer screens showing the day's fluctuating rates. It felt electrifying, and, to compound the sense of power, the floor-to-ceiling windows on all sides showed a backdrop of the City in all its glory. Nick showed me into one of the glass-walled meeting rooms that clung to the edge of the trading floor. The magnificent dome of St Paul's and the jostling scrum of buildings at the economic heart of Britain stretched beneath us. It was hard not to be impressed. This was a world I knew so well. Whether I was truly comfortable in it was another matter.

As a teenager, I had wanted to join the British Army and to use that route to be a force for good in the world. There was a strong military history in my family, and I had grown up with my ancestors' medals from Waterloo, the Crimea and other notable campaigns on my bedroom wall. That military tradition had exerted an undeniable attraction for me, but then I had gone to Loughborough University to study Politics and International Relations and discovered a new passion – for political activism. I am guided by my principles rather than by any one political party, but at university, I was drawn to David Cameron's compassionate Conservatives and their bid for the aspirational centre ground, and I quickly found that being involved as an activist was extremely rewarding. I even stood for election as a Conservative councillor in a ward where the Conservatives had previously come a distant fourth. True-blue territory this was not! Nevertheless, I threw myself into the challenge, knocked on doors, took the trouble to speak to people – and to listen to them – and came second in the poll, not far behind Labour. My new-found love for politics soon morphed into a desire to help people on a more human level. During my second year at university I went to Zimbabwe to work for the centre-left Movement for Democratic Change – the MDC. It was an extraordinary summer as I watched a country falling to pieces around me, but it only bolstered my determination to work harder for human rights. I had left university with so many different plans and aspirations – how swiftly everything had changed. I graduated in 2009, at the height of the recession, with people tightening their belts and knuckling down to work, if they had it. My sense of independence and a fierce determination to succeed at whatever I did meant that I wanted to show I could support myself financially. Before I really knew it, I had entered the rat race. After a couple of years working my way up the corporate ladder and broadening my knowledge of world trade, I joined a major currency company and then moved to a smaller, boutique currency house, where I was really on the up. I should have felt fulfilled, but my heart was not really in my new job, which was why I was looking around for a different challenge; something to make my pulse race a little faster.

The door swung open and Nick and I were joined by the bank's head of foreign exchange. Over the next hour we discussed everything from the market place to new regulation and, above all, me. When it was time to go, Nick guided me down to the lobby and shook my hand. Then, with a quick smile at the very attractive receptionist, he was gone. It had only been an hour and a half since I had entered the building but it felt like I'd run a marathon. The interview had gone well. I should have been feeling enthused and excited. So why did I feel so dejected?

Before long, I was on a tube train heading west from St Paul's and glancing at the newspaper being read by a woman sat next to me. 'Hero in the face of evil,' declared the headline above the image of a man in an orange jumpsuit. 'Oh my God, the Islamic State must have executed another prisoner,' I realised. These people really were animals. Every day for months the papers and news channels had been full of the growing crisis in the Middle East. The rise of a terrorist group declaring itself the Islamic State had taken everybody by surprise. The first time I had heard about them was in June 2014, when they had captured Mosul, Iraq's second city, with just 300 men. Every day since then, their fighters had cut an increasingly bloody swathe through Iraq and Syria, mercilessly killing their prisoners, whether men, women or children. Thousands of Syrian and Iraqi soldiers who had surrendered had been mowed down in cold blood. Much more public had been the trend of parading captured journalists and humanitarian workers and, in front of the camera, cutting off their heads.

By the time I got home, I had already received an email from the bank wanting to know my pay expectations. It seemed like I was one step closer to that dream job. Before I replied, however, I flicked on the TV, morbidly anticipating more news about the Islamic State. The next few weeks after the interview were punctuated by a number of emails and calls telling me about the continued interested from the major bank, and from a foreign bank I had also had an interview with. Both seemed keen to recruit me. On the face of it, I had plenty of reasons to feel self-satisfied, but neither of my suitors might have been so enthusiastic if they had known that my work at the currency house had been suffering for months, and that things were coming to a head. It didn't help that as soon as I got to my desk each morning I spent an hour reading the news. Don't get me wrong, my work in foreign exchange meant I needed a grasp of global current affairs, but I was becoming addicted to the horrendous stories of torture, murder and rape perpetuated by the terrorists in Syria and Iraq. The Western media publicised every sick video that the ISIS propaganda machine churned out, and I was part of the rapt audience. The stories were a hot topic in the office and among my friends and family, but while others were simply shocked, I became consumed by a burning hatred for everything that ISIS represented. I couldn't sleep at night for thinking about the thousands of women and girls – many under ten – being sold into sexual slavery or thrown down wells by the terrorists, and yet people – including hundreds of Britons – were rushing to join this death cult. They made my skin crawl. How could they want to become involved in such bestiality? An estimated 20,000 foreign fighters – including as many as 1000 British men – had flocked to the black banner of jihad.

I couldn't understand the lack of reaction from the governments of Britain and America. Why weren't they doing more to counter ISIS before the region was torn apart? It took weeks for the Americans to start bombing in support of the Iraqi government forces and the Iraqi Kurd military, the Peshmerga. In the meantime, ISIS fighters had reportedly reached within fifty kilometres of Baghdad. The horrific scenes of thousands of Yazidi people trapped on Mount Sinjar, in Iraqi Kurdistan, was especially distressing to me. If only I could take some time off work and raise money for the refugee camps or, better still, actually visit Iraq and work on the ground. It was a fantasy, though. I had a job and a girlfriend and neither would allow me to go. My girlfriend, Anna, was a fiery Russian I had met at a conference just a few months before. A twenty-two-year-old former model from Latvia, she had been employed by the currency house to greet people and guide them to our stand. She had just graduated from university with a first-class degree and was looking for a full-time job. I had plucked up the courage to ask her on a date and we had been together since. Every Wednesday I would go round to her flat with a movie and a bottle of wine, or she would come to mine. As we lay in bed or relaxed on the sofa, I would try to tell her about my frustrations at work and wanting to do more for charities in the Middle East, but it wasn't what she wanted to talk about. She particularly couldn't bear to talk about ISIS. The subject was becoming increasingly important to me but I understood it was shocking to her. The daily reports were grim.

While I struggled at work, the world seemed to burn. I watched the Islamic State grow in power and tried to understand how it had started. Most people I knew blamed the Americans and the British for invading Iraq and 'creating the conditions' that allowed the Islamic State to rise, but the more I looked into the conflict, the more I disagreed. When the Americans had left Iraq at the end of 2011, the country was a relatively peaceful democracy, compared to the war zone it once was, with a chance of success – but the Iraqi government's disenfranchisement of the Sunnis had gifted them to the terrorists, and now extreme conservative Muslims throughout the world were flocking to Iraq and Syria to take up jihad in the name of ISIS, prepared to kill anyone who did not share their fundamentalist views. It was, to my mind, as dangerous a threat to the world as the rise of Hitler's Nazis had been. Back in the 1930s and 40s, principled Britons had stood up to fascism and fought for the liberty of others. Now, in the twenty-first century, I was witnessing the rise of an organisation that had a genocidal wish to rid the world of all diversity. I knew in my heart it was not something the British people would be prepared to accept, if only the government would see this and take steps to help stop it. If I got a new job offer, I speculated, I could use my gardening leave from my current employer to take a few weeks out and volunteer in Iraqi Kurdistan.

I could even try to raise some publicity. Done properly, I could not only make a difference but hopefully impress my new employer as well.

The weather began to get colder as December approached, but I barely noticed. I had two potential job offers from two separate banks. If things panned out as I hoped, I could end the year satisfying my urge to do humanitarian work and start the new year with a new career. Everyone was preparing for Christmas, and I was only too happy to throw myself into the annual festive frenzy. I was living for the weekend, boozing with friends, enjoying my time with Anna, seeing plenty of my family and saving for my first property. Then the unexpected happened.

# Lions of Rojava

It was my own fault. If spending hours reading the news was not bad enough, I'd become blasé in my search for another job and had been responding to job enquiries from my work computer. It was only a matter of time before my work ethic was called into question. That moment arrived on a Friday afternoon when I was called in for a performance review. My call statistics were dismal, and over the course of the meeting it became impossible to hide how lacklustre my work effort had been. I thought I was too well liked by my bosses to be fired, but when I turned up on the Monday for a disciplinary hearing, there was no second chance and, after an hour's meeting, I was sacked. My overconfidence was shattered.

In spite of the shock of my sacking, my thoughts were still in Iraq and Syria. The day before, I had seen an article about a young American called Jordan Matson who had been injured in Syria while fighting the Islamic State. I looked again and saw a number of pieces in the US media on Matson and a group called the Lions of Rojava. Apparently, a few American veterans had been so disgusted by what was going on in the Middle East that they had contacted a Syrian militia called the YPG (People's Protection Units) and offered their services. Matson, a twenty-eight-year-old former soldier from Wisconsin, was one of them. He had been hit by mortar shrapnel on the front line and, while recuperating, had created the Lions of Rojava web page, to spread the word about the foreign volunteers and to get more people to join up. It was as if a light had suddenly been switched on in my head. Why not actually go out to Syria and fight the Islamic State? I wasn't a soldier but nor was George Orwell when he went to Spain to fight the fascists. Nor were the thousands of people from all around the world flocking to the so-called Islamic State. If mindless animals with no military training could join ISIS to kill women and children, why couldn't good men fight against them? It was an idea that scared the hell out of me, but I could already see the potential in it. I suppose there was a restlessness in me at the time, like a dormant gene waiting to rise up.

As the days passed, I continued to look into the idea of fighting. It was clear the Kurds were allowing foreigners to join the YPG because it attracted international attention. The Westerners were seemingly being used as propaganda tools, but that was fine by me. Getting to fight would be the ideal, but the thought that I could help to embarrass the British government into doing more just by being seen to be in Syria was something that appealed to me. Further research told me that the YPG was a local militia in Rojava, a region of north-eastern Syria bordering Turkey. It had evolved following a 2004 uprising in Qamishli against the regime of President Bashar al-Assad. The rioting had ended disastrously when the Syrian Army crushed the insurrection and forced thousands of Syrian Kurds to flee their homes, but when the Islamic State swept north towards Rojava, the YPG was the only force in the region to put up any meaningful resistance, quickly drawing widespread support and recruits. They became locked in a brutal war of attrition with ISIS on a number of different fronts, most famously in the besieged city of Kobane, where the defenders were still holding out. Of Rojava's three administrative regions, or 'cantons', Kobane and Afrin were almost impossible to get to for a Western fighter because of the tight border controls by Turkey and heavy attacks from the Islamic State. The Jazira canton was largely overrun with ISIS fighters but that was where the foreign volunteers were fighting. The more I read about what the YPG was up against, the more sobering my research became. Months into Islamic State's genocidal campaign, and in spite of the West's belated air attacks and US President Obama's promise to 'degrade and destroy them', ISIS still controlled more than 100,000 square kilometres of Iraq and Syria, an area bigger than Cuba. They had created their own armies, their own police force and a judicial system based on a perverted view of Sharia law. This self-declared state, built on thirteenth-century values of extreme violence and the basest human urges, had more than $2 billion in assets and an annual income of nearly $1 billion from usurped oil revenues, stolen bank money and taxes imposed on the eight million people under its control. The 30,000 fanatical jihadists and their families who had flocked from eighty-five different countries had joined thousands of hard-core fighters already in Syria and Iraq. In contrast, there seemed to be only twenty or thirty foreigners – Americans, British, Germans and Iranians – fighting for the YPG in Rojava. The Kurds' position looked hopeless, but the more I read of their values of secularism, democracy and multi-culturalism, the more it seemed like the clearest battle lines between good and evil since the Second World War.

I agonised long and hard over whether I might be an asset or a liability to the YPG. What I knew about fighting boiled down to some basic tactics I had learned in the cadets at school, plus an ability to handle and strip an AK-47 that I had learned from guards employed by charities to protect us in Zimbabwe, and that was it. Yet that was probably more than many of the young local fighters who were travelling from mountain villages and small towns ready to die to defend their homes and their people against the ISIS death cult. I was young and healthy, with the ability to articulate the Kurdish cause, and fighting alongside them in their hour of need would be the ultimate act of solidarity. I could feel the righteous fervour rising within me, but I had to consider the impact it would have on my family. If I were to die in Rojava it would be a devastating blow to my parents. My father had had a pacemaker fitted after a second heart attack and just the thought of me being out in Syria, I knew, would cause him distress. To make matters worse, my grandmother had been diagnosed with cancer just a few months before and was going through chemotherapy. So how could I square the desire to help the people of Rojava with a wish not to upset my family? And, of course, there was Anna. The more I thought about it, the more I knew how horribly selfish it would be.

As it happened, I got an offer to start a new job in the foreign exchange department of the major bank in January. I'm not sure exactly when I decided I would definitely go to Syria. The many deliberations I had gone through in my head made it feel like several weeks after I had lost my job but, in reality, is was probably little more than a fortnight. By then I was so blinkered in my determination that I didn't even bother to tell the recruitment agent that

I would not be taking up the bank's job offer. When I eventually told my family I was going to help the Kurds, they were understandably horrified. 'Why give up everything that you have worked for in the UK for an unpaid job in the Middle East?' they asked. And that wasn't the worst of it. I was honest about my intention to highlight the Kurdish cause, but I didn't tell them that I intended to fight on the front line. To my mind, I was sparing them the worry, though I wasn't kidding myself that, with little military training, I would be some kind of Kurdish Lawrence of Arabia. I would just be happy if I could use any publicity generated by being in Syria to shine a light on the conflict.

It was 6 December when I decided to join the Lions of Rojava, and I created a fake Facebook identity for the purpose. I chose the name Macer Gifford – a National Hunt jockey from the 1970s who died tragically young from motor neurone disease. I had spotted his name in an old racing magazine and it had leapt out at me as being unusual. I knew that if, in a tight situation in Syria, someone called out 'Macer' I would realise they were talking to me. I was messaged back with instructions to go to Sulaymaniyah in Iraqi Kurdistan. I was told people would pick me up from the airport and take me to a safe house. I wanted to know details such as whether my contact would be in uniform, what equipment I should bring and what would be provided, but they gave only curt answers, plus a warning about the seriousness of the situation and that it was not for anyone who was not fit to go, who had any doubts or who was not prepared to fight until the end. Eventually they said that one of the administrators for the group could answer more of my personal and security questions. The administrator duly copied and pasted conversations she had had with previous recruits and sent them over to me. They seemed genuine, had the same questions as me and the conversations ended with the international volunteers successfully entering Syria, and yet . . . I was petrified that this was some sort of elaborate ISIS scam to get a naive British citizen out to Iraq and to capture him at the airport. I researched the other recruits and went as far as to try to find their families online. It took me a few days to trust them enough to send a photo of my passport, but once I did, I had taken the first step on the road to Syria, and I could feel the anticipation and excitement building. This was really going to happen. The next big problem I had to face was how I was going to tell Anna. Now that I had decided to go to Syria I had to explain that there would be no holiday; that, in fact, I was going to leave her behind to go to fight in a foreign war.

The fact that I had delayed saying anything for a couple of weeks was purely down to cowardice. Deep down, I knew my decision would end our relationship. When I finally arranged to meet her for dinner I waited until our food was in front of us before I started to talk about Syria, telling her about the suffering there. She was full of sympathy for the Kurdish people but, even as I discussed the different ways the international community could help, there was a suspicious look in her eye that conveyed, 'And exactly what has this got to do with me?' There was no avoiding the moment of truth any longer, and that was when I told her that I was going to leave London and volunteer with the YPG. It took a second for my words to sink in, then, with a flash of anger, she demanded, 'Why?' I told her again that I was no longer able to watch the suffering in the Middle East without at least trying to do something myself.

I had deluded myself into thinking that I was prepared for her reaction. I expected her fiery temper to blow, and I was ready for the volcanic eruption, but none came. Instead, I saw her eyes filling with tears and heard her voice breaking as she asked more questions. After a few minutes of silence, the look of pain subsided and she reached across the table, took my hand and asked if there was anything that would keep me in the UK. When I told her that nothing was going to stop me going, she nodded and sank back into her seat. There was no more anger, no more tears, just a look of sadness and defeat. I would have preferred it if she had slapped me in the face, told me she hated me and that she never wanted to see me again. I really didn't want to hurt her. I was ready to offer myself to the Kurds, and risk my life, in the hope that I might inspire others, but why did the people who loved me most have to bear the pain of my decision?

Something had passed between us and the relationship was clearly gone. After a few minutes, we got up and walked to the door. As we stepped out into the cold, I threw my arm around her shoulders and hugged her. She still had questions for me, asking how soon I might come back, how dangerous it would be out there and whether I would be safe, but I didn't truthfully know the answers. If I had known it was going to be the last time I would see Anna, I would have tried harder to comfort her, but the finality of the moment hardened my own resolve. While I felt anger with myself, and regret that I had killed our relationship, I could at least use the emotions to quash any misgivings I had. Knowing what I had given up, and not wanting the loss to be in vain, had given me the determination to book my flight as soon as possible. The next morning, I messaged the Lions of Rojava to say I would fly out as soon as I had spent Christmas with my family. Once I clicked 'send', I felt a surge of adrenaline. This was it: the first step had been taken, and I was physically and emotionally ready to go to Syria. It was also the moment the YPG knew I was serious. They instantly had a prepared list of questions for me. 'Have you committed a crime? If yes, what? You take drugs? Have you sold drugs? You sat in jail? If yes, when, and for how long and why? Have you killed a human being? If so, why? Do you have a military experience?' They explained: 'Because YPG will have no criminal. And there are some who want to escape and want to find refuge.' They told me not to bring any military equipment – just good boots and warm clothes.

It was 15 December and all my bags were packed ready to go home for Christmas. It might be the last time I would ever see my parents so I was determined to make the most of the next two weeks. I was quite surprised that, after their initial shock, they did not raise many objections to me going out, but, of course, they still didn't know the full details. As soon as The Lions of Rojava responded that they were ready to take me on, I booked my flights. The cheapest flight I found had a long stopover in Istanbul. It wasn't perfect, but I had to be wary about what I was spending my money on. In any ordinary year, Christmas is a wonderful time, but there was something about knowing I was going to fight, and that it could be my last one, that made that Christmas particularly special. I pushed all thoughts of my mortality out of my mind and lived in the moment, drinking with my brothers, laughing with my family and inviting friends over, having a great time while hiding my great secret. My only regret was that I couldn't stay for longer, but just a couple of days after Christmas, on 27 December, I packed my bags for my flight the next day. I kissed my family goodbye in the hallway of our family house and promised to give them a call from Istanbul. My mum took me to the station to catch a train to London. She put on a brave face, but what I didn't know was that she had discussed with my dad why he thought I would have given up my career to go to Turkey to help refugees and he had told her, 'Well, I don't know that, but the one thing that we do know is that Harry would not lie to us.' What I also didn't know was that, as soon as I had got out of the car and waved mum goodbye, she had sat and wept.

En route to the airport, I asked myself again if I was being too impetuous. Was there more that I could do in the UK to raise the profile of the YPG and the fight against ISIS? If I was trying to talk myself out of going then I was doing a pretty poor job. The longer I thought about fighting, the more comfortable I became. Some things in life really are worth fighting for and there's no way I could live with myself if I didn't seize the opportunity. I decided that when I got there, I would settle in for a few months and experience what was happening on the ground. I could then start to write media articles. I felt sure the British press would be eager to focus on a Briton out in Syria fighting ISIS and that I could quickly gain some notoriety which would help me draw attention to the Kurds. Already, refugees were flooding into Europe, so Britain could not ignore what was happening on the ground in Rojava. I needed to cultivate the righteous anger of the public and use it to get Britain out of its slumber. I couldn't afford to think about the personal cost – the loss of a relationship and the misery I might force my family through. I might have to kill, and I would risk my life in a war many miles from home. I wouldn't be paid, nor would I receive a medal for my efforts. In fact, I would risk arrest on my return. I had a grandiose plan in my mind of what I wanted to achieve, but how realistic was it? All I could keep telling myself was that it felt like the right thing to do. It just felt right.

# Rain on Syrian Fields

The light was starting to fade, and the spectacular Zagros mountain views I had enjoyed just hours earlier were already lost to the dusk as we were ushered back to the 4x4s that had brought us to the Iraqi hillside camp. It was a little after 5 p.m. and the Kurds had received word from contacts at the Syrian border that there was an opportunity for us to cross. Now they were hastily rearranging bags of ammunition, RPG rockets and cling film-wrapped AK-47 assault rifles, which I noticed had appeared in the back of each car. Blankets and our personal bags were placed on top, and I was told to keep quiet as we drove off. We headed northwest for about an hour, looking out for checkpoints manned by the Kurdish Peshmerga militia, who had political differences with the YPG leadership and had been known to shoot those trying to cross the border. So, this was my New Year's Day? Sitting in the back of the smart new 4x4, everyone in casual civilian clothes, with Western tunes filling the air, it felt like I could have been on my way to the pub with mates . . . apart from the lack of chatter, the Iraqi road signs and a boot full of deadly weaponry!

In the darkness, our small convoy lurched off the road and we bumped along a rough track until we reached a large river. The Tigris, I reckoned. There was a flurry of activity and raised whispers as everyone piled out of the vehicles and began unloading the weapons. I had three

AKs thrust into my arms and I ran down to the water's edge with the others, then . . . nothing. People were milling around, anxiously looking across the river. I looked downstream, and just 300 meters away a spotlight began to lazily scan the water. Shit! It was a Peshmerga sentry post. If they didn't know we were there at that moment, they soon would. Just then, I heard the thrum of an engine and saw a boat emerging from the gloom. It was followed by others, all full of people and making slow progress towards us until they finally made landfall and the frantic activity on our riverbank sparked up again. It was clear we were meant to load the weapons onto the boats, but first we had to help the people out of them. It was only then that I realised they were all injured fighters, hobbling ashore. Most had gunshot wounds to their legs and arms, and some had been shot multiple times.

The weapons were placed aboard, and when the boats headed back into the gloom, I took the arm of one of the wounded fighters and guided him over the rough ground towards the cars. He leaned heavily on me and winced when I tried to put my hand on his back for support. He'd been shot in the hip, stomach and shoulder. I was amazed he could walk at all. By the time I got him to a car, the boats had delivered their loads and were coming back for us. I got in first, followed by a few other fresh recruits. I glanced again in the direction of the spotlight downstream and heard loud voices in the distance. I was sure someone had spotted us and was shouting a warning. Suddenly, I heard the revving of diesel engines, but I was relieved to see it was the cars that had delivered us now reversing quickly off the bank and towards the track with their new passengers. At the same time, we neared the opposite bank and I could see the bags and weapons piled there and a crowd of YPG fighters waiting to greet us. I had made it. I was in Syria.

My journey had begun five long days before, in a state of anxiety at Luton airport, as I clutched my travel documents and waited to pass through security checks, expecting at any moment that someone from the authorities, having monitored the Lions of Rojava page, would put a hand on my shoulder. The Border Force officer swapping wisecracks with holidaymakers bound for Ibiza or the ski slopes of Europe had stopped smiling as he took a long look at my ticket and saw the onward journey to Sulaymaniyah. 'I hope you're not going anywhere near Mosul,' the officer said, but he accepted the various visas in my passport as evidence I was heading for Iraq because I was an adventurous traveller, not because I was a would-be fighter. At Istanbul, I managed a few hours exploring the Blue Mosque and other tourist sites, making sure to take plenty of photographs to send to my family as part of the pretence that I was staying in Turkey. My paranoia levels had risen once more on arrival in Iraq, as I watched my bags, with knife, boots and compass hidden in the clothing, go through the X-ray machine, but the security officials seemed more interested in going for their lunch than quizzing me. So far, so good, but I still couldn't relax. As I stood in the taxi queue outside the small provincial airport I was alarmed when a small man in glasses grabbed my arm and demanded, 'You are Mazzer?' It was surely my Lions of Rojava contact, but I had needed to be sure. 'No, my name is John,' I lied. Confused, he showed me the photo I had sent to the Lions of Rojava and, with a smile, I confessed

I was indeed Macer Gifford, and followed him to his car. Even then, I had been like a coiled spring, ready to leap from the moving vehicle if 'Mr Short', or the two other stocky men who were waiting for us in the car, tried anything, but arriving at the safe house to find it decorated with Kurdish flags finally quelled my distrust. I spent the evening trying to make friends with the other occupants of the house with smiles but few words. The next day, a car and driver had arrived to take me to the Syrian border. A hair-raising, high-speed road journey was followed by a 4x4 drive across mountain tracks and then a walk with three other recruits to a YPG border post, before, the next day, we were driven to the banks of the Tigris.

On the Syrian side of the river, I helped the guys carry the bags of ammunition to a line of waiting minivans, and we were driven in the darkness to a guardhouse at the top of a rocky hill, where a sentry waved us in. There were about half a dozen people huddled in there on seats around an oil stove. I began to greet them in English and most grinned back blankly, but the third person I came to looked European. 'Well, it's clear you're definitely not Kurdish,' I said. He laughed and said his name was David. He was American, and I proceeded to try to rinse him for information. He told me that he had arrived in the country two weeks before with another group of foreigners, but he said they were all former military and had ganged up on him from the start. He said he had been a medic in the US military but the others had looked down on him for his comparative lack of military experience as they jockeyed for position within the small group. With my own lack of military experience, this was not something I wanted to hear. I gathered that David had been kicked out of the group and sent back to this holding camp on the hill, where all new foreign recruits were processed. So, this was my introduction to the 'international brigade', and my initial impressions were not good. I said goodnight to David and was shown to a steel shipping container that had been converted into accommodation. The new recruits I had arrived with were already snoring loudly by the time I lay down.

I woke at 6 a.m. and wandered out into a dark, grey morning so cold I could see my breath. I don't know why but I hadn't expected that of Syria. And then it started to drizzle. 'Baran!' I thought. Baran was the Kurdish nom-de-guerre I had been given by the Lions of Rojava. It had sounded noble when I first heard it, but if I had expected something heroic like Mountain, or Warrior, I was disappointed. 'Baran', I was told, meant 'Rain'. In the daylight, I was aware the buildings around me were part of an oil installation, but it was the view from the precipitously steep hill we were on that will stay with me for the rest of my life. To the north, I could see the beautiful mountains of Turkey; to the west, I could see Rojava below, a patchwork of flat green fields that stretched more than 300 kilometres to Kobane, where the Kurds were still fighting for their lives. Less than 130 kilometres to the south-west, I could see Mount Sinjar, and 400 kilometres beyond that, I knew, was Raqqa, the capital of the so-called Islamic State. ISIS was very much the dominant force in the area; the most well-armed, well-funded terrorist organisation there had ever been. It had tanks, mortars and armoured personnel carriers (APCs); it had heavy weaponry it had looted from the Iraqi and Syrian military; it had equipment from Saudi

Arabia and Turkey and even from the US and UK, given to the rebels fighting Assad, which it had either purchased or stolen. I looked around me at the YPG soldiers in their cheap cotton uniforms, armed only with old AK-47s. There would be victories ahead for the YPG, and I hoped to be part of them, but at that moment they were still in their infancy, desperately defending their homeland against the barbarians killing their countrymen and selling their women and children into sexual slavery.

Within an hour or so, I was joined by others who directed me to a vehicle canopy. It kept the rain off us but not the chill, as we gathered for a Kurdish breakfast that would come to be my daily staple – chunks of tomatoes and cheese, flat bread and olives, and tea. The day passed slowly as I watched in anguish the comings and goings of wounded fighters, some from Kobane on their way to Iraq for treatment. In the afternoon, I learned that the Kurdish recruits I had arrived with would be shipping out soon to the front line. They were issued with uniforms and AK-47s, and David and I sat in a corner of the container room and watched, smoking, listening to music and practising Kurdish phrases, as they cleaned their rifles and checked through their bullets. At least, as volunteers, we had chosen to be there. For them, it was a struggle for their lives and their homeland.

Suddenly, there was an almighty bang that was amplified by the steel walls, and David cried out in shock. Bewildered, I looked around and realised one of the Kurds had fired his weapon and he was now looking sheepish while his friends laughed at the hole in the top of the container and re-enacted David's frightened screech. David, I learned, considered himself a philosopher, downloading the spoken works of Aristotle on his phone to listen to through his headphones, and as we chatted about politics and life at home he told me that he was in the military for three years. On another occasion, when he admitted he lasted just one year, he initially said he was discharged for opposing the War on Terror and being a conscientious objector, and then he said he was medically discharged for psychiatric problems. He changed his story on so many occasions I didn't even bother calling him out on it, but I couldn't help liking him and his absurd, booming laugh. At least the Kurds continued to be friendly, and, as night fell at the end of my second day, they cajoled me into joining in their dancing. One would start singing and then everyone would stand, stomp their feet, hold hands and sway in a line to the song. I did my best to get involved, and then, as I was saying my 'goodnights', I was called over to the guardhouse. When I walked through the door, I was delighted to meet a new British volunteer. Nathan had been in the French Foreign Legion until just four weeks before, having served for seven years in their parachute regiment and reaching the rank of corporal. He and I were the same age and, although at first I felt like he was quite reserved with me, he soon relaxed and we chatted happily. He seemed like a nice guy, and we talked and laughed late into the night.

On my fourth full day in the country, we were visited by a Kurdish General who asked us about our experiences and what we wanted to achieve in Rojava. I told him: 'I want to experience what the Kurds are experiencing. I am here in solidarity to fight ISIS and to protect local people but I also want to raise awareness in the West, so anything I can do to help, I will.' He seemed happy with my answer. He told us we would be split into two groups and that mine would go to the training camp that day and the other would join us the following night. When we got back to our accommodation, we had uniforms and weapons waiting for us. As I am 6'3" tall, it took me a while to find a uniform that fitted. My magazine belt would have looked less out of place in the Vietnam War than in a twenty-first century conflict, and my AK-47 rifle, by no means the oldest, was Romanian and made in 1988. I was ordered into a vehicle with others and, while Nathan was left with David at the hill camp, we were driven to a deserted-looking building in the middle of the Syrian countryside. Inside, as we unloaded our kit, were yet more foreign volunteers. They included two Americans, Jack and Mark; an Australian, Ash; and a Dutchman, Rick. Within a couple of minutes of talking to them, two things were clear: one, that this was David's former group; two, that they were not the morons he had portrayed them to be, and they were probably right to have kicked him out over his repeated lies about being an army medic. They were a nice crowd and all had a good amount of experience in their respective country's armies or in the French Foreign Legion. We spent the rest of the day practising stripping the PKM heavy machine gun, having lectures on the aims of the YPG and getting to know one another. We were asked our Kurdish names and I told the trainers I had been given the name 'Baran', at which they nodded more respectfully than I had expected. 'And what about a surname?' they asked. Since I had not been given one, they told me I would be 'Amed' − named after a major city in northern Kurdistan. So now I was Baran Amed.

That night, our 'classroom' doubled as our sleeping quarters, so we threw a few thin mattresses on the floor and carried on sharing experiences from our travels. We were a young group, mostly in our twenties – apart from Jack, a gnarled Texan truck driver, who was in his forties – and the banter inevitably reflected that. The Australian's full name was Ashley. He was a postman and former army reservist from Queensland who was about the same age as me, and we soon had each other in stitches talking about girls and that joker David. 'Ash' told me it had got to the point where they couldn't trust David with a rifle, so they had sneaked into his room one night and took the bolt out of his weapon while he was sleeping. He had spent four days patrolling with a boltless AK-47!

The next day's training started early, with a long day on the shooting range and more lessons on the history of the YPG and the sort of government they hope to create in Rojava. After years of persecution at the hands of the Syrian regime, the Kurds finally had a chance to create a functioning democracy, and they were determined to make a success of it. A car arrived that evening with fresh supplies for the camp and took away three of the guys – Ash, Mark and Rick – who had already been in the country for a few weeks and were bound for the front line. I was going to miss them. The driver was keen to get going but Ash ran back to find me, as he was eager to Bluetooth me a message he wanted me to pass on to the Lions of Rojava. He had been so disgusted by David's lying that he was keen for the Lions to post a message on their website for any would be recruits: 'Don't lie or you'll either get yourself or someone else killed.'

I felt envious that the guys were heading off so soon, but I had only been in the training camp for two days and there was more that I needed to learn. I was also keen to see Nathan again. Not only had we got on well but he was probably the best-trained person I had met in Syria. Sure enough, an hour or so later, Nathan and David turned up at the training camp. The next few days involved more 5.30 a.m. starts in the freezing cold and hour upon hour of weapons training or lectures on how the YPG wanted to build a bottom-up democracy where control is in the hands of the people, and national government only focuses on national issues – a sort of devolution max where secular communities ran their own affairs and tolerance was built into the very fabric of society.

On the fifth day, we woke before dawn to find the ground blanketed in snow. We mobilised ourselves into two groups of foreigners, emptied our rifles, wrapped scarves around our faces and watched the young Kurds from the training camp walk to their large classroom 400 metres away from our quarters. When we were satisfied they were well into their lesson, we took up positions behind the building and, on the pre-arranged signal of a burst of AK fire from one of the instructors, I kicked down the door and we stormed the building. More instructors fired their AKs in the air as we screamed at the terrified young recruits, who had piled their weapons in the corner of the room and were totally unprepared for a surprise attack. It was a valuable lesson for them, but for us the training was over.

The instructors decided we were all fit for the front line. Even David, who had spent most of his time with his head in the clouds, infuriating his fellow American, Jack. After a few hours a minivan arrived to pick us up and all the young Kurdish recruits came out to say goodbye. As we drove away, I turned and wiped the condensation from the window and looked back at our Kurdish instructors. I would bump into them a few more times over the next five months on the front line and we would greet each other warmly. I would learn later that they were all killed in heavy fighting further up the line.

# The Palace

After a night back at the oil installation, we were driven
towards Sinjar Mountain and separated into two groups.
A steady drizzle was turning the countryside all around us
into a quagmire of sandy mud as Nathan, David and I were
sent south to an old farmhouse at the edge of an abandoned
village. The *tabur* (unit) of young Kurds based there were
mostly aged between eighteen and twenty-two, and were
clearly surprised to see foreigners, but we quickly got to
know our new comrades, pulling guard duty with them
or sitting indoors, playing chess and smoking, to keep out
of the persistent rain. We might have finished our basic
training but we were clearly not being thrown straight into
action. The nearest ISIS positions were just a smudge on
the horizon. Sensing our frustration, the tabur commander
Agir piled us into a vehicle for a tour of a different part
of the front line, first at a fortified village to the west and
then at a school converted to a YPG base. My first sight
of ISIS – the fearsome enemy I had come to take on –
was through binoculars. I watched one jihadist wander to
the edge of an ISIS-held village about 800 metres from
our lines, yawn or belch, then urinate in our direction.
He clearly wasn't worried about the threat of being shot
by one of our snipers mid-piss, and I gathered the lines
there hadn't moved in a year or so. It was very different
from the all-out fighting to the south in Sinjar, where Ash,

Mark and Rick were helping the YPG and the Peshmerga lay siege to the ISIS-held town.

Back at our farmhouse position a few days later, Nathan was sitting on some sandbags on the roof, tapping away at his phone, when I joined him for guard duty. 'What's up, buddy,' I said as I shouldered my rifle, but he continued staring at his phone. 'Have you heard the news?' he asked. 'Rick's been injured. He's been hit by an RPG and sent to Germany for treatment.' I struggled to take in the information. 'Fuck! I don't believe it. What happened?' I asked. Nathan looked up from his phone with a grim expression. 'He was running for cover in Sinjar when an RPG hit the wall next to him. A piece of shrapnel hit him in the head and now he's paralysed,' he said. I went cold. It felt like only days ago we had all been laughing and joking in the training camp, and now Rick had been sent home with life-changing injuries.

I didn't have time to dwell on it for long before we were loading the cars and heading further south to a deserted village, close to the Iraqi border, that had been turned into a sizeable military base. The boys of the YPG had been billeted in a compound of administrative buildings with a large courtyard. The girls of their sister force, the YPJ, were in a fortified house on the other side of the village, with their female commander, Heval Ulcum. They seemed so young but were well-trained, passionate and committed about what they were doing. ISIS, which had once held the village before they were forced back, were about a mile distant. So this was our new home. We were an odd little group. David spent much of his time reading or talking philosophical nonsense. Nathan was the most suitable of all of us to be there. Super-fit and from a military family, his father was an ex-officer and his brother was a paratrooper who had fought in Afghanistan with the British military. Nathan had also fought in Afghanistan as a paratrooper but in the Legion's famous 2nd REP. He had decided to leave the Legion just when he was due for promotion to Sergeant, but the military ethos was still strong in him. He would boot me awake in the morning and conscript me into joining him for building projects around the camp in order for the Kurds to see us pulling our weight. Nathan, who was fluent in French, had already picked up a decent amount of Kurmanji (Northern Kurdish) and had, in a way, become our de facto leader. His vanity projects, building furniture and other stuff for the camp, including a rifle range for him to practise with the Dragunov sniper rifle he had been issued, helped us to forge bonds with the thirty or so young YPG lads in our tabur. It also improved our surroundings so they were comfortable enough for Nathan and me to nickname the base 'The Palace'.

As the days went by, we became particularly close to our democratically elected commander, Heval Agir, and his second-in-command, Heval Dilivar. The word 'heval' was virtually the first word of Kurmanji we learned as international volunteers and was the most important. It meant 'friend' or 'comrade' and went to the heart of the incredibly strong bond of brotherhood. We were all hevals. Both Agir and Dilivar were from the mountains and as hard as nails. Agir, who had spent ten years fighting the Turks, seemed the more intellectual, and I would often get called over and, since neither of us could speak the other's language, join him for a silent game of chess, which he won every time.

The lack of action over the winter months was perhaps to be expected but was still frustrating. There were a few times when we were rushed to pack our kit ready to fight, only to be stood down after a few hours, and it was during one of these frantic false alarms that my twenty-eighth birthday came and went. The following evening, we were sitting around talking when a young Kurd rushed into the room, announced, 'Foreigners!' and pointed excitedly at the compound gates. Stepping outside to where two cars had pulled up in the dark, I could hear a variety of accents. There was an Australian, Ronnie; two Brits, Jim and Jac; an American by the name of Bruce; a Greek guy, Gregor; and a Frenchman. All were big guys and even in the darkness I could see they were heavily armed. On the orders of the Kurds, 'Greg' and Bruce would be joining our group and the others would be going to a village half a kilometre to the south. If I thought the lads were intimidating outside, they were even more so inside. Bruce was six-feet tall and stocky. Aged around forty, he had done four years in the US Rangers, another few years in the National Guard, and had deployed to Afghanistan and Somalia in his time. Even more imposing was Greg, who stood 6'5" inches tall, and was one of the biggest guys I'd ever seen. If his frame wasn't menacing enough, he had a thick black beard, a Mohawk haircut and piercing dark eyes. He had served five years in the Greek marines and a year in the French Foreign Legion. The young Kurds, who had been impressed by the size of Bruce and I, looked with awe at Greg, as if he was going to eat them!

Over the next few days, we helped the new lads to zero their gun sights on the range. They had arrived straight from the training camp and had been issued their Russian weaponry on their way over to us. Bruce had requested a Dragunov, because he was an avid hunter and it had been his weapon of choice in the US military. Greg chose the PKM, which, in the hands of the young Kurds, looked like the heavy machine gun it was, but in Greg's hands looked like a toy. I would sit down-range, just to the right of the target, and we devised a series of hand signals to indicate to Nathan and Bruce, 600, 800 or even 1000 metres away, whether the bullets were hitting high or low, left or right. The crack, snap and whirr of the rounds passing so close to me was fairly sobering. Greg was a real character, straight out of a Greek mythological story. Still a young guy at twenty-five, he had been a wrestling champion at home, and when it came to combat, he told me he thought guns were 'cheating' and he regretted the passing of the days when warriors felt their enemies die at the end of their blade. We used to take it in turns to wrestle with him, but he always kicked the crap out of us. Bruce was a real outdoors guy. He was part Native American, I think, and after leaving the military he had joined the police force for a reservation in Wisconsin. He was a real pillar of the group, and not just because of his age. He seemed professional in everything he did, solid and immovable, but friendly and funny, the kind of guy you never thought would have any low moments. His stoicism, however, hid a tragic truth, and I learned that he had suffered from demons ever since his brother had been killed when his army helicopter was shot down in Iraq in 2009. When Bruce had learned that the militants who claimed credit for shooting down his brother were joining ISIS, he left home without telling his wife and young daughter where he was going and flew to Istanbul, intent on reaching Kirkuk. When that wasn't going to happen, he agreed to join the YPG, to try to get some closure.

With the run of the entire village, Nathan and Bruce got us up to speed with house clearance drills and awareness of improvised explosive devices (IEDs) until we felt like a well-trained team. By the end of the week, I had come clean with my parents and started to drip-feed them information on where I was and that I was safe. Since I was not actually fighting, I also thought it was time to do what I could to raise awareness by writing a few articles on the conflict for British newspapers. I called a news desk in London. I insisted I didn't want to be the focus of any article, I just wanted to provide some freelance articles. Two days later, I was relaxing with the guys after lunch when I got a text from my mother and was horrified to read, 'Hi sweetie, just having tea with a tabloid journalist. Did you know anything about this?' Fearing a hatchet job, I agreed to an interview so long as my identity was hidden and that the story was focused on the Kurds. Suffice to say the article focused far too much on me, but I had learned a valuable lesson. The furore was not helped by other papers reprinting the story, or by the fact that it coincided with ISIS burning to death a Jordanian pilot they had captured, which spooked my family further.

January turned into February, and, as the weather improved, it could no longer be used as an excuse for the lack of any military operations. We were taken by trucks to patrol Sinjar Mountain and to see for ourselves the utter devastation wrought on villages in the area by heavy gunfire and air strikes. The views from the mountain were spectacular, but it felt strange to be at the scene of the heart-rending exile of some 50,000 Yazidis that had so motivated me to come to this country. At last, we started to see significant movement among the Kurds and we were ordered several times to pack our bags and get in the vehicles. On one occasion, 100 Kurds showed up with APCs fitted with heavy machine guns. The Soviet-era 50-calibre DShK was capable of firing 600 108-mm rounds a minute and was known as a *dushka* – ironically a Russian word for 'darling' – but they would not see action on this occasion as we were soon stood down. Another few weeks of training passed, then, out of the blue, Jack came to 'The Palace' and said he would be moving in with us, as the other foreigners with him had either gone home or moved to other taburs. There was distressing news, too, of two of the YPJ girls from his camp who had ignored an order not to stray out of their village and had tripped an IED. It took a while to get both girls to hospital and one bled to death before she got there, while the other lost her leg. I was still nowhere near seeing any fighting and already the casualties were mounting among the people I had grown to call friends.

By mid-February, the lads from the village just to the south of us – Jac and Ronnie – moved to join us too, and though they were in a different tabur, we were all moved to another part of the compound where we were given our own rooms and an area of the village to patrol during guard duty. It felt good to be part of a large group of foreigners. Nathan, Bruce and Ronnie took control. They had us build an inside toilet, shower and kitchen, and Bruce and Greg built a gym. We had our own fire, which we stocked with wood, and the shower was heated with water from the kettle. The Palace was finally beginning to live up to its nickname.

Ronnie, a former army medic, was a typical Aussie, very down-to-earth and practical. The English kid Jac was probably the most chilled-out guy I had ever met. He liked his sleep – a lot – and at twenty-two, he was the baby of the group and had left behind a job as a part-time IT technician in Bournemouth to come to fight. I was cleaning the rooms around 11 a.m. one morning when I heard snoring from under one of the mounds of bedclothes. 'What the fuck?' I asked one of the other guys, who shrugged and said Jac would sleep until the afternoon if you let him. 'Oi!' I yelled, and the mound of bedclothes muttered an expletive before a bleary-eyed figure emerged, lit up a cigarette and sat for several minutes, trying to acclimatise to the world before stumbling off in search of tea. Jac had no military experience and I thought to myself, 'He's not going to be sticking around for long.' How wrong time would prove me to be.

Rumours that we were there only for propaganda abounded, and Greg was threatening to go home, but we carried on making The Palace as habitable as possible. Our long wait for action, however, was nearly over. On 21 February we were told that the first big operation to free Rojava was about to begin and that we should pack our bags and ditch all non-essential items. The YPG had launched an operation the year before to try to seize the town of Tel Hamees, but ISIS had counter-attacked with tanks and artillery, leaving hundreds of YPG fighters killed or injured. It had been a massive failure which had jeopardised the entire front line. The Kurds had spent a year preparing and mobilising for a fresh attempt. The new Tel Hamees Operation was going to be huge, with thousands of YPG fighters, heavy weapons and armoured vehicles and, for the first time, American air support. I didn't know whether to be excited or scared. Or both.

It was the afternoon before our tabur saddled up, and eleven foreigners piled into one truck. After an hour's drive we reached a deserted town just west of Sinjar Mountain, and pulled off the road and into the car park of an abandoned elementary school. Another tabur had arrived before us and half of them were having a noisy dinner while the rest prepared sleeping quarters. We all piled into the makeshift dining room and were surprised to see Ash and Mark. They looked tired and had clearly had a much worse time over the past month than most of us. The fighting in Sinjar had been constant, and they had endured firefights at night and mortar attacks during the day. 'Mate, we're lucky to be here,' Ash told me. 'One mortar brought down the whole building we were firing from and buried us alive. If the Kurds had not dug us out with their bare hands we'd have been fucked.' The knot in my stomach was growing. This was a long way from target practice on the range, or guard duty miles from the nearest ISIS position. This was getting real.

As we waited, we were joined by British ex-soldier Jim. He had apparently demanded to be sent to fight or be sent home, and the Kurds had acceded and sent him to Sinjar. Many of the lads disappeared upstairs to find a bed, but I stayed with Mark, Ash and Nathan, who were deep in conversation about what the guys had seen in Sinjar. After a while, I walked outside and watched the Kurds piling up a load of wooden desks from the classroom into the middle of the courtyard. They doused the pile in petrol and set it alight, then turned on some music and began dancing. Ash came out to join me and said the Kurds in his unit always danced before a fight. With that, one of the Kurds grabbed Ash by the hand and dragged him away to join the revelry. 'Come, Heval Bagok,' they called, using his Kurdish nom-de-guerre. I made my escape, but as I was walking along one of the open-air corridors on the second floor, I glanced back down at the Kurds dancing in the courtyard. They had grabbed Mark too, and were now performing the traditional line dancing I had already come to know, stamping their feet as they danced around the flames. It felt like everything up to this point in Syria had been a dream. Now, as the heat and the smell of the fire, the music, and the cries of my dancing friends assaulted my senses, I knew I was very much awake. Though apprehensive about the deadly fight with ISIS, I was determined and raring to go.

# The Battle for Tel Hamees

Thoughts of what the coming day might bring danced in my head like the flames of the fire until exhaustion finally overcame me, but even then, it was a fitful rest. In spite of the thirty or so fighters wedged into the small room, it was bitterly cold, with just a single thin blanket each. I shivered in and out of sleep until dawn brought the dull roar of low-flying jets and the distant sound of explosions. I curled myself into a ball and tried for a few more minutes to ignore the bomb blasts that were vibrating through the concrete classroom floor and the snores that reverberated through the air.

In the early morning light, we began loading up the cars. The other tabur, with Ash and Mark, had already left, but a steady stream of Kurds was arriving until there were more than 200 young YPG and YPJ fighters milling in the car park in front of the school. We were soon joined by a Kurdish commander who sat us in a semicircle to thank us for our willingness to defend the people of Rojava. He told us again how they hoped to build a secular democracy in which every community had an equal say in how the country was run, and he warned us that the coming fight would truly test our mettle. There were thousands of ISIS fighters across the region, he said, but he was sure we would be triumphant and he warned us we must never harm any whom surrendered to us. Any soldier mistreating prisoners, desecrating bodies or caught stealing would be arrested and jailed, he added. The commander said the assault on Tel Hamees would be a surprise attack that would go around many of the east-facing ISIS defences in Syria. We would assist the Peshmerga the next day in clearing some villages on the western edge of Sinjar Mountain and then we would swing north across the border and come upon Tel Hamees from the south. We would get full air cover from the Americans while in Iraq, and then partial cover in Syria.

The sun was beating down by the time we set off behind a vast column of trucks and heavy weapons, and I spotted two familiar faces among the Kurds. Ash and Mark were clinging on to the back of a particularly large dushka-mounted APC and I grinned and waved at them. They had already seen plenty of action, but I was finally on my way to help strike a blow against the hated Islamic State. The thirty or so Hilux pick-up trucks, with hundreds of YPG fighters, pulled up on the edge of a hamlet, and I just had time for a brief chat with Mark and Ash before the huge force was split into two and their column rumbled into formation. Heval Agir, meanwhile, beckoned us to help clear a large Iraqi village which ISIS had not long since abandoned. There were still uniforms hanging in some of the bedroom wardrobes, breakfast bubbling on stoves and tea spilled on the floor where the ISIS fighters had left in haste after being taken totally by surprise by our attack. I felt frustrated to be so close to the action yet still not involved. The noise of the other YPG convoy, cheering and beeping their horns as they headed west to the fighting, didn't help. Jac and Aussie Ronnie were with them and almost as excited as the Kurds, whose enthusiasm and laughter was at odds with the danger we all faced. For many of them, like me, it would be their first taste of action, and I was more than a little envious they would experience it before me. Agir told us that the other taburs were going to attack an ISIS-held village about a mile away, and as soon as they had successfully done that, we would head north, beyond them, to take an ISIS-held hamlet on the Iraq/Syria border. We would then leapfrog each other, taking other villages, until we reached Tel Hamees. At the same time, a third column would be attacking ISIS positions at Tell Brak, further west. It was about forty minutes later when we heard the sound of heavy fighting a mile away. There were so many distant gunshots, tank blasts and explosions it was clear the lads had walked into a firestorm, but we could only listen and wonder.

We were distracted by the arrival of civilian vehicles entering our village. Now that the fighting had moved on, the looters came out in force. They kicked down doors and helped themselves to TVs, generators, home appliances and furniture. Disgusted, I asked for permission to disperse the thieves, but Agir rolled his eyes. This wasn't Rojava, and the YPG was subordinate to the Peshmerga here, so we were not allowed to intervene. Only as dusk settled, and the looters began to set fire to the houses they had stripped of all valuables, did Heval Dilivar order them gone. As I prepared to sleep, the sound of fighting in the distance was only just dying down after seven hours.

The next morning, Nathan found some eggs in one of the sheds and we fried them over a fire while the Kurds sat in a circle relaxing and joking around. One of the comedians of the group found a donkey in one of the fields and amused us by riding it around the yard. The laughter soon stopped, however, when one of the Kurds began scrolling through the videos and pictures on ISIS phones that Nathan and I had found the day before. Among the Rambo poses by ISIS fighters with ammo belts draped around their necks were numerous videos of executions – of mostly men but also of women and children. There were images, too, of decapitated bodies with the heads tucked under their arms or resting between their shoulders. The same, or similar, videos and photos appeared on other phones and it was clear they had been shared like pornography.

After breakfast, we drove north-west before unloading from the Toyota Hiluxes at a small deserted village. I gripped my rifle nervously as we spread out and advanced on foot, and I scanned every doorway and window I could for any sign of ISIS snipers. Tufan, a senior Kurdish fighter, called for David and I to join him, to secure the left flank, and we were heading out to a defendable mound of earth in a field on the outskirts of the village when I heard a growl to my left and spun round to see a huge dog bounding towards us. Its hackles were raised and its lip was curled back in a vicious snarl. I put my rifle to my shoulder and, after a second's hesitation, shot it in the chest. A bright red jet of blood sprayed out onto the floor and suddenly the rabid dog looked harmless as it gave out a pitiful whine. Its left leg curled into its body and its chest was wet with blood as it turned on its good legs and limped away. It wasn't the first shot in anger I had imagined.

We rejoined the rest of the tabur at a small graveyard on the northern edge of the village, with a commanding view over the wide open, flat fields between us and a larger village about one kilometre away. Even without binoculars I could see a lot of ISIS movement and, sure enough, when the top of our hill was crowded with YPG fighters, there was the crack of an ISIS sniper round and a few optimistic AK shots. Agir called up a dushka, which began hitting the village and any cars that came within range. Moments later, another dushka arrived and was ordered to a group of farm buildings on our left flank. A small detachment of YPG fighters, led by Bruce and 'the Beast', Greg, were sent to defend it. As they ran across the open ground, the enemy positions opened up with PKM rounds, most of which hit the ground fifty metres short of the lads. For the next two hours, as the dushkas peppered the ISIS positions, we waited for the order to move forward. A YPJ commander told Agir that there were probably ISIS tanks in the village and that we should wait for American planes to bomb before making an assault. The hours dragged, and Nathan swore in frustration. If ISIS had tanks or even dushkas in the village they would probably have used them, he argued.

By 4 p.m., with the light soon to fade, we faced the prospect of spending a cold night in the graveyard. Another half an hour passed before a YPG tank arrived and started to shell the village, targeting the school, where there was supposed to be a high concentration of ISIS fighters. The YPJ commander finally conceded that no US air cover was coming, and she ordered Agir to attack. Bruce's team was called back and the tabur was divided into three groups. Realising what was about to happen, Nathan appealed to Agir not to try a direct assault. It was inviting disaster, he said, because there was no cover, the open fields could well be mined and ISIS had had all day to prepare their defences, but his advice was ignored. He and Greg were ordered to go with fifteen Kurds in the first group to flank from the right; a second group of twenty Kurds was ordered to attack head-on; and Bruce, David and I were in the third group kept in reserve. I felt cheated to be left out of the initial attack but, at the same time, I was glad not to be in the group carrying out the frontal assault as I watched Dilivar lead the twenty girls and boys in a run towards a small stone shed 200 metres from the target village. They hadn't gone fifty metres before the first shots rang out, and by the time they reached halfway, the ISIS PKMs had opened up, sending clods of earth flying right in front of the lead man. They hit the deck and began to return fire, but they were well and truly pinned down by the entrenched enemy machine guns while still too far away for their AKs to be in the least bit effective. 'Fuck!' I muttered, as I watched their predicament and looked to see if Nathan and Greg's group might be able to help, but they still had a long way to go to be in range and were coming under fire themselves. It was fast turning into the kind of clusterfuck that Nathan had warned of and Dilivar's group faced being wiped out unless something was done. I could see consternation among the Kurdish commanders and they soon ordered the rest of the tabur, including Bruce and me, to get into two Hiluxes.

My relief that we were going to try to do something to help turned to horror when I realised we were accelerating down the hill straight towards the ISIS positions. I couldn't believe it. We were in a soft-skin Toyota Hilux, not an armoured vehicle. One burst of heavy gunfire would tear right through us. That's if we didn't hit a mine first. Still we sped forwards, with about ten of us wedged in the back of the vehicle, being violently bounced around. I could see Dilivar's group to the left of us, pinned down, and above the roar of the engine and the rush of the wind I could hear the crack of rounds splitting the air around us. I was just waiting for the next round to pass through the vehicle and possibly through me. Still we rushed onwards until, suddenly, the driver slammed on the brakes and we ground to a halt. 'Fuck! Fuck! Fuck!' I thought. It was bad enough driving headlong into the teeth of the enemy guns but this was even worse. We were now sitting ducks! I braced for the inevitable incoming fire and feared my first taste of action might also be the last thing I ever did. That's when I saw the cavalry arriving. Two APCs were speeding past us, the Kurdish gunners, with shemaghs wrapped around their heads like twin Lawrences of Arabia, blasting away at the enemy positions with their 50-cal weapons. I was still dreading the ISIS barrage but quickly realised there was none. At the sight of the APCs, the ISIS fighters had abandoned their positions and run. The fight was over.

We drove fast to catch up with the APCs and when we got into the village, we jumped out and began searching the streets. But they were clear, and the Kurds immediately began firing in the air in celebration. As I walked over to speak to Greg, I could see 'the Beast' deep in conversation with one of the Kurd gunners who was clambering off the APC except that, when he unwrapped his shemagh, the gunner exposed a shaven white head. He wasn't a Kurd at all but a British former Royal Marine called Kosta, who I had heard about. 'Hi, I'm Macer. We've been watching this village all bloody day and then you swoop in at the last minute and take it for us!' I said, with mock indignation. 'But I'm bloody glad you did,' I added. 'You're welcome, mate,' he said. We chatted for a few minutes and he explained that he had volunteered for the armoured unit and that, because their two vehicles were the only two APCs on this part of the line, they had been flat out running backwards and forwards with supplies and ammunition and ferrying casualties away from the battles. He had been involved in the heavy fighting and his APC gunner had been shot dead, which was why he was now manning the dushka. The lads had indeed run into hell. 'The fighting's vicious on the left flank. We've got to head back there shortly to help out,' Kosta said. It told me a lot about the kind of guy Kosta was that he had taken over the gunner's position so soon after seeing his comrade killed doing the job. Though he was British, from Nottingham, he was clearly very proud of his Greek roots and keen for a quick chat to our own Greek warrior, Greg, before he headed back to the left flank, so I left them to it.

The following evening, I was woken by the sound of hell being unleashed. It was about 10 p.m., and the night air was full of AK fire and Kurdish shouts. I dived for my boots in a panic and grabbed my rifle. Apparently, not all of the ISIS fighters had managed to get out of the village during our initial attack, and they had waited until darkness before hotwiring a car and driving out of the village under heavy fire from our sentries. By the time I got out of the building, I could just see a set of tail lights in the distance, but since I was now awake I was asked to take over guard duty. At that point, the heavens opened, and I spent the next two hours on the roof in the teeming rain. The downpour had finished by the morning, but the mud was back with a vengeance, and the day was about to get much darker. As I pulled another guard duty, my mobile buzzed into life and it was a reporter from Sky

News asking me what I knew about the first Western volunteer to die with the YPG? 'The what?' I asked. 'I don't know anything about it. Who told you this?' He said the Kurds had announced the 'martyrdom'. 'It's an Australian by the name of Ashley Johnson . . .' he began. The words hit me like a freight train. Ash? Dead? I'd only seen him three days earlier. I told the others and we sat around in stunned silence. I remembered Ash laughing, fit to burst as we had talked about girls and about David unwittingly patrolling with his disarmed rifle; I could see him dancing round the fire with the Kurds from his tabur; and I pictured him smiling as he and Mark rode into battle just days before. There is something about shared danger that brings people together, and lifelong friendships can form in a day. I had definitely lost a friend, but it was Ash's family and Mark that I couldn't help thinking about. Ash and Mark had become blood brothers, and I knew Mark would be devastated to have lost his mate. I thought of Ash's mother, too. He had told her he was only going to do 'humanitarian work' to support the Kurds, and it reminded me of my initial deception towards my own family, and how much it would have hurt them to learn the truth in such awful circumstances.

We woke the next morning to the sound of tanks rumbling past the village, with at least 200 Kurds on the back of twenty Hiluxes following the armoured vehicles. Three kilometres further on, we could see Tel Hamees spread out before us just the other side of the flat, featureless countryside. The town – our key objective – was taking a pounding from the Kurds' heavy artillery, and US Spectre gunships were joining in. We were told to wait while the softening up continued. Nathan and I spent a tense night doing a long guard duty in a farmhouse just 800 metres from Tel Hamees – and clearly within attacking range of any ISIS patrols.

When we rejoined the rest of our tabur and lined up for the big attack on Tel Hamees, it felt even more as I imagined it must have done before a First World War advance. Bruce was sent ahead with at least forty Kurds, to run around the field and charge the right flank, and, while at least half a dozen other taburs attacked the town from multiple directions, several APCs were tasked with taking twenty or so guys from our tabur, including Greg, to attack the power station on the left flank. Once again I found myself in the remaining group, held back ready to support house clearance. I steeled myself for the cacophony of battle and for the part I would eventually play, but there was noticeably little gunfire and the air strikes were off in the distance. We drove across the field and caught up with Bruce's team on the right flank just as they were arriving at the first few buildings. Hundreds of Kurds were pouring into the town, but there seemed to be very little evidence of any ISIS defence. 'There were a few snipers who put up a fight, but you should have seen those bastards run when they knew there was no stopping us,' said Bruce. We parked up next to a couple of APCs and as I climbed off the back of my Hilux I noticed Kosta and his crew relaxing in the shade. He said a large group of ISIS fighters had been seen fleeing the town just an hour before and an air strike had pulverised at least one of their vehicles. It seemed like the town had fallen without too much of a fight.

As Kurdish media teams arrived to document the victory, and Bruce and Nathan pushed me forward as the inter-national volunteers' 'media man', a car pulled up with

Jordan Matson and Mark inside, and all of us gathered around to commiserate. Mark had a thousand-yard stare and didn't really say much. He was on his way to collect his stuff and to accompany Ash's body to Australia. We also learned that ten Kurds from our column had died in the last few days of fighting.

That night, the Kurds in our tabur built a fire and stayed up late talking and smoking. Standing on top of our sleeping quarters and looking out over the town on guard duty, I could see the glow of dozens of fires from other taburs celebrating their victory. The Palace seemed like a world away. We had come so far in a few days. The fight for Tel Hamees was over, but the fight for Rojava was only just beginning.

# Cat and Mouse

Greg lay motionless amid the rubble, his face a deathly white beneath his bushy black beard. I had thought it would take a cruise missile to fell 'the Beast'. In the end, it had just taken some loose bricks. He had been standing on them to try to reach a shed roof when they gave way and he badly twisted his ankle. Now he was moaning in pain and cursing in Greek as he prepared to go to hospital. Having to leave Tel Hamees without him, we split our column, with the armour heading south to chase a large ISIS force into Iraq and our tabur heading west to hunt down ISIS stragglers. I just had time to grab a quick chat with Kosta before we went our separate ways. He was speaking with Kurdish friends and I was amazed at his Kurmanji. He was just the kind of guy I had hoped I would be surrounded by among the international volunteers in Rojava – I had met enough chancers already to appreciate guys like Kosta all the more.

From Tel Hamees, we spent days clearing village after village by the simple expedient of driving into them to see if we attracted an ISIS ambush, in spite of our protest-ations to Agir that our three Toyotas weren't bulletproof, and neither were we! The only good thing was that in one abandoned building Nathan found me a perfect set of abandoned body armour with level-four plates that could stop multiple AK-47 rounds. We also found a huge stash of IEDs, the second in a few days. It was a sign of how fast we had advanced that ISIS had not had time to deploy them against us. Nathan and Bruce had already handed me Greg's PKM. Now that the Beast was gone, I would have to take the crucial support weapon. I spent a day training on it and making sure I was as familiar with it as I was with the AK-47. I set to work cleaning my new weapon and when I ran into our accommodation room to grab a cloth I noticed the flash of a message coming in on my phone with a text from my mother. 'Kosta's been killed,' she informed me. She had been regularly checking the Lions of Rojava Facebook page and had been alarmed to see the 'martyrdom' announced of the first Briton. I felt numb. It was terrible news. I learned that the armoured units had caught up with the fleeing ISIS fighters as they headed for their Sunni strongholds in the south and met with fierce resistance in a village near to the Iraqi border. Kosta had fired an RPG and was about to climb back inside the APC when an ISIS RPG hit the front of the vehicle, spraying shrapnel everywhere, and he was hit in the chest. Even his normally stoic YPG comrades had been in tears, but we had precious little time to grieve.

The ISIS counter-attack was well underway, with 3000 ISIS fighters launched against the villages around Tell Nasri to our west, capturing hundreds of Christian civilians. We were moved west to meet them, and travelled to a huge hill on the southern edge of Tell Brak, where the third YPG column had ousted ISIS from defensive positions over-looking the Iraq border. Several YPG commanders visited the base there to see the fortifications, and they invited me to join them for lunch and a chat, which was recorded by a Kurdish photographer. I learned that during the Tel

Hamees operation, ISIS had launched a massive diversionary attack of their own on the village of Tell Nasri, to the west. The lunch was clearly a PR opportunity, and I took advantage by asking about our role in the coming operations. None of us wanted to be stuck on the windswept hill for weeks while the key fighting went on elsewhere. Later that night, the senior commander promised to stick us on the front line as soon as possible. The Kurds were delighted and a beaming Dilivar promised to reward us with a meat stew, then recruited me to help him prepare it. After two months in Rojava, I had halalled my share of sheep, but it never got easier, and now that we were so close to ISIS-held territory it took on greater significance for me. I sensed more keenly than ever the animal writhing under my grip as I pinned it down, its eyes swivelling in its head as it stared up at me, and its shock at the first cut of the blade. I couldn't help but picture myself bound and gagged on the floor, staring up at an ISIS fighter above me. In the UK, we are so far removed from the possibility of dying, but in Syria, we had deep conversations about it, long into the night. The conditions were harsh, but there is something particularly egalitarian about war. Everything, from our food to our problems, was shared, and I couldn't help feeling a sense of fulfilment that I had not experienced in London. In a small way, it made me uncomfortable to find myself enjoying the experience. With so much pain and suffering around me, I had no right to, and yet the closer you are to death, the more alive you feel.

The following day, we were joined by Jim, the British ex-soldier who I'd last met at the school near Sinjar Mountain. Well-educated and desperately keen to fight, he had leapt at the opportunity to join Agir's tabur, as it was clear we were headed for the front. That afternoon, we drove south-west for about an hour, and the local people waved as we passed, as if we were conquering heroes. Towards dusk, we reached the Khabur River and drove through a series of Assyrian Christian villages until we reached our destination near the village of Tal Erphan, south of Tell Tamer. It was a YPG base set up in the office buildings of the local reservoir, and we were invited to curl up on the concrete floor to sleep. I shifted uncomfortably in the semi-darkness for what felt like ages and was finally close to sleep when I felt a hand shake me. It was Nathan, and he whispered to me to quietly follow him outside. When I got there, Bruce, Nathan, Agir and Ulcum were in deep discussion. They needed a team to go on a perilous mission behind ISIS lines. It was just what I wanted to hear. The plan was for the main tabur to attack the ISIS-held Syriac village of Tell Fweidat to the west of us the following day, but the YPG did not want any ISIS fighters there to escape in the night. They wanted to trap them rather than allow them to reinforce a larger ISIS force that was well-entrenched a few kilometres north and already under sustained attack by half a dozen different taburs. Our job was to take up a position to the north of Tell Fweidat and ambush any ISIS fighters trying to flee under cover of darkness.

The five of us were driven west for fifteen minutes until we reached the beautiful monastery of Morth Maryam – St Mary the Virgin – at Tel Wardiat, where the doors were opened by YPG fighters. Another 100 metres down the road we met with a further dozen or so YPG fighters, who I was glad to hear would be taking up a position near us.

We climbed into the back of two cars, loaded with water, ammunition and food, and continued north-west as fast as we dared with no headlights on. The cold night air whipped my face as I peered through the darkness at a small group of houses just 300 metres away. 'Shh! *Daesh!*' whispered one of the Kurds pointing to the enemy-held buildings and using the derogatory Arabic term for ISIS. A short distance further on, we came to a silent halt at the side of the road, grabbed our bags, and followed one of the Kurds into a field, through the knee-high grass, towards a small hill with a great vantage point over the ISIS-held positions. Making my way through the pitch-black with the weight of my body armour, bag and PKM, I struggled to keep my breathing as quiet as possible. Realising just how close we were to the ISIS positions, I wondered if there might be someone out there in the darkness with me in their sights, just waiting to kill me, and my knees nearly buckled when a single gunshot rang out. Almost immediately, a barrage of gunfire shattered the night air and I could hear the whirr of bullets overhead. We ran as fast as we could to reach the lee of the hill and threw ourselves to the ground, our panting breath clouding the cold night air. Ulcum made a few radio calls and it became apparent that a Kurdish sentry from another tabur had heard us creeping around in the darkness and had fired an aimless shot, which only sparked off the equally jumpy ISIS sentries. Within half an hour, the firing had died down and the village was quiet once more.

I was given night-vision goggles and asked to do the first watch from 10 p.m. to 2 a.m. There was nothing moving in the village, but watching the distant battle for the ISIS fortress to our north was like having my own personal fireworks display as dushka and tank shells exploded, tracer rounds stitched patterns into the night sky and the shockwaves of distant blasts pulsated through the air. Very quickly, the cold earth and the freezing wind began to suck the heat from my body and I shivered violently. The hours ticked past and I watched the others sleeping with envy. As I maintained my vigilance for any sign of ISIS fighters, every hedge and every tree seemed like it might conceal an enemy fighter. I was finally relieved by Bruce, who complained that he had not managed to get a wink of sleep, though I was sure I'd heard him gently snoring, and I crawled down the steep mud bank, my limbs stiff with cold. Wrapping myself in Bruce's sleeping blanket did nothing to warm me up, as it was not wide enough to go around my body and my feet stuck out the ends, so I managed to snatch only a few moments of sleep over the next two hours as my body shivered uncontrollably. By 4 a.m. I was in agony. I could no longer feel my feet and my hands were so stiff I could not flex my fingers. I was forced to stand up in an attempt to get the blood flowing around my body, and it felt like I was walking on clubfeet. Seeing me awake, Heval Ulcum called me over to do another guard duty – until dawn!

With the sun slowly rising, revealing frost on the ground, I was joined by Tufan, who sat next to me to share a tray of cold rice and mutton as the others began waking or returning from other guard positions. The expected ISIS escape attempt had not happened and so, after a few more hours of watching, a commander arrived with half a dozen Kurds and told us that the operation to take the village was about to begin and that we would be part of the first attack. We followed a local guide through a field towards the village as the sound of gunfire erupted from a number of different directions. The ammunition in my ammo box was rattling as I stumbled over the uneven ground, but at least the feeling in my feet was beginning to return. A YPG Humvee tore past us as we ran up the main street of the village, and we took shelter behind it with a number of Kurds as bullets flew just over our heads. Nathan and Bruce called me onto the roof of a nearby house, and from our new vantage point we could see the layout of the battlefield. A beautiful church lay on a hill 400 metres ahead of us on the western side of the village, with a number of houses and outbuildings below it, all occupied by ISIS fighters. The elevation and the thick stone walls made it a formidable defensive position. When a couple of dushkas were moved up and began bombarding the ISIS positions, I was ordered to give covering fire for the Kurds who were trying to get within AK-range. With Nathan's help to get the weapon ranged, my PKM was having a devastating effect as I hammered every window and doorway I could see. Within a few minutes, I was drawing ISIS fire, and the air was soon full of the zing and whirr of deadly missiles. There were AK rounds, M16 sniper rounds, 50-cals and, every now and then, a mortar. The noise and the smell of burning were horrendous. For the next hour I continued to cover the advancing Kurd fighters while the dushkas pounded the enemy. Nathan and Bruce were causing havoc with their sniper fire, putting rounds through even the smallest of gaps with deadly accuracy. At one point, Bruce spotted three ISIS fighters running between the buildings. The first caught his attention; he fired at the second a moment later, but missed; the third unfortunate soul had only taken one step into the alleyway before Bruce put a round through his stomach and out of his back. He keeled over and, before Bruce could shoot him again, rolled back behind the wall to die.

It was just before lunch that we took our first casualty. Time and again, the Kurds trying to close on the ISIS-held houses had been forced back by the intensity of the ISIS fire and then, in a daring assault, Heval Kendal, one of the Kurdish commanders, led his men across the field and was shot in the head. With that, every dushka and every PKM was ordered to open up on the ISIS positions at the same time, to keep them pinned down while Kendal's body was retrieved. Thereafter, I was ordered to conserve ammunition as we waited for a possible night assault. Mid-afternoon, we were joined by British Jim, a twenty-nine-year-old former US Marine called Jamie and his fellow American, David, who had all spent a more comfortable night at the reservoir while we shivered in the field. Jamie took his M16 to join Bruce in sniping at the enemy, and Jim joined me on the roof.

Utterly exhausted by late afternoon, I went downstairs and climbed into the house through a broken window. I was surprised to find an immaculate home, otherwise untouched by war, and a crucifix and a picture of the Virgin Mary on the wall. Two of our fighters followed me through the window and smiled when they saw what I was looking at. One took a small crucifix from around his neck and held it up, while the other reached into his pocket and pulled out some Muslim prayer beads. If I needed an example of the multi-faith, multi-ethnic composition of the YPG, I didn't need to look any further.

When we rejoined the Kurds on the roof after a night of hellish guard duty, they signalled for us to crawl. Apparently, the ISIS fighters had left the church and flanked us in the night, and since first light, a sniper in the graveyard 300 metres away had been targeting them. I asked one of the lads to hold up a dummy they had made to see if I could get an indication of where the sniper was and, sure enough, when the dummy was lifted, there was the snap of a shot above our heads. The dummy was flung backwards with a small, perfectly round hole in its chest where the heart would be. I had seen no sign of where the shot had come from, and nor had anyone else. The sniper was going to be hard to shift and posed a huge threat to our ability to move around.

Later in the morning, I joined Bruce, Nathan and Jamie in search of the sniper. The next three hours were like a game of cat and mouse, as the lads set up a succession of sniper nests, looking for movement, and the ISIS marksman regularly changed his position. At one point, they located him among the graves, but after a barrage of fire, he managed to crawl away. My AK didn't have the range to be much help, and trying to loose off rounds from my PKM would have got my head blown off, so Jamie and I did our best to assist Nathan and Bruce by building a dummy and drawing as much fire as possible. At other times, Jamie would fire his M16 in an attempt to coax out the sniper, and, if I had so much as an inkling of where the sniper might be, I would run to either Bruce or Nathan and guide them. As we moved between the buildings, there were spots where we were briefly visible to the enemy, and I was only too well aware of how Bruce had nailed the ISIS fighter the day before, so it became a joke between Jamie and I as to who would go first when moving. Being the coward that I am, I usually ran ahead and laughed at Jamie's attempts to keep up. It was tempting fate. We tried to stop and go irregularly so the sniper couldn't accurately gauge our movements, but we were playing with fire, and it was only a matter of time before our luck ran out.

# Under Siege

Inevitably, by the late afternoon we got complacent, and for once we didn't stop to break our movement. We just kept running, and the ISIS sniper, watching us flit between the buildings, and judging the speed and direction, must have hazarded a decent guess as to when we would next be exposed. Sure enough, as I ran laughing between two buildings there was the violent crack of a shot passing a foot behind my head. I staggered forwards and nearly fell, with Jamie stumbling and nearly landing on top of me. One of the Kurds then told us that Agir had ordered the tabur to pull out. Pissed off though we were that the sniper had survived, ISIS were counter-attacking to our north and we were clearly needed, so there was a sense of urgency about our departure. When we arrived at the YPG base in an enormous former cattle auction yard at Tell Tamer, we were divided into three groups. Bruce and Nathan were placed in the first group, Jamie in the second, and I was placed with David and Jim in the third group, which was ordered to stay behind while the other two groups went on patrol. I settled down to sleep that night, annoyed that I was missing out on whatever action the others had been sent to, but still sobered by the image that persisted in my head of Kendal's dead body wrapped in a blood-soaked blanket, with a scarf hiding his shattered head.

The hours dragged by the following day as I waited in vain for the others to return, unaware that barely a mile to the south of me they were involved in fierce house-to-house combat, driving back the ISIS counter-attack. At least I had a chance to use a bucket to wash myself and my clothes, which was a blessed relief after weeks of sleeping rough. As the evening approached I heard Western voices, and when I investigated, I found it was Quentin Sommerville, the BBC's Middle East correspondent, with his American cameraman and team. We did a quick interview about our reasons for being there, about Kosta's death and what we thought of Britain's stance on the conflict. Then they took some shots of us sitting around the fire, chatting and singing with the Kurds. Even as the rest of the tabur were in the thick of the fighting, I felt I was contributing to the cause in a very real way by educating people about the conflict.

The next day, a minivan turned up at lunchtime with six more foreigners. An Australian and one of the Americans were both in a particularly foul mood, swearing and muttering that they wanted to go home, but they all seemed dejected. Apparently they had left the training camp a fortnight before and gone straight to the front line, where they were very quickly involved in some heavy fighting and managed to kill eleven enemy fighters before ISIS retreated. They must have got the distorted impression that this was exactly the kind of action they had come in search of, but Syria was not like that. It was hours, days, weeks of boredom with the occasional glimpse of hell; waiting interminably for a contact that would either be terrifying or a huge anticlimax. After being posted for less than a week in another village where nothing happened, the guys had got bored and decided to walk off in search of action. Now, the YPG may be a militia, rather than a standing army, but these guys had not clicked that deserting their post was an offence. Needless to say, they had got chewed out by the commanders and sent to our camp while the Kurds decided their fate. I was glad when they were all called away. Jim clearly shared my opinion. 'Thank fuck they're not with us,' he said.

That night, Jim, David and I were driven to a town about a mile north-west of the cattle yards. Even in the dark, with the streets empty, the houses of Tell Jemaah would not have looked out of place in a smart Southern European town, but if I thought we were going to get to sleep in one of them I was wrong. We were led across country, forded a river, then walked some more until we reached an earthen wall around the top of a hill manned by Kurdish fighters. In a large open building they had a fire going, but there was precious little shelter. It was a bleak outpost, and a Swedish Kurd told us the guard duties there were four hours long and that they were on high alert for ISIS attacks. A translator immediately took us to our guard posts around the perimeter, and when we passed a hole in the ground leading to a concrete pipe he told me, 'You will sleep in there, but first you need to do guard duty.'

In the morning light, I could tell we were in an agricultural complex converted to a fort by the building of the berms, but the protection from snipers lessened the further you ventured from the perimeter wall, so I ended up running to the farm building in the centre, where the bonfire had been the night before. Others were brewing tea and having breakfast, and I got the opportunity to get to know the new foreigners a little better. There was an American, Levi, who was a bit of a joker and began doing Monty Python impressions. I was embarrassed as he went through his 'dead parrot' routine, to the bemusement of the Kurds I had already made friends with, but his inane chatter was suddenly interrupted by the sound of gunfire, and a Kurd messenger came running around the corner of the building, followed by the crack of two bullets just above his head. Before he could say anything, more gunfire broke out, but this time from positions all along the perimeter. Everyone jumped up and grabbed their weapons as we were ordered to our positions. I ran to the concrete pipe, grabbed my body armour and spare magazines, and joined a Kurd in manning the nearby gun emplacement. There was a lot more firing now. I looked out and could see the ISIS positions behind trees on the other side of an orchard. Apparently a squad of Kurds had struck out to the trees the previous night to act as a warning party, with orders to ambush any ISIS fighters trying to sneak into the compound. They were now engaged in a fierce firefight and it was clear we were under a determined attack.

The Kurd next to me must have been no more than eighteen, and he was clearly terrified. A few high rounds whirred faintly above our heads and every time he heard one, he flinched and ducked down behind the sandbags. I gave him a big grin and made as if to dance to the rhythmic beat of the dushka fire to try to ease his nerves. I then ran back to the sleeping quarters to get my PKM, set it up in the dugout and yanked back the cocking handle. It felt good to be locked and loaded with a fresh 100-bullet belt, but, just then, there was a massive bang. I threw myself to the floor – a split second later we were showered in dirt. I was numb with shock and about to sit up when there was a mighty 'CRACK!' above our heads. Fuck! The dushka was now very definitely aimed at us. 'CRACK! CRACK! CRACK!' I looked back at the building behind us and saw holes the size of dessert plates being blasted into the bricks. We crouched as low as we could into the sandbag emplacement, and the young lad didn't dare move a muscle. His teeth were gritted, his eyes wide with fear. The sound was incredible. Mortars, tanks, dushkas and small arms fire were all adding to the cacophony of noise. After an hour, the rounds were still cracking overhead and hitting the building and three tall trees behind our camp. Every so often, a branch as thick as my thigh would drop from the trees as if snipped by some giant invisible hand. There was so much sniper and dushka fire coming our way that I could hear the shrapnel landing all around me – a gentle tinkling sound of falling metal audible even above the explosions. One red-hot piece even landed in my lap. It was literally raining lead. Mercifully, the ISIS fighters were being prevented from storming our base by our Kurdish hevals, but the barrage of incoming rounds did not let up.

After four hours of fire, one of the YPJ girls was trying to bring some tea to the guys on guard duty when a bullet struck the wall behind her and shattered. Her legs buckled and she dropped like a stone as she clamped her hand to her head, with blood pouring between her fingers. The bullet fragments had torn a vicious gash in her scalp but, fortunately, had not penetrated her skull, and she was able to stagger back with the help of one of the sentries.

The sky was dark and thunderous, which seemed apt. As the battle raged, I thought of the young lives being snuffed out on both sides around me and other pale hands clawing at wounds, trying to plug the gush of crimson blood. It was utterly wretched. It was only the onset of rain which, eventually, lessened the rate of fire. We stayed on guard duty late into the afternoon, long after the last shot was fired. When I finally got the opportunity to head back to my sewer pipe, I made my way via the kitchen area behind the building and found a few crusts of stale bread so old and hard that they broke like crackers, though I was able to soften them with some jam I found in a tin. It was an injection of sugar I desperately needed. It was not just the ferocity of the sustained attack we had come under, the constant need for alertness or the oppressive weather. The whole place seemed to suck all spirit out of you, and I could feel my morale ebbing away. I missed the camaraderie of my old tabur, and I was not the only one. Others seemed just as depressed. David spent all day moping around, refusing to speak to me and looking utterly miserable. Dense fog had replaced the rain, and over breakfast of mouldy bread and some tinned tuna, we were told our guard duty was to be doubled in anticipation of another attack. I was not the only one to think we were being punished. I could understand why the new lads were there. They had left their post without permission. What had *I* done? I thought the Kurds from my tabur loved me. I was always the first to volunteer and I would follow Agir into hell if he asked me. What had I done to deserve this foggy purgatory? My foul mood was compounded when I heard David hadn't turned up for his guard duty the previous night. When I confronted him, he made no effort to defend himself. His shoulders were sagging and the tone of his voice was flat. He seemed a broken man. He told me his paranoia was driving him to despair and that he felt rejected by the group. He told me he was going to leave. An hour or so later, David began following one of the younger Kurds down towards the river. I raised my hand in farewell but he never looked back. I was surprised to find how much I would miss him. He was eccentric, but he had been the first international volunteer I had met.

Another night of long guard duties and shivering attempts to sleep through the bitter cold eventually brought a morning of warm sunshine and then the welcome arrival of US aircraft, which circled and repeatedly swooped, unleashing their deadly missiles. When they left, I was surprised to receive a text message from Bruce's wife, who was worried that she hadn't heard from him in a week. I replied that I hadn't seen him in days but that I had been sent away to the arse end of nowhere, and that Bruce was almost certainly in a better place than me and she shouldn't worry. Her concern became clearer when she told me that young Jac from Bournemouth had been shot in the arm in the fighting in which they had both been involved. Jac wasn't a big lad, so I imagined a bullet in his arm would be a horrendous wound. I had bumped into enough Kurds who had been shot in the arm and whose injured limb hung uselessly by their side. Poor immediate care often meant that being shot in the arm or the leg could result in death from blood loss or complete loss of limb function. Either way, I was sure Jac would be on a one-way flight back to the UK to get proper treatment. It depressed me that it would be one more familiar face that I wouldn't be seeing around. All I could do for the rest of the day was kill time before another freezing night on guard duty, this time with Jim.

I rose at 6 a.m. after very little sleep and went in search of food. We hadn't eaten or slept properly in four days, and there was mutiny in the air. While everyone hatched plans to get out, I was doing the opposite. If it was true that Agir had sent me away then I resolved to accept this tabur as my new group and knuckle down, but we were eventually called together and told we would be leaving our temporary unit.

The Christian village was even more beautiful in daylight, and by the time cars arrived to take us back, my mood was already brightening. Within minutes, we were all in high spirits – but it wouldn't last.

# Reality Check

As we pulled into the cattle yard at Tell Tamer, I was relieved to see a huddle of Westerners by one of the barracks. I could see Nathan's unmistakable outline, and Aussie Ronnie and others talking privately with serious looks on their faces. There was little reaction from the others and I called out to Nathan, 'Mate, where's the love? I was expecting a fucking hug!' He glanced at me and silently shook his head like he didn't know what to say. I looked around. 'Where's Bruce?' I asked, afraid of the answer. 'It's not Bruce. He's OK. He left yesterday,' Nathan said. 'Left?' I exclaimed. 'As in gone home?' Nathan nodded. 'Yeah, he's gone and I'm not far behind. Mate, we've been fucked! Half the tabur's injured and Ulcum's dead.' I looked around for familiar faces in the tabur but so many were missing. I felt distraught. Yes, we had endured our own firefight, holding the line, but I felt I should have been with my tabur while my friends were fighting and dying. I needed to speak to Agir.

It turned out that three days earlier, they had launched a day assault on the ISIS-captured town of Tell Nasri, just north of where we had been in Tell Fweidat and just south of where we were now, in Tell Tamer. With the support of armoured vehicles, they had been involved in some fierce urban combat until they had recaptured half of the town. Another tabur – with young Jac and Aussie Ronnie – had attacked from a different side of the village. That's when

Jac had been shot. He had been eager to stay and continue fighting but was ordered to hospital for treatment. He clearly had more about him than I had initially given him credit for. Inexplicably, after they had used the element of surprise and superior numbers to get the upper hand over ISIS, they were ordered to stop and to take the rest of the town the next day. Bruce and Nathan had tried to warn Agir that they should take the whole town while they had the advantage, then build defences in case of a counter-attack, but Agir was adamant. Inevitably, they came under sustained sniper fire throughout the night, and though the younger members of the YPG showed enormous courage, they also showed naivety in the face of the full ISIS counter-attack the next morning, and several were injured.

Apparently, Dilivar was going through the village like a man possessed, spurring them on. Bruce was dropping plenty of ISIS fighters with his sniper rifle, but more and more Kurds were also getting hit, and the ISIS onslaught continued, with their fighters getting close enough to throw grenades. Soon the guys were having to fall back, and what should have been an ordered retreat descended into chaos. The lack of body armour and poor medical facilities meant that manpower was dropping fast. Even the indestructible Dilivar took a bullet to the hand and some shrapnel to the face. He simply walked to a car and waited patiently for the driver to take him to hospital, while Aussie Ronnie was busy treating wounded YPG fighters and villagers alike. It was in the confusion of the retreat that Ulcum was shot as she made sure her girls got out. The fire was so intense that the rest of the tabur were unable to retrieve her body. Bruce was hit by a bullet which took the heel off his boot but luckily missed his foot.

When he met up with the others at the rallying point, the enormity of the shambles hit home, and Bruce, Jamie and Nathan, who were used to fighting with all the discipline and all the protection of soldiers in a Western army, decided that they had done enough for the Kurdish cause and were going to go home before they were killed on another failed mission. They had been sent back to the cattle yard to meet senior commanders and to collect their stuff. They had already met up with a weeping David who told them he felt 'dishonoured' at being left behind. Bruce, Jamie and David had all left together. Nathan, Texan Jack and Aussie Ronnie would be going home in a few days, as soon as a car was sorted.

To see the lads so despondent and to know they had all fought without me was hard to take, and was made even more so when I knew that so many young, inexperienced Kurds had fought too. The battle would have been the first terrifying taste of action for the young YPJ girls Ada and Shemal, who I felt so protective towards, and both had been wounded: Ada shot in the lower arm and Shemal in the upper thigh. When I was told by Nathan that Shemal had wept as she struggled to reload her AK magazine in spite of her injury, I thought my heart would break. Why hadn't Agir realised how fierce the fighting would be and that he would need his whole tabur? I felt bereft and there was an awkward silence in the room as I sat away from the others, until Jack said, in his deep Texan drawl, 'He's suffering from non-combat stress disorder!' His quip cut through the tension in the room. I turned to the wall, not wanting them to see the smile on my lips, or the hurt in my eyes.

★

The next day, after breakfast in the morning sun, Ronnie was keen to leave me his medic's kit. Very early on, the lads had impressed on me the importance of having a proper IFAK – individual first aid kit – and taught me how to plug a wound and stem bleeding, as well as showing me how to improvise a tourniquet from an AK-47 rifle strap. Now Ronnie left me his bandages, QuikClot combat gauze and proper tourniquets, and gave me an hour-long crash course on combat medicine. I volunteered to drive the lads to the rendezvous point for the supply lorry that would take them east.

I drove through Tell Tamer and further eastwards until we reached the reservoir base where we had arrived a long week ago, and the lads jumped out. I was keen not to shoot off straight away, and filled up the car with petrol at the nearby fuel depot. The lads joined me to offer unhelpful advice, and we sat on the back of the truck and drank a glass of chai as we talked about the past few months. When I hopped off to go and take a piss under a tree, Jack sneaked up behind me and kicked me in the back, which caused me to piss all over my leg, and we all laughed. 'Damn, I'm going to miss you bastards,' I said. Before long I didn't have any more excuses to stay, and when the lads went inside to get some lunch, I dished out some last-minute hugs and walked off.

There was a young Kurd standing next to the car with his friend and both chirped, 'Helllooo'. I smiled and said 'Hello' back but didn't break my stride. 'How are you?' said the nearest lad. I wasn't in the mood to help a couple of Kurds practise their limited English. 'I'm fine thanks,' I said, and reached for the car door. 'Are you an American?' the one Kurd persevered. I stopped and grinned at him.

'You speak English?' I asked. He told me he was from Kobane and that his elder brother had taught him to speak English. He said he was likely to be posted to Tell Tamer. 'Well, perhaps you'll see me there,' I said. 'What's your name?' 'Kendal,' he replied. I waved goodbye and drove off without giving the encounter much thought.

Back at the cattle yard, I spent the rest of the day in deep melancholy at the departure of my friends and in contemplation of the new group of foreigners. Jim, from Stoke-on-Trent, I had already begun to get on with. He was a sound lad and, as an ex-military guy, he really knew his stuff. He had studied philosophy and literature at university after his military service and then taught English to military cadets in Saudi Arabia. He had been inspired to join the fight in Syria after seeing a photo of an ISIS fighter waving around a woman's decapitated head. In the absence of Nathan, Bruce and Jamie, I felt I could learn a lot from Jim's military experience. That left Levi the joker, who had been in the Marines. He had done his basic training but only spent two years in the military and had never deployed. Levi said he had been discharged after being hit by a car. Syria, I guessed, was the chance to see the action that he never got before. Levi's zany impressions grated slightly less on me as I got to know him. Then there was Mario, the Portuguese lad who was apparently a military deserter who had gone AWOL from his country's air force because he felt compelled to fight against ISIS. I say 'military', but he was a cook and had about as much fighting experience as me. Apart from Jim, I had kept them at arm's length until now. However, at the back of my mind I was considering leaving my new group at the earliest opportunity. I felt like it would be a good time to be in a tabur as the only foreigner, to further demonstrate my solidarity with the Kurds, and I determined that, after I had spoken to Agir, I would request a transfer.

The next morning, we drove from the cattle yard at Tell Tamer to a village less than two kilometres to the south, where we were met by Tufan from my old tabur. I greeted him with a hug and he led us through a maze of alleyways and holes in the sides of buildings because we were clearly within range of a large ISIS village about 400 metres away. Ducking below the top of a huge earthen berm to avoid sniper fire, we reached the garden of a small house, where I saw Agir sitting with a few Kurds under a tree. '*Roj bos* [Good morning], Baran,' he said, but I carried on following Tufan into the house, where we dropped our bags. Apparently the large village I could see beyond the berm was in fact the town of Tell Nasri, where the tabur had suffered so many casualties and where Ulcum's body still lay. It was hard to look at the place. I walked back into the garden and made sure I had a translator with me when I finally got the chance to speak to Agir, because I wanted to be sure he understood the extent of my hurt. I demanded to know why he had taken Shemal and Ada to attack Tell Nasri when he could have taken me. His answer was simple: he had been ordered to. They knew they were likely to take casualties and a Kurdish general had especially requested that not all of the foreigners from our tabur should fight. They had already lost Ash and Kosta, and if they lost a big group of foreigners in one go, then it would be a major triumph for ISIS and a PR disaster for the YPG. Agir was asked to take only three foreigners, so he took the three most experienced. He didn't include

Jim, since Jim had not long since arrived, and he was never going to take David. 'If I had been allowed four foreigners you would have been there, Baran,' he said. The wind was taken out of my sails because I knew he was right. I regretted not having been with my friends, but there was a bigger picture. Now I was more determined than ever to carry on.

'Baran . . .' he said after a while. 'It's a good name.' I looked puzzled. 'What, "Rain"?' I asked. Agir smiled. 'It is the giver of life. It is what brings the hope of new growth. And we shall have new life in Rojava,' he said. I apologised to Agir for doubting him. He assured me that he wanted me by his side whenever they attacked again. We shook hands and had a try at some small talk. Someone brought over some tea and he watched patiently while I stirred in my sugar. When I had finished, I passed the tub of sugar over and he leaned forward to take it. 'I have more news for you, Heval,' he said, and his eyes glinted with mischief. 'You won't have to wait long to fight with me.' He smiled and leaned back with the sugar in his hands. 'We will attack again tonight. There are many enemy, but we will use the darkness! You and me Baran! We will go and destroy Daesh together!'

# Attack on Tell Nasri

My mind was in a whirl as I carefully organised my assault pack, then emptied it and tried again. The plan was to attack Tell Nasri at night, which meant all day to think about what lay ahead. I ditched my clothing and non-essentials but packed all my grenades and Ronnie's medical equipment, in anguish over what else to take and what to leave. With my body armour and extra ammo, I would have a huge amount of weight just when I needed to be light on my feet. With fumbling fingers, I reorganised my pack again. Nathan had left me his Dragunov sniper rifle, and I had passed on my PKM to Jim, but, as we would be attacking in darkness, my sniper rifle would be useless, so I opted for my AK-47 and stored the Dragunov.

At around 8 p.m. I was asked to do an hour's guard duty. Another tabur had arrived and more and more fighters were now milling around the camp. It was dark, but I still had no idea where I fitted into the plan of attack and the uncertainty was gnawing at me. All I knew was that Jim and I would be the only foreigners fighting and the others would have to pull guard duty and watch out for a counter-attack. It bothered me, too, that my desert camouflage trousers stood out in the moonlight. I had pulled a black top over my shirt, but my legs were too long for any of the Kurds' green uniforms. Without greater support from the West, the Kurds could only afford so many sizes of cheap uniforms. I had managed to find better quality US-made fatigues among stolen Iraqi Army gear abandoned by ISIS, but that suddenly didn't feel like a good thing.

Shortly after midnight, a Kurdish fighter motioned for me to follow him and led me to the other side of the village, where we joined a line of around thirty heavily armed fighters facing the earth wall, on the other side of which was the approach to Tell Nasri. 'Macer, is that you?' I could just make out Jim in the darkness. He joined me and immediately remarked on my trousers. 'You'll stand out like a target in those,' he said. 'Thanks for that re-assurance, mate,' I replied. There were about fifty of us by the time a Kurdish commander hissed, 'Move!' I looked at my watch. It was 12.10 a.m. as we climbed the soft soil of the berm and silently lowered ourselves into no-man's land.

About thirty metres ahead lay the ruins of a small hamlet, which presumably had been tactically levelled by the diggers that had built our defensive wall, but the piles of bricks and wood still gave some cover as we approached the enemy-held town beyond. 'Clang!' My stomach tightened as one of the Kurds accidentally knocked an old metal water tank with the butt of his rifle and the noise reverberated through the night air. I held my breath, waiting for ISIS sentries to open fire, but the silence was restored and we pressed on in single file, bunching up as we reached the other side of the ruined hamlet. Over a low wall, I could see the dark silhouette of Tell Nasri, no more than 300 metres away and well within small arms range. At that moment, the silence was shattered again, this time by the roar of an engine and the metallic crunch of tank tracks behind us. 'Fuck!' I thought. If our approach hadn't already alerted ISIS then this surely would. As we all moved forward, still in single file, the YPG tank drove past us and stopped in the middle of the field, about 180 metres from the enemy town. My heart was pounding. Why weren't ISIS firing? I was sure I would hear the snap of bullets any second. The Kurds headed towards the tank, which was the only available cover. If ISIS opened up now, a dozen of us would be cut down before we could hit the deck. Then came the roar of a second tank, this time with a dirty great headlight. With a sound of screaming metal, it roared into the field, its light bucking and swaying, one minute shining on the enemy positions, the next illuminating our column of fighters for all to see. 'Fuck, fuck, fuck!' The seconds it took us to reach the shelter of the first tank felt like hours, but still no sound came from the enemy. The second tank roared past us and came to a halt ten metres to our right. The driver cut the engine and the sudden silence was nearly as shocking as the noise.

The Kurds separated into small, prearranged groups behind the tanks, and I saw Agir clutching an M16 in one hand while talking into a radio in his other hand. He beckoned me closer. The back of our tank – an old Russian T-72 – was hot and stank of diesel. The other, I could now make out, was clearly home-made; a brutal mess of metal welded onto an old tractor. Its main weapon appeared to be a heavy machine gun. Agir asked me to join a small group of Kurds a short distance away. As I crouched among the semicircle of young YPG fighters and tried to memorise their faces in the dark, there was an almighty 'BANG!' Our tank rolled back a few feet as a flash of light erupted from its gun barrel. A second later, a massive explosion tore through one of the buildings in the enemy town and flames licked through its windows.

My ears rang with the percussion as the tank fired twice more, with equally devastating effect, but still there was no response. We ran forward in open-line formation and I followed the most senior-looking Kurd in my fire team. After about fifty metres I could see a ditch, which the Kurds were jumping in then forming a line on the far bank. I jumped down into it and I, too, levelled my rifle at the town in front, my heart still pounding. The home-made tank rumbled forwards and tried to cross the ditch but came up hard against the other side. The driver revved the engine, then stuck it into reverse and revved again. With a screech, the tank went a few feet up the ditch before rolling back down. 'Fuck, I don't believe this. The sodding tank's stuck!'

Directly ahead I could see a walled compound, with a big steel gate, and several two-storey buildings. There were dozens of windows and small sheds – all places for ISIS to hide – and we still had another sixty metres of open ground to cross. 'BANG!' Our T-72 decided to fire again, while the Kurds struggled to get the other tank out of the ditch. There was a flash of light, the 'Pammh!' of an explosion, then the sound of falling rubble as the entire corner of one of the enemy houses collapsed. With a roar, the home-made tank surged out of the ditch and didn't slow down as it rushed towards the walled compound.

Like something out of a First World War newsreel, the Kurds leapt from the ditch and charged towards the village – and I was up with them, running as fast as my legs could carry me. The tractor tank smashed straight into the wall of the compound, dust swirling in the light of its headlight beam. Seeing a piece of farm machinery ahead of me, I dived behind it for cover, followed by six Kurds.

I listened for the sound of gunfire above the noise of the tank, but still there was none. The tank roared backwards out of the compound and I jumped to my feet and gripped my rifle to my chest. This was it. I was going in!

I led the Kurds across the last bit of open ground towards the tank and the new 'entrance' it had made into the compound, but just as we were joined by another group of ten Kurds , the tank commander decided to go back into the compound! 'Shit!' I wouldn't have left my cover if I had known I would have to stand in the open, waiting for the fucking tank to come back out again. The noise was so loud I could barely think straight, as my eyes darted from window to window in the two-storey building, looking for signs of ISIS defenders. Then, with another roar, the tank came speeding back out of the compound and I noticed the front was a shower of sparks and flame. 'FUCK! WE'RE UNDER FIRE!' ISIS had waited for us to get within thirty metres before opening up, and we were sitting ducks. Almost the entire tabur had bunched up, ready to get into the compound, and there was no cover. I threw my rifle to my shoulder and fired at the building. I could see a thousand flashes in the darkness but could not tell if they were enemy muzzle flashes or our ricochets. Still standing, I put bullets into every window I could see. I must have fired a dozen rounds in just a few seconds and, above the pandemonium, I was suddenly aware of a different sound – the dull 'Thump! Thump! Thump!' of bullets striking the ground around me! I threw myself to the floor and resumed firing. Everyone else had done the same and we all blasted away in the darkness.

The tank was only ten metres away from me but was thankfully attracting most of the enemy fire. The bullets were bouncing off its makeshift steel armour in a steady stream of sparks. I looked around at the Kurds, expecting one of the commanders to take advantage. We needed to get up and run to the compound because the longer we stayed in the open, the greater the chance of us being decimated. A few of the Kurds had managed to get as far as the wall but there were too few to storm the compound by themselves, and they were staring back at us, clearly expecting to be reinforced. I stopped firing and reassessed the situation. I needed cover, and not just from the stream of rounds coming from the ISIS positions. My lungs were vibrating with the percussion of a Kurdish PKM that had opened up just a few metres behind me and the rounds were passing about two feet from my left shoulder. I immediately rolled to my right, belly-crawled for a few feet, then rolled again. I fired my rifle a few more times at the nearest window, then rolled again until I came up against something hard. I reached out with my hand and realised it was a tarmac road. It was only a few inches high, but it was some cover. Another roar, and the tank reversed backwards at speed out of the compound and kept going. The driver had presumably tired of being a bullet magnet and was probably afraid of being hit by an RPG. As the sound of the engine receded I was momentarily glad to be spared the noise, but then I realised the fire that had been hitting the tank was now being directed into the field. At us.

The sound of the bullets hitting the ground made my stomach churn with fear, as rounds smacked into the tarmac and whirred away. The Kurds behind us were giving fire support, but we were getting hit from the front and from the left flank. Then I saw muzzle flashes from the window of a building on my right and I thought, 'If we get hit from three sides, ISIS is going to turn this field into a meat grinder.' I swung round and put a few rounds into the window and, thankfully, the Kurds behind me had also seen the flashes and added a few dushka rounds. The air was buzzing with projectiles, and the fire was so intense that neither I nor anyone around me could shoot back. I began frantically pushing soil away with my hands – desperate to get a tiny bit lower to the ground. Even through my own terror I was blown away by the bravery of the Kurds. In spite of our predicament, not a single one of them was about to flinch without orders to do so. In the hailstorm of lead, one young YPJ girl next to me stood up and fired an RPG before hitting the deck once more. It was a wonder she was not gunned down. Our collective prayers were answered when another Kurdish dushka opened up from behind us and the rate of ISIS fire slackened significantly as the enemy was forced to take cover. With that, I saw groups of Kurds beginning to withdraw. It was a blessed relief to hear my name being called from behind me, and I joined the stream of shadows running back to the YPG lines. The ISIS fighters whistled and jeered at us as we ran.

Any thought of rallying back at the ruined village and trying again was put paid to by the 'Crack!' of dushka fire coming from the ISIS lines. 'Jim, is that you?' I asked as I saw a small group taking cover behind a levelled house and heard some muttered swearing in English. 'Yeah. What the fuck's going on?' he said. 'We're under dushka fire,' I replied. 'I FUCKING KNOW THAT! ARE WE ATTACKING OR WHAT?' he yelled in frustration. 'Oh,' I said, 'I don't think so. I think we're done here.' Moments later, our group joined the rest of the tabur heading back to our village. Clambering over mounds of rubble and exposing ourselves to the terrifying dushka rounds had not helped my own sense of confusion.

After a nervous hour of waiting for any ISIS counter-attack, I fell asleep outside in my kit before waking at 5.30 a.m. and finding a house with an electric heater for a few more hours of sleep. The rest of the morning was spent chatting with the other guys about the night's events before ISIS gave their own response to our failed attack with a salvo of mortars in the afternoon. There were only four, all off target, but the two-fingered message was clear. The only bright spot in the day was when Jac returned from the hospital. It seemed he had been incredibly lucky. An M16 bullet had gone straight through his arm, missing the bone and artery, but Jac was furious to learn the others had gone home in his absence. I hadn't got to spend much time with Jac during our week together at 'The Palace', but over the course of the rest of the day and the next, he and I were able to get to know each other better, and I found him a really good guy. I was seriously impressed that he was willing to stay and continue fighting even after being shot. He and I spent some time moving around our village with the sniper rifle, taking potshots at the ISIS-occupied Tell Nasri. I guess we riled ISIS a little because, after an hour, we took a few mortars, but they would become a daily occurrence anyway. We frequently had to take cover when we heard the ominous whistling of an incoming shell, including one time when I had to hang up on a call to my mother. I didn't want her to hear the sound of the shell going off, and I certainly didn't want her to hear me diving for cover.

To make things easier for translating, all the foreigners were asked to live together in one house at the northern end of the village. We were a motley crew – Jim, Jac and I from the UK, Levi from America, Mario from Portugal, and a few others. Whatever reservations I had harboured before about the guys were beginning to evaporate. Levi liked to compare his fight against ISIS to that of the Eagle Squadrons of American pilots who made their way to Britain during the Second World War and flew with the RAF before the US had joined the war. He would say that the American Eagles couldn't sit back and watch the Fascists roll over Europe, and nor could he stay at home and watch ISIS rape and murder their way across Syria.

That night we were ordered to prepare for another attack on Tell Nasri. There had barely been a moment in the two days since the failed attack when I had not relived the experience, and the idea of doing it again so soon made me feel physically sick. Naturally, I didn't let it show. I couldn't lose face in front of the guys, so outwardly I pretended I was ready for another go, but in reality I was utterly convinced that this time I was going to die. As I unpacked and reorganised my assault pack once more, my mind was racing. I couldn't stop thinking about my family and about the friends I would leave behind. I thought about an entire lifetime of happiness I was about to deprive myself of; the chance to marry and have a family. 'Oh God,' I thought, 'it would be so easy to fake illness.' No one at home would ever know that I had bottled it and ran away. I cleaned my rifle and checked my bullets. In my mind, I was a quivering coward, but I had no intention of leaving. We were told we were waiting for an American air strike and to try to get some sleep. At midnight I was shaken awake and my heart leapt in anticipation, but it was an order to go on guard duty and I stumbled outside. It was raining, and there was no cover as I sat on the earth wall freezing my ass off for the next two hours. Just as I got back to bed, I was told the attack had been called off, but my stress continued for the next week as every few days we were told to prepare for an imminent attack, only to be stood down each time.

The rain was becoming intolerable and the position had taken on a First World War feel as we waded through wide puddles and ankle-deep mud. The misery was compounded by the constant mortar attacks and the threat of sniper fire, and I was not able to stand properly outside, having to go everywhere bent double. The only relief came when I was either in bed or standing inside a building. Our situation changed after a week when Agir and my old tabur were moved back behind the lines and we had to join a new tabur. They seemed like a better-organised unit with better-trained fighters, led by a very capable young commander called Serxwebun. To my surprise, the first Kurd I saw in the new group was the young lad I had met when I dropped off Nathan and the others at the reservoir base. Kendal was a good lad and extremely funny. He had a strong 'don't give a shit' attitude that made his dealings with grumpy Jim amusing to watch. It didn't take long for me to become firm friends with Kendal, and with other Kurds in the tabur, such as Munzur the translator, an unlikely soldier who looked more like a professor than a YPG fighter.

Every day would bring false rumours of an imminent enemy attack, and at night I would do guard duty from 7 p.m. until midnight and then, after an hour's sleep, be woken to do another four hours. If we weren't listening to the enemy in Tell Nasri chanting from the Koran or singing Arabic songs, or to the Kurds whistling and jeering back at them, then we were listening to the nightly battles for the village to our north. In the morning, we would hear the reported death tolls from the attacks, and while we rested during the day, we would feel the room shake with the blast of another mortar attack. It felt like I, too, could die at any moment. I just wanted to get out of there, but not before we had achieved something tangible. Once we had taken Tell Nasri, the plan was to go Mount Abdulaziz and take the major ISIS base on top, opening up the road to Raqqa. Looking south from our position, I could just see the blue tinge of the mountain against the skyline, and I knew the magnitude of the task ahead.

Soon enough, there was a new plan to take Tell Nasri. In the middle of the night, Jim, Mario and I were taken off to join a separate fire team and to await the order to assault. Everyone was in good spirits, and even I was over my previous fears and eager to move forward. We sat around smoking and waiting while listening to a YPG artillery barrage, the scream of aircraft engines and the rattle of small arms fire. In the darkness, I suddenly felt Mario's hand reach out for mine. I was shocked and about to pull away until I felt a rough scrap of paper being forced into my hand. 'Can you give this to my family if I die?' Mario whispered, as the tank parked just outside our house fired another deafening salvo that shook the room. 'Of course,' I said, as I fumbled to put it into my pocket.

# On the Move

It was daytime. I could hear all hell kicking off a kilometre further down the line and knew that people would be dying, or being horribly injured; but, as I sipped my tea, all was quiet at our position and I could hear the birds singing. It felt as I imagined the trenches must have done in the First World War, with the routine of smoking, cleaning weapons and waiting for rubbish food, while elsewhere the fighting was murderous. And then the peace would suddenly be disturbed by the horrifying whistling of a mortar and we would take to our slit trenches in fear for our lives again as another building in our village was destroyed by the blast. The last planned assault had been cancelled because a preliminary attack by another tabur had been ambushed by hidden ISIS fighters, with the loss of seven YPG guys, and we settled into a brutal routine of night-long guard duties and tedious days punctuated by nervous patrols into no-man's land, enemy sniper fire and mortar rounds. One mortar exploded just outside the room in which we slept and we all stumbled out of the building coughing from the noxious smoke.

After a month of inactivity, the Kurds had begun to allow us shopping trips into Tell Tamer to try to build up morale. It was costing me a fortune to make sure the tabur shared in the treats of cakes and cola. During one trip, I managed to email Bruce and Jamie. Bruce was back with his family and Jamie was with a girlfriend in Erbil. The word on the grapevine was that the next big operation was imminent and, keen to help, Bruce and Jamie managed to supply us with some decent aerial shots of the villages we expected to be fighting in. Just before he signed off, Jamie suggested I join him in Erbil. 'Don't go to Tell Nasri, Macer,' he said. 'We nearly died in that place and, by the sounds of it, so did you. I've got a bad feeling about it.' He was not only a good soldier but a good friend, and if a former Marine who fought in Fallujah suggests you should stay away from somewhere, it's probably worth taking his advice, but I couldn't allow myself to turn away without having accomplished something for the Kurds.

Towards the end of April, we were told we would be moving to another position further down the line. The change of scenery would do us good and relieve some of the growing tension. People were falling out frequently, and I'd had a few clashes with Jim. He was dour but a good soldier, and I really liked him, but we were different personalities. He was a real anarchist – a natural protestor – and we argued furiously over many things, but there was no lasting animosity. It had been a weird existence, living with the constant fear of ISIS attack, dodging the snipers and dreading the mortars that were slowly destroying the village and churning up the fields around, but we had become used to the place, so it felt odd to climb into the truck and wave goodbye to the base. Our next position was a line of brick houses straddling the main road south of Tell Tamer. About 800 metres away were three ISIS positions – a small village on the left flank, another small village in the centre, and Tell Nasri on the far right. I was proud to be asked to organise the internationals for guard duty, so when I organised the sentry positions, I made sure to give myself the unpopular stints. Kendal often came over for a chat. We would sit together for hours talking about home, our past lives, our hopes for Kurdistan and our shared hatred of ISIS. The Kurds called the guard duty *nobat*, but since they could be six hours long, we christened them 'no-bed'. On this particular occasion, Kendal pointed out the ISIS positions and updated me on the new plan. The northern part of Tell Nasri had been too well defended. By taking us south, the commanders hoped to take the two smaller villages and then swing upwards through Tell Nasri's soft underbelly, but there was no saying when the next operation would take place.

April had become May before we met Heval Simko, the senior YPG commander for our entire front line. I had met him when I first entered the country, but after the success of the Tel Hamees operation, he had been promoted. He came round to chat to the foreigners, but first he took me aside and, through a translator, he said, 'Heval Macer, the friends want to thank you for the work that you have been doing in the media.' During our six weeks facing Tell Nasri I had been writing to newspapers in Britain about the Kurdish struggle against ISIS, and it seemed my efforts had been noted. When we were all gathered together, Simko thanked us all for fighting. He said the Americans had been staggered by the recent successes and were beginning to make the YPG central to their plans to destroy ISIS. In fifteen days' time, he said, the US would give 24/7 air support for an operation to liberate Mount

Abdulaziz. It would be a massive step forward in the fight to open a land route to Kobane and to the ISIS de facto capital in Raqqa. 'Then we won't be on the defensive all the time,' said the tabur's German Kurd translator, Dilsoz. 'So it will be our turn to strike at the heart of ISIS!' I said with a smile. 'Yes, we will go to Raqqa soon, but this mountain needs to fall first. It is like a door, a doorway to Raqqa,' he said.

Back on the front line, the YPG diggers built a huge berm to protect our position from ISIS snipers, and things started to become a little more relaxed. Once upon a time, a gunshot whirring over my head would have sent my heart pounding, but now I simply shuffled lower into my seat and resumed my silent watch of the ISIS positions. The sudden release of adrenaline didn't seem to come to me anymore – it didn't surprise me that many people describe war as a drug. I could see how old soldiers could become war junkies, having slowly built up a tolerance to the horrors of combat and thirsting for greater quantities of action to push their boundaries. I'd even come to enjoy guard duties and with the warmer nights I had taken to sleeping outside.

We were visited again by Simko, who told us the Americans had got their act together a lot sooner than predicted. With action imminent, we foreigners began training to sharpen up our drills, and Jim put us through our paces practising patrolling to contact, working in fire teams and house clearing. We also did more Kurdish training with the entire tabur. As we sat for days waiting, I could see and hear the sights and sounds of battle all around us; the distant thud of shell and air strikes; the flashes of light; the roar of US jets and the hum of Spectre gunships overhead.

Poor Kendal was becoming exhausted with the extra guard shifts. As one of the more senior Kurds – even at his young age – he was usually in charge of the night guard and had to roam the perimeter with night-vision goggles, checking the sentries were all alert. When he passed my guard position, I liked to surprise him with an energy drink, which he needed more than me. He had become such a good friend. While on guard duty he could be moody and serious, but at other times he was full of fun. We found some old rollerblades in one of the houses and I laughed until I cried at the antics of my Kurdish friends. Kendal on rollerblades was like Bambi on ice. It was crazy to think both Kendal and Dilsoz were only twenty-two. The men and women of the YPG and YPJ were inspirational to me: an entire generation mobilised towards the liberation of their country and the foundation of a democracy.

As I lay on my bed on the afternoon of 14 May, Jac popped his head around the door and smiled. 'Have you heard? We're leaving tomorrow. *Roj bos*! We're going!' Our tabur was going to swing north to join the forces heading south-west from Sari Kani, bypassing Tell Nasri and liberating the countryside west of Tell Tamer from behind. After all that had happened in Tell Nasri, I had hoped to be part of the force that finally liberated it, but there was a new plan.

In the early morning, we hit the road, heading north through Tell Tamer, then west from Sari Kani, through villages reduced to rubble and past burnt-out vehicles at the side of the road. As we swung south, we were joined by two other taburs, so there were now twelve Hiluxes in our convoy, with at least 120 YPG and YPJ fighters on board. In one of the vehicles, I noticed Agir sitting in the front seat and we both burst into grins and waved at each other. When we pulled off the road into a field and disembarked, there must have been more than 200 Kurds. There were ISIS prisoners too, handcuffed and blindfolded in the back of vehicles coming back from positions to the south. They were of fighting age but not in uniform, and they pleaded that they were just local shepherds, although when quizzed, they could not name any of the local places any more than I could. Around us, tanks and APCs were parking up in the field, the sky was full of US planes, and every so often an enormous explosion would rip through some of the houses to the south.

At around 11 a.m. the next morning, we separated into two groups for an assault on the village ahead of us. Some YPG taburs had tried to take the place the day before but had come under intense fire, so this time we were going to go further around the flank to approach it from the East. Jim and I were with the Kurds in one group, Jac in the other. We drove in Hiluxes to a group of houses where a huge anti-aircraft gun was firing at the enemy village around 900 metres away and Simko was scanning the ISIS positions, looking for movement and weighing up his options. Eventually he called our tabur commander over to him. Serxwebun was one of the youngest tabur commanders in the YPG at barely twenty-five, but he was renowned for his bravery and good humour. A brilliant soldier who expected the most out of people around him but was quick to smile if something amused him. With a wave of his hand, Serxwebun began to walk into the stomach-high wheat and grass of the fields that surrounded the enemy village. Our eleven-man fire team followed in single file towards a group of farmhouses 400 metres ahead. We soon split into three fire teams of four, ten metres apart. My heart was racing, but otherwise I felt oddly calm. I wouldn't know if I was in somebody's rifle sights until it was too late, and I could imagine someone looking at me right at that moment, just waiting for me to get into range, but there was not much I could do about it.

We made our way across the fields at a jog, and the weight of my assault pack and armour made me pant, as my eyes darted back and forth from the horizon to my feet, looking out for ISIS fighters ahead and IEDs below. I zigzagged around any slight disturbance in the ground, but that became almost impossible when we reached the last fifty metres of the field, which had been ploughed, and my stomach tightened with every tentative step. We cleared the buildings, then Serxwebun decided to send two lads across the 500 metres of open ground that lay between us and the enemy village to reach an earthen reservoir in the centre. It was just a circular berm, fifteen metres across, that trapped rainwater, but it offered some cover for our final approach. No sooner had the lads got halfway to it, however, than we heard the snapping and whirring of rounds, and they had to dive behind the berm and start returning fire, while the rest of us took cover in one of the farmhouse sheds. Another two lads were sent across the open ground to reinforce the guys at the reservoir. 'Fuck!' Even if we all made it to the reservoir alive, we still had a few hundred metres of open ground to cover before we reached the village, I reasoned.

Jim and Dilsoz were sent forward to the reservoir next, and I scanned the village with my binoculars. I could see no signs of ISIS, though I knew from the rounds pinging all around me that they were definitely there. I looked to my left, and a YPG T-72 rumbled into position among the buildings and – 'BANG!' – with a flash from the gun barrel, one of the houses in the ISIS village collapsed in a cloud of dust, smoke and flames. Moments later, there were loud snaps in the air as the YPG behind us levelled the anti-aircraft gun at the same spot in the village. A couple more hours of sniping and shelling followed before American air cover arrived, and with a massive 'Whhhhooooopppppp! Whhhhooooopppppp!', two missiles smashed into the ISIS village. The shockwave hit us like a gust of wind and all firing stopped, as a huge mushroom cloud rose above the enemy position. I grinned and was about to move forward when the ISIS firing started up again. 'How the fuck did they survive that?' I yelled above the noise of the barrage.

After a difficult night guarding the farmhouse against counter-attack, we were roused at 7 a.m. by the fresh sound of gunfire, and soon a small squad of Kurds piled into the back of a tank and roared towards the village, with Jim giving covering fire with his PKM. Twenty minutes later, the tank returned, and we piled into the back ourselves. There were ten of us in a space big enough for eight, and I was half lying on Dilsoz, my head and knee bashing against the sharp metal interior of the tank as we bumped violently across the rough ground at speed. The stink of sweat and diesel was almost overpowering, but did nothing to dull the sharp pain that shot through my body with every bump. After what felt like an age, we ground to an abrupt halt, and the driver screamed at us to get out. I emerged blinking into the bright sunlight, the air buzzing with rounds coming from all directions. The tank had parked just five metres from the walled courtyard of a house on the edge of the village, which gave good cover from the fire coming from within the village to our right, but, to my confusion, there were also rounds snapping just above my head from the left. I ran as fast as I could into the courtyard and threw myself behind an old metal water tank. 'Why the fuck are we taking fire from the left? ISIS aren't supposed to be there.' Just then I heard a cry of pain and saw one of the YPJ girls rolling in agony on the porch of a house. I grabbed my assault pack, with Chris's medical kit, and made my way over to her as fast as I could, ducking behind walls as the rounds zinged and cracked into the masonry. By the time I reached her, she was already in a bad way. A bullet had struck her in the stomach and come out of her side. One of the other girls had removed her scarf and tied it around the wounded girl's waist, but it had done nothing to stop the bleeding and there was a bright crimson pool congealing around her. When I went to dress the wound properly, the wounded girl cried out and pushed my hand away, and another YPJ girl told me to leave her alone. I had heard from other foreigners that some of the YPJ would refuse treatment from a man in order to protect their modesty. It seemed crazy to me. She was going to bleed to death if she didn't accept treatment, so I reached inside my bag for some gauze, but again she shook her head and cried out – a mixture of pain and protest. Thankfully, Serxwebun arrived and shouted into his radio for the tank commander to bring his vehicle inside the compound. Realising they were about to evacuate the girl, I decided to join Jim in giving covering fire. By the time the tank was reversing across the field with the casualty, the gunfire and noise was dying down, until it became oddly silent. One of the

Kurds tossed me the injured girl's bag, which was full of spare ammunition and grenades. It was still wet with her blood, which covered my hands.

The lack of gunfire, it seemed, was because ISIS had been forced out of the village to a school some 200 metres to the south. I was ordered to join a few Kurds guarding the left flank while Serxwebûn prepared for the main assault on the school building. It turned out to be a walk-over, but I spent an uncomfortable night behind a petrol station wall, staring out across the open field in case of an ISIS counter-attack. Half of the effectiveness of the ISIS fighters wasn't their military prowess but their carelessness for life. The wild and aggressive tactics of the death cult could cause confusion and fear in undisciplined troops, which was why they had experienced such success against the Iraqi and Syrian conscripts. Eventually I was relieved, and went to lie under a tree five metres from the sentry position. I curled up under a blanket next to my rifle and, with my spare hand, took a grenade out of my assault pack and pushed it into my trouser pocket. If ISIS did get over that wall, then I would use my rifle to fight them back and, as a last resort, I always had my grenade.

# The Doorway to Raqqa

I woke early the next morning, did the first guard duty, then took the opportunity to explore our surroundings. The discovery of a mud-brick dwelling piled high with pressure plates, car batteries, home-made Claymore mines and suicide vests near to where I had been sleeping reminded me of the continuing ISIS threat. Minutes later I got another reminder — a text from a UK journalist informing me that ISIS had attacked Ramadi in Iraq and routed a large Iraqi Army contingent. There were videos circulating of burning Humvees, Iraqi soldiers lying dead in ditches and ISIS fighters grinning into the camera as they found soldiers hiding among the ruins and dragged the crying conscripts to a pile of their comrades' bodies then shot them in the back of the head. It all seemed a world away from my war against ISIS, where they were retreating from Kurdish forces and cowered pathetically when caught. I texted defiant messages to any journalists that contacted me for comment and once again urged UK political and military support for the YPG, before we were on the move again.

We arrived for the night at a hamlet in the middle of nowhere, and were joined by some Kurdish lads from a different tabur, who insisted on sharing a box of cakes. Our new Kurdish mates made us laugh until we cried by dressing up one of their number in clothes they found lying around in one of the houses. However, an hour or so later the mood was much more sombre as the Kurds gathered to hear accusations that one of our tabur had been killed the day before by friendly fire. A young lad in the same attack group as Jac admitted that he had thought our tank was an ISIS vehicle. Since he had fired at us, and because one of our comrades had been hit by a PKM round through the guts, the lad had a potential manslaughter charge hanging over him. I felt tremendously sorry for him, even though I, too, could have been killed by his bullets. I had previously spent many an evening laughing and joking with him, and it was tough to see him stripped of his weapon and under armed guard. In the end, he was deemed to have been negligent in the extreme and ordered to leave the front line immediately. He looked devastated as he was put into a car and driven away. Tragically, it was the last time I saw him. He was allowed to return to duty in another tabur but was killed just two months later in a gun battle with ISIS.

With the impromptu court martial over, we were ordered into the cars and told we would be advancing towards the distant Mount Abdulaziz. Twenty minutes later we roared into a deserted village, where I realised the three Hiluxes already parked up belonged to my old tabur. Our car had not even come to a complete standstill before I jumped off and began embracing my old friends, Agir Tufan and Chia. These were guys I had spent months – and countless guard duties – with. We had laughed by campfires, shivered in the cold, sweated in the heat and dodged ISIS bullets together. Since my Kurdish was still so bad and their English was non-existent, I'm fairly sure that so much love has rarely been shared with so few words. With a cup of tea in hand, and Dilsoz to translate, Tufan explained how hundreds, if not thousands, of ISIS fighters had been fleeing in cars and on foot even before we chased them out of the last village, and they were now streaming in disarray back to their regional HQ at the mountain. With many caught in the open by the American planes, Tufan spoke of fields littered with ISIS body parts and burning cars on roadsides. His tabur – my old unit – had counted 140 ISIS bodies in different places. The shambolic ISIS retreat was a world away from the images that had convinced me I had to come to Syria. Maybe I had fallen then for the propaganda that this death cult was organised and unstoppable, but I'd chased these bastards for nearly five months and quickly learned that they were nothing more than knuckle-dragging thugs with guns, happy to shoot unarmed women and children in a ditch, or take a knife to a kneeling humanitarian, but were powerless in the face of a determined, superior force.

The next morning, more taburs began to arrive, followed by several tanks and half a dozen dushkas, and at 11 a.m. we were ordered to saddle up and move out. 'Hurry, Baran!' shouted Kendal from one of the cars, and I ran to jump on the bumper of the nearest vehicle, which was a dushka with eight people already clinging on to the back. We bumped west, then swung on to a tarmac road heading south. I could see in the distance Mount Abdulaziz in all its glory, a formidable feature, and if it did indeed contain ISIS's main base for the region, it was surely going to be very well defended. We were by now part of a vast convoy, but we had to move slowly because of the very real fear of IEDs. When we passed the last village and there was only flat desert between us and the lower slopes of the mountain a few kilometres away, Commander Simko directed the taburs to spread out into battle formations. The drivers revved their engines and two dozen vehicles, in a line 500-metres wide, accelerated towards the mountain and our first target – a small steep-sided hill, the plateau top of which was well positioned to prepare an attack on the ISIS positions. We were so close now, but if the approach was mined, or the ISIS PKMs were waiting for us, then I knew not all of us were going to make it.

The mountain was a lot wider than I thought, stretching east to west for several kilometres, and at the bottom were a number of settlements where ISIS were likely preparing to make a stand. We skidded to a halt in the shelter of the hill and I was out of the vehicle in half a second, my rifle cocked and ready to fire. I stopped to grab my sniper rifle and a couple of its short magazines, but, with my adrenaline pumping, I soon caught up with the others and was among the first wave to reach the summit, then ran, stooping, the fifty metres or so to the far side. We were about a kilometre short of the mountain and even with the naked eye I could see people running among the houses of the ribbon settlement at its base. To get a better look at the enemy, I pulled out my sniper rifle and scanned the village through the sight. The ISIS fighters were in disarray. Most were already fleeing up the mountain slope. One of our APCs and two dushkas arrived and began harassing the village with 50-calibre fire. The sun was baking hot and my position on the ground felt like I was lying in a frying pan. A huge explosion erupted ahead of us, then more. American planes were smashing any resistance on the slopes and more and more of the terrorists were running in all directions as they sought a way up the mountain. I was desperate that we should move forward quickly. The Kurds were expert mountain fighters and would massacre the undisciplined ISIS stragglers, I thought, but, as usual, caution was the prevailing tactic. Only when we had been watching, frustrated, for four hours did we get the order to advance.

The APC rumbled forwards to draw any fire, and we followed in our Hiluxes, closing quickly on the ISIS position. But the village was empty. The terrorists had escaped, and the next few hours involved nothing but house clearance. From the distant noise, it was clear any fighting was going on elsewhere. As night fell, I stuffed a black ISIS flag into my bag as a trophy before we travelled west along the base of the mountain to an area of desert where the taburs were coming together once more. We were briefed that there was a town halfway up the mountain that had a large contingent of ISIS fighters hidden among the houses. Even further up at the summit, perched at the top of a sheer cliff, was the main ISIS base for Rojava. It seemed we would get our big clash with the cornered terrorists after all. There were to be two main attack groups with the first, all-Kurdish group going a mile up the road to the town. They set off on foot and soon disappeared into the night. Jim and I were the only foreigners assigned to the second, support group while the others were told to get their heads down and sleep wherever they could find shelter. Nearly two hours passed before one of the APCs turned up at midnight, and we climbed into the back with eight Kurds. It took an agonising ten minutes of lurching around hairpin bends in the pitch black interior of the claustrophobic steel box, fearing at any minute we could be incinerated by an RPG, before we came to a jarring halt and the doors swung open to reveal we were in the target town.

I could hear the shout of Kurdish voices and the crash of doors being kicked in, but there was no gunfire. Serxwebun was there and ordered us to help clear the last few streets. It was obvious that the town, like the village below, was empty. Our expectations that the ISIS thugs might stay and fight had proved wrong. It was just as well. I was by then staggering with fatigue. We had been running around since 6 a.m. and it was nearly 2 a.m. before I was able to get my head down.

I was woken by the morning sun on the back of my head. I was lying on my front and could taste dirt in my mouth. I rolled onto my back and looked up at the blue sky. There were birds chirping merrily around me as I staggered to my feet and tried to get my bearings. I felt groggy, like I'd been on the booze all night and woken up in someone's garden – something that I'd certainly done in my previous life, which now felt like a hundred years ago. The rest of the international volunteers had arrived in the town in the early hours, and Jim and I were about to join them when we were told we were needed for a renewed mission to storm the ISIS base at the top of the mountain. I didn't have time to feel apprehensive. I got my kit together and we jumped in the back of a couple of Hiluxes with twenty YPG and YPJ fighters. The mood was tense. This would surely be ISIS's last stand on the mountain. They had nowhere left to defend.

# Mountain Men

The main ISIS base was now within sight, but, as we passed an old farmhouse, we were stopped by a couple of Kurds who told us that another tabur had gone on ahead of us to clear the summit and we were no long needed. The battle for Mount Abdulaziz was apparently over, and Jazira Canton had been liberated. The ISIS base at the summit had been devastated by US air strikes and had been captured without a fight. Any surviving ISIS fighters had fled down the southern slopes.

As soon as we were able, Jac and I hitched a lift in a car taking water to the guys and girls at the top of the mountain, so that we could see for ourselves. At the summit, there was a brand new tarmac road leading to a huge radio facility which had been badly damaged. Among the ruins were a number of dead ISIS fighters – or the remains of them, at least. The bodies were lying with a wrecked motorcycle among what was left of some trees. It looked like the men had been in the process of fleeing when a missile had struck. There was no crater. Instead it looked like someone had gone through the area with the most enormous hedge cutter and sliced everything, the ISIS fighters included. Only two of the four bodies were still intact, and one was a lad no older than fifteen. His body barely had a mark on it. His face was like marble, unblemished and serene. His long brown hair gently flickered in the breeze. I would have sworn he was asleep had I not realised the back of his head had been cleaved away and his brains were hanging out. The boy was in better condition than the two guys who had been sitting on the bike. They were literally in pieces, the largest of which was a leg. I felt some pity, for the boy in particular, but I had seen plenty of bodies and was becoming immune to the horror. More important to me, as we wandered around their wrecked HQ, was the proof that ISIS's grip on Jazira Canton had been ended, and it was a symbolic moment I wanted to treasure. I had promised to fight ISIS until they had fled Rojava. When I had arrived they were everywhere, and it was the YPG that was losing. Just five months had passed and now, with US air support, our little army had liberated an area of land the size of Rhode Island or Wales, and the YPG had emerged as a serious player in the Syrian War; a player that could bring peace not only to Kurds but all Syrians, regardless of their faith or ethnicity.

There was still a long way to go to win the war, I knew, but once we came down from the mountain it was clear that, for the rest of the foreigners, the fight was over. People were tired; they had endured six months of nothing but bad food and stress. Jim, Jac and Levi all wanted to head to Erbil and then home. I would be the only foreigner left with this tabur and it was going to feel strange, but I was acutely aware that while we could go home, the Kurds could not, and I wanted to show some solidarity for a while longer. As the others left, I joined my tabur in a minor operation to arrest ISIS stragglers below the mountain. One, in particular, gave the lie to their fearsome reputation. He looked about twenty and had been found hiding in a shed. He was hungry, dirty and scared, with the wide-eyed look of a man who had not eaten or drunk properly for days. He was wearing a ragged ISIS uniform and clearly hadn't washed in weeks. If he was expecting to be executed or, at the very least, beaten up, then he was mightily relieved. Seeing the Kurds put a bottle of water in the prisoner's hands made me realise that, amid all the carnage of this war, some decency still prevailed. I helped the handcuffed man onto the flatbed of a Hilux, and watched as he was driven away to be handed over to the police. In all, we managed to round up seven ISIS stragglers without a fight before night approached, when we headed back up the mountain and settled down to sleep wherever we could find any shelter on a windblown outcrop.

I woke the next morning to find that only a low stone wall was separating me from the edge of a thirty-metre cliff. Further exploration of our surroundings revealed it had been a major air-defence installation for the Assad regime before it was taken over by ISIS, but US missiles and bunker-busting bombs had completely destroyed it, and the smell of decaying bodies was emanating from the rubble. With about fifty YPG fighters and fifteen or so YPJ at the base, finding any shade was at a premium, but finding food – and especially water – was even harder. It was no surprise, then, that in the first few days, half the fighters went down with stomach problems and I, too, became ill with diarrhoea. With stomach cramps and nothing but liquid pouring out of me in sweat and shit, I was spending most of my day lying on the hot earth and under the scant shade. After five appalling days, a commander turned up and saw that our exposed, unsupplied position was untenable, and we were ordered into trucks. Unfortunately, where we were going was even worse.

After a thirty-minute drive along mountain tracks, I recognised the new tarmac road and realised we were at the ISIS base I had seen with Jac. At least it was a pleasant surprise to see my tabur in full strength, manning the defences and setting up camp in the only three buildings that had survived the US air strikes. Although the water situation had improved slightly, the tabur's morale was at a new low. There was a belief that this position was going to be our new home for at least a month or two. The food was appalling. There was no gas delivered to us to cook with, and the mountain had so few trees that gathering firewood was near impossible. We had tinned meat and stale bread every day, and the flies descended on us like one of the great plagues of Egypt. They got everywhere, forcing their way into the packets of bread and into our eyes and mouths. The thought that they had been feeding on the remains of the dead ISIS fighters was enough to explain why my crippling diarrhoea was not getting any better. When we weren't breaking our backs building better defences around the camp, we lay almost comatose on the concrete floor of our building, exhausted from our guard duty, thirsty, hungry and sick. And this was victory!

The bodies of the dead ISIS fighters I had seen had been removed, but the stench of decay was still in the air. I put this down to the remaining lumps of flesh and offal that still littered the ground. In the heat, the blood had fried and stained the ground an oily black, and the flesh had blackened and shrivelled. The nights were especially uncomfortable, with no mattresses, and each blanket had to be shared by three people. We were warned constantly that ISIS would counter-attack in force, so our guard duties were doubled, putting extra stress on morale. It took me a few days of sitting on guard duty to work out that the stench of decay was worst when the wind was blowing in my face, meaning it was probably coming from the bottom of a gorge away from the camp. Eventually, I and a few others went to explore, and we saw four body-shaped blankets at the bottom of the gorge. Whoever had been tasked with burying the dead ISIS fighters had presumably realised very quickly it was impossible to dig a hole in the rock and had just dumped the remains. As we approached, a blue cloud of flies rose with a hum from the nearest blanket. Black liquid was oozing out of the sides, crawling with maggots, and the rotten smell clawed at the back of our throats. The Kurdish lad next to me doubled up and retched loudly. Our smelly, windswept hell was made worse later, when one of the lads on my sentry position disappeared with a can of petrol and soon a black cloud of smoke rose from the gorge. I swore, jumped up and ran to stop him, but it was too late. The bodies were all burning furiously. My worst fears were realised when, for the rest of the day, the wind blew the thick black smoke and the smell of roasting flesh directly into our camp. It was the final straw.

I was tired to the very marrow of my bones. My nerves had been stretched raw, I was sick and getting weaker by the day and my body weight had started to plummet. I was well overdue a break at home, to spread the word about what I had seen. I was not the only one struggling. On the day I put in the request to leave the YPG, the Kurds held a series of meetings to discuss the recent operation, singling out for praise those who had performed well and fiercely criticising those who had misbehaved. One of the younger guys in the tabur, another Agir, was well liked by everyone, but he refused to accept criticism of his arrogant behaviour so, in the end, he had his rifle confiscated and was sent to sit in shame in an empty room for a few days. It hardly seemed an extreme punishment to me, but at the end of the first day, and while the guard was distracted, he walked downstairs, picked up someone else's rifle and, in front of a shocked tabur, placed the muzzle under his chin and pulled the trigger. Although his face was a mask of blood, he was still breathing. I was told later that he had angled the shot so it came out of his cheek and, though he survived the experience, I never saw or heard of him again.

I felt like shit. This mountainside was tearing the tabur apart, and yet there were some brighter moments. As the only international volunteer left in the group, I became even closer to the English speakers, Rem, Dilsoz and Kendal. Kendal and I spent hours drinking chai, smoking and talking politics, or dozing in the sun only to be frequently disturbed by explosions. The YPG sabotage squads had buried defensive mines but the heat would set them off, and on one occasion such a blast had had me leaping from my bed and grabbing my rifle. I was about to return to my bed, having discovered it was not an ISIS counter-attack, when I saw Kendal coming up the road with an enormous eagle wrapped in a blanket. 'Look, heval, I have a pet,' he said with a grin. 'It was injured by the mine.' Kendal warily put the animal on the floor and leapt backwards out of the way. The blanket fell away and the fearsome-looking bird fixed us with a glare from behind its vicious, curved yellow beak, but made no attempt to move, swaying slightly on its weak legs. Its left eye was badly damaged and there was blood dripping from its wing. It was still a beautiful animal, but if the blast had damaged its balance or its ability to fly, then it would surely starve to death. Kendal opened a can of meat and tossed lumps to the bird, which stared at the closest morsel before returning its glare to us. 'See, this meat is so bad not even the animals will eat it,' said Kendal with a laugh. 'I will call him Shaheen.' It meant 'hawk', and the bird became something to distract us from the hardships we were suffering. The following day, it ate some of the food and managed to walk around, though it was no friendlier and still tried to bite any of us who dared to go too close. After a few days of care, Kendal was able to touch the bird. He gently cleaned the blood off the wing, but was always ready to jump backwards if the bird went for him.

After several weeks on the mountain, we were finally told we would be moving back behind the lines for a rest. I was still sick and losing weight, and I was keen to get back to the UK to see my family. I knew that Quentin Sommerville and his crew were at the training camp, and I thought I could make an impact in the UK if they documented my journey home and highlighted what I had been doing.

In the meantime, and with only days before we were due to be relieved from our mountain posting, Kendal stepped up his efforts to get Shaheen airborne. We took the bird outside, stretched its wings and pushed it to fly, but it was having none of it. That night, I saw a hint of desperation in Kendal's efforts to feed the eagle. The next morning, once the trucks were packed up, Kendal and I took Shaheen out for a final attempt at getting him to fly. I could hear the orders for us to join the trucks and Kendal swore in Kurdish, picked up Shaheen and tossed him a foot in the air. The bird didn't have a chance to react, let alone bite him. It fluttered its wings in a panic but landed back on the floor in a heap of indignant feathers. 'Heval Baran!' Rem called out to me. 'Fast, fast! We go!' Perhaps realising his time with us was over, Shaheen suddenly stretched his huge wings and, with a few flaps, began to fly at head height, with Kendal running after him. I felt a surge of adrenaline and joy and ran after them. I heard Rem give a shout of protest behind me but I didn't stop. I wanted to catch Kendal and the fast-disappearing bird. We followed the road out of the camp and down the hill, past the place I saw the burning bodies, away from all the mines, the flies and the rancid smells. The bird swung away from the road to the edge of the mountain, where the rock fell away in a 100-metre-high cliff, then suddenly it felt the familiar surge of thermal currents under its wings and quickly soared fifty metres above us. Kendal and I stopped, panting, just a few metres short of the cliff edge, and stared in wonder at the bird and at the breathtaking view of Rojava stretching out beneath us.

# Return to Rojava

I placed a comforting arm on Jordan Matson's shoulder as we looked down at the recently dug grave and he fought not to shed a tear. A small olive tree adorned with ribbons and a simple wooden patriarchal cross wrapped in a colourful shemagh marked the mound of sun-baked earth that was Kosta's final resting place. Around us were hundreds of gravestones, not on the parched summer plains of Rojava but amid the greenery of a Nottingham cemetery. Kosta was home. I felt privileged to be there, to lay flowers with Jordan and Jac and Kosta's mum and dad, Vasiliki and Chris, and to leave a personal note for Kosta. A temporary memorial plaque to Erik Konstandinos Scurfield bore the legend '02.03.2015' – the date of his death five months earlier – but already it seemed like a lifetime ago.

I had hit the ground running on my return to the UK in June. The BBC team had travelled back with me on the flights to England, so the day I arrived back it was headline news on TV. There were no police waiting to arrest me because the YPG was not a terror group and I had broken no laws. I had been very open about what I had been doing in Syria, but it felt surreal to watch the coverage over a cold beer with my parents, who were so grateful to have me home. As they witnessed my journey, my guilt at going away had quickly evaporated. I had so much to tell them about the Kurds. 'There is something special in Rojava,' I told them. 'There is a genuine chance to have a renaissance right in the heart of the Middle East.' I was interviewed on Radio 4 and Radio 5 in the week that followed; I did articles for the *Telegraph* and the *Guardian*; one of my videos got a million views; and I found an ISIS jihadist pictured on Facebook, on a Turkish beach surrounded by British tourists, which made the *Daily Mail* and Channel 4. My social media following was growing fast on the back of a documentary made by three former British army officers who had spent time with us, and I was determined to capitalise on my fifteen minutes of fame to spread the word and educate people about the Kurdish cause. I had no illusion that I had been the greatest fighter or that I had been through the hell that some others had, but I had a voice and an opportunity to use it, and that was as powerful as any gun.

I was brought down to earth by the most sickening of blows. As I celebrated word from Syria that my first tabur had been involved in liberating villages around the strategically important town of Tell Abyad, the dreadful news about Heval Agir came. My friend, my first commander, was dead, killed by an IED blast that had also killed one of the YPJ girls. I struggled to take it in. I pictured him drinking tea with me and playing chess, promising with a twinkle in his eye that we would fight side by side together against Daesh. Now he would never again take the fight to the terrorists, or see the sun rise on a free Rojava. I remembered the girl, too. Just nineteen, she had joined the YPJ straight from school and was one of the kindest-hearted girls in the YPJ. She had once grabbed me by the scruff of the neck and dragged me into the back of a

Hilux because I was in danger of slipping off the back of the truck as we were moved quickly between battlefield positions. She had apparently been killed instantly by the blast which blew off Agir's leg, and he had bled to death. I could feel my seething hatred of ISIS rise anew, and I felt so angry and so helpless, so far away from my friends who were still fighting and dying. I wanted to be with them to help. I consoled myself that what I was doing to promote their cause in the media was my contribution.

It became a habit for me to check the YPG website daily, dreading the faces I might recognise among the şehîds – martyrs – listed as killed in action. It was torture to open the page each time, but I had to know. About a month after my return, and shortly before I visited Kosta's grave, my fears were realised. First I learned that my German friend Dilsoz had been killed by an IED as my old tabur, led by Heval Serxwebun, had made their way to Tell Abyad, and that Cher, another guy in the tabur, had been shot dead by a sniper. Worse was to follow. After the Tell Abyad offensive, the rest of the tabur had been sent to seize a village between Al-Hasakah and Mount Abdulaziz and had been almost wiped out in an ISIS counter-attack. I don't know if someone fell asleep on guard duty, but somehow scores of ISIS fighters got back into the village at night as the bulk of the tabur slept. My translator friend, Munzur, had been shot in the stomach and the arm, though he had survived. Rem had been killed after getting other members of the tabur to safety, and so had two of the YPJ girls. I forced myself to read on, and the final blow was perhaps the hardest to bear. Kendal, too, had been killed in the attack. I felt the pain like a knife to the guts. I stared at my friend's martyrdom pose on screen with tears in my eyes. I would learn later that he had fought off the ISIS invaders to the end, though badly wounded, and had saved a grenade for himself and for his attackers when they finally closed in on him. It was scant consolation to me that he had died as he would have wanted, and that the tabur eventually fought off the ISIS counter-attack. He and Rem had told me they would one day take me to see the bright blue flowers that carpeted their beloved mountains in summer, but Kendal had told me, too, that he was sure he would eventually be şehîd. The only mountain flowers I could now imagine were on his grave, and I felt like I would never feel such sadness again.

It made me all the more determined to champion the cause of my friends, and I threw myself into my public speaking with yet more passion. I travelled to America to raise awareness of the struggle going on in Rojava, and gave lectures at universities there and in the UK. In New York, I met senior representatives of the PYD (Kurdish Democratic Union Party) and the SDF (Syrian Democratic Forces). In London, I met senior members of the British Government with links to the security services and told them about the Kurds and how important it was to support them. I went with Kosta's mum, Vasiliki, to the Foreign Office to lobby the head of the ISIS taskforce, who we were able to educate about the YPG. The response was not too encouraging, but it felt to me that at least the Kurds and the YPG had a proper voice in the UK. For the first time, they actually had people sitting down in front of the BBC and in front of major politicians saying, 'Let me tell you what I saw out in Syria; let me tell you about the Kurds and what they are fighting for.' I felt I had really come into my own. At the same time, I always knew that

I would be going back to Syria and that I would fight again. The job wasn't done.

I started to wonder what I could do differently that would help the Kurds the next time I went. The YPG was becoming more professional and the US had helped to create the SDF, but Ronnie had ignited a spark in me when he gave me his medical equipment in Tell Tamer and bemoaned the number of Kurdish casualties who were bleeding to death unnecessarily from survivable wounds. I decided I needed combat medics and individual first aid kits (IFAKs) – like those used by the British and American military – which I could hand out to the Kurds and train them how to use them. My first recruit was a giant New Zealander, Big T, who I met at one of the university lectures I gave about the Kurdish cause. Big T had served in the British Army and was clearly a well-trained soldier with combat medic experience. Ryan was next to join me after he answered my online appeal for experienced combat medics. He was a former US soldier from Kentucky who had fought in Iraq in 2005. I spoke to him via Skype and he was a really good guy – very intelligent, very eloquent and very knowledgeable about the Middle East. He put a lot of effort into sourcing the right IFAKs, which I bought, along with other medical equipment and a drone, with the £7000 or so that I had managed to raise from family and friends. My final recruit was another American, Chris, who was prepared to fund his own way in order to be involved. I arranged with the YPG for Big T and Ryan to go on ahead, because they would have to go through the Kurds' training camp in spite of their military experience, while I carried on trying to drum up support from the UK. Eventually, I, too, headed East.

There was an air of déjà vu as I exited the Sulaymaniyah airport building into the bustle of the Iraqi streets and jumped in a taxi to rendezvous with my YPG contact. He walked me to the new safe house and there, asleep in the front room, was Mario. I had last seen him before the Abdulaziz operation and it was so good to see a familiar face. He grinned sheepishly when he woke and saw me. The Iraqi/Syria border was still controlled by the Peshmerga, and the Kurdish Regional Government had ordered the stopping of all traffic in and out of Rojava. It had been a nightmare getting out of Rojava in June. Now, to avoid arrest and certain deportation, we were going to have to find a different way to get in. Fortunately, our YPG friends were nothing if not resourceful. I was wedged between two other volunteers – Mario on my right and an American guy called Jordan MacTaggart on my left – on the back seat of a 4x4 as we were driven in civilian clothes westwards, towards the border. As far as any Peshmerga checkpoints were concerned, we were simply heading for the town of Duhok on business. After a while, however, we pulled off the road and changed into Peshmerga uniforms, and then headed north-west towards the Sinjar Mountains, being waved through roadblocks with barely a cursory glance inside by the guards. It would have taken only one Peshmerga soldier to ask for my ID, or even to speak to me in Sorani (the Kurdish language in Iraq), and we would have been found out. Fortunately, they didn't.

I was impressed by Jordan. He was young and pugnacious despite never having been in the military – he'd been something of a rebellious punk teenager, I'd gathered – and he had already gained a reputation for fearlessness among the YPG and his fellow internationals. He had been fighting in Syria in 2015, aged just twenty, when he had been shot in the thigh during a firefight near Suluk and inadvertently left for dead by his comrades. Alone in a field, he risked being shot by ISIS if he broke cover and was in danger of being mistaken in the dark as an enemy fighter if he crawled towards his own lines. Bleeding badly from the wound in his leg, he feared he would not survive the night, so he recorded a last message on his phone, saying goodbye to his family, saying how he didn't regret fighting or dying, and urging the Kurds to carry on their revolution. It was heroic stuff. Obviously, Jordan didn't die, and the next morning he crawled back to safety, to the amazement of his YPG comrades. He had been evacuated home to America, recovered, and was now on his way to rejoin the YPG. I found him to be good company on the long drive – sensitive in spite of his bluntness. He was an anarchist who had found that the Kurdish cause chimed with his sense of allegiance to anyone who didn't have a fixed place in the world, and it was because of that same sense of fairness that he was determined to help stop the relentless and merciless spread of ISIS. As we drove, we talked politics and about our shared belief in the Kurdish fight for Rojava. The Kurds had given Jordan the nom-de-guerre Cîwan Firat but, in spite of their admiration for his bravery, the YPG fighters affectionately called him 'Jin' – Kurdish for 'woman' – because of the gauge earrings he wore. Jordan found it hilarious. Since he routinely referred to his colleagues with insulting nicknames, he wore his own like a badge of honour. Mario, I obviously already knew. He had come to Syria aged twenty-one to try to impress his father and uncles, who were all either in the army or security forces, and he had told a Portuguese magazine he did not regard himself as a mercenary because money was not his motivation.

Before too long the rocky shape of Mount Sinjar emerged on the skyline, and it was as beautiful as I remembered it. We skirted around it, through more Peshmerga checkpoints, and finally arrived in YPG territory. It felt strange to drive past familiar landmarks, including our old position at 'The Palace', but good to see women hanging out washing and children playing at the side of the road in peaceful surroundings. What was also clear to me was an increased Coalition presence, with US Special Forces bases and US helicopters overhead. As we drove from the plains up into the hills, towards the new academy for YPG internationals, there were signs of the oil industry everywhere, and I couldn't help feeling a flair of anger at the world. If only these people would be allowed to export their natural assets as a sovereign state they wouldn't be so reliant on food aid from the West. People just assumed all of Syria was broken and dysfunctional. Aid was only being sent to refugees in third countries like Turkey and Jordan, yet here, in front of my eyes, was a functioning state that no one wanted to help.

It was good to catch up with Big T and to meet Ryan face to face. He was a solid-looking guy, about six-feet tall, muscly, with brown hair and a strong Kentucky accent, and he was keen to get on with the job. Now I just had to get all the necessary permissions for our medical team. I spent weeks writing endless reports and asking for meetings with various commanders, but they didn't like the autonomy I was asking for, travelling up and down the front lines giving medical classes and handing out IFAKs. Things had changed since my first year, and the more professional YPG had introduced a 'note' system that controlled troop movements. It made sense but was unpopular with the internationals, because it meant we were more tightly controlled. For me, it also took away some of the endearing amateurishness of the early conflict when the YPG were fighting for survival.

It helped that, in late January, I had a chance meeting with another international volunteer, Joe Akerman, who had an excellent reputation with the Kurds and foreigners alike. 'Keep it simple,' he told me. 'Mould your unit around the structures the YPG already has.' With that, I dropped the idea of a small independent training unit and instead began asking for my own YPG tabur. Our aim was to completely reinvent the way that front-line casualty care was offered in Rojava. The Kurdish commanders were keen to improve the care for their soldiers so I started to make better progress, but we still needed vehicles, a barracks and permission to recruit a few more members for the team. In the meantime, I took Big T and Ryan to the former cattle station at Tell Tamer in the vague hope that I would be able to bump into a major YPG field commander. Chris joined us there.

Hundreds of YPG fighters were mobilising for a rumoured major offensive against an ISIS stronghold in the town of Ash Shaddadi, near Al-Hasakah, to the south of us. There was also an all-foreigner tabur led by an American called Servan Amriki, and I was delighted to see Mario with them. He seemed to be in his element. They called themselves the 223 tabur – in honour of the date (23 February) when Ashley Johnson had become the first international volunteer killed. In return for a few hours of medical training – our first 'customers' – and the promise of some IFAKs, they allowed us to stay at their base in the cowsheds, which they had transformed into first-rate accommodation. By the time the Shaddadi offensive was launched, I was in a dilemma. Should I attach our small team to the YPG column in the hope that we could make ourselves useful in action, or should I keep negotiating for official recognition and for the vehicles we would need to be effective? I decided to send Big T, Ryan and Chris on the Shaddadi operation while I went to Mount Qarachogh for a meeting with the YPG's senior command. It was gut-wrenching to watch the guys hitch a ride to the front line on the back of a truck, knowing that I wanted to be with them, but I wasn't just a fighter any more. I was trying to build something long-lasting.

The slopes of Mount Qarachogh were where I had spent my first few days in Syria, at the oil installation the previous year, but further up at the top of the mountain was the nerve centre of the YPG – its command base, barracks, weapons store and media hub. The press centre when I arrived was a hive of activity, full of dedicated teams of reporters, cameramen and fixers, all in uniform. Most of the young men and women had served on the front line. They included my friend Munzur, who was working in the media team providing local news in Arabic and Kurdish. He had talked to me while we were in Serxwebun's tabur together about his media training and his aspirations to be a journalist, so it was great to see him alive, in spite of his injuries, and following his dreams. I was so damn busy during my first week on the mountain that I felt like one of the team. When I wasn't writing a detailed report requesting my own tabur, and getting it translated into Kurdish for the commanders to read, I was doing Skype interviews with broadcasters as varied as Sky News and Russia Today. I was expected by many media outlets in the UK to give a running commentary on the unfolding Shaddadi operation and, as I was in the main military HQ, I was perfectly placed to do that. I messaged Big T on a few occasions but got nothing back. Thankfully, the YPG were making good progress and the ISIS forces in Ash Shaddadi were in retreat. Finally, I was called to a meeting with my friend Mo, who dealt with the English-speaking press and who had good news for me. A senior commander was due to arrive at the mountain that evening. He would not have time to see me but was aware of my plans, and Mo said he would hand him my report. A few hours later I was in the media building, texting my mother, when Mo walked in waving an official-looking document. It had the seal of the YPG High Command at the bottom. It was written in Arabic but Mo quickly translated it for me. 'It says you have permission for a vehicle, a facility in Tell Tamer and that you must report to the YPG HQ in Al-Hasakah,' he said with a grin. I leapt to my feet and gave him a hug. I was a tabur commander! Only the American Servan Amriki had previously achieved that as a foreigner.

To make things better, I finally got word from the guys who had managed to make themselves useful on the Shaddadi operation. They were now waiting for me at a hospital in Al-Hasakah. The next day, I was put in a luxury minivan that was clearly used by VIPs. I felt pretty damn good being driven in style all the way to Al-Hasakah to see my team.

# Medicine Man

The hospital was a military facility for YPG and YPJ casualties coming in from the Shaddadi operation. Big T and Ryan had built an excellent relationship with the hospital management and had been trusted enough by the Kurds to assist with patients coming in from the front line. They had been given quarters in a bungalow on the roof and were full of praise for the hospital staff, but frustrated at the failure of the front-line fighters to stabilise their wounded colleagues. Time and again the injured weren't getting fluids, pain relief or even having their wounds dressed properly before arriving in Al-Hasakah. This meant people were bleeding out somewhere along the hour-long journey from the front line to the hospital and arriving dead or beyond help. The lads had received one particular casualty who had been shot in the chest. Someone had tried to plug the entry wound but not the exit, so when he arrived at Al-Hasakah, he was pulled out of a blood-filled vehicle and was dead before he made it to the operating table. He couldn't have been much older than eighteen. It was proof that what we were offering – in front-line IFAKs and training – was desperately needed, and if we could grow the unit and acquire ambulances, I knew we could save dozens of lives.

★

A few days passed while I waited to be seen by the top YPG commander in Al-Hasakah, and we got into a routine at the hospital, with Big T and Ryan assisting the doctors and me focusing on my media work. The Shaddadi operation had been declared over, but ISIS commanders had switched tactics and began sending small teams of snipers to the town and surrounding villages. The casualties of these attacks were coming to us in a steady trickle. As my confidence grew, I began helping out the hospital staff, redressing wounds or cleaning up.

As well as the YPG casualties, there were other reminders of the war being waged a few kilometres south of us. I was surprised to find that Big T had helped to rush an ISIS casualty into the operating theatre with multiple gunshot wounds. The next day, one of the doctors invited us to the room where he was being held with a rifle-toting guard on the door. I looked down at the injured enemy fighter. He looked like a child and could not have been much older than fifteen. 'He's been shot in the head and the wrist,' said Big T, pointing out the injuries. 'He'll be dead soon.' The boy's face was indeed yellowish and he had dark bruises around his eyes. 'His organs are failing. I'd be surprised if the kid lasts more than a few hours,' Big T added. The lad reminded me of the dead ISIS kid on the mountain, and I felt a glimmer of sympathy. I was sat on my bed the following morning reading emails when Big T walked in after an early shift. 'Kid's dead,' he said, picking his own phone off his bed. 'Died at some point in the night.' He turned and went outside to sit in the sun, and I was surprised to realise how sad I felt. He hadn't been some evil killer. It was the so-called Islamic State that had stuck him in a uniform and sent him to die.

We needed a translator, and Ryan recommended a Kurd from Sweden who had fought at Ash Shaddadi. Firat was a badass character with a shaved head and a fat cigar in his mouth when we met him, which had earned him the nickname 'Kurd Diesel', after the movie star Vin Diesel. He was a welcome addition to our growing team and an important cultural link with the Kurds. We were soon invited to the Al-Hasakah YPG HQ and led into a living room where a senior commander was waiting for us. As tea was poured I launched into a description of our unit and showed him my documents signed by the YPG High Command. He nodded and said he would sort out accommodation and a vehicle. I told him we only had a couple of AK-47s between us and that we needed better weaponry, but he frowned and asked why ambulance drivers needed guns. I insisted again that we weren't paramedics but combat medics, and the first job of a combat medic was not to become a casualty. We needed to make sure the enemy kept their heads down while we tried to get a casualty out. He didn't seem convinced, so I got Chris to show him some video he had taken of the guys during the Shaddadi operation. Unfortunately, the only footage of note was of Big T treating a guy who had managed to shoot himself in the foot quite a way back from the front line. I tried to play up the importance of the treatment and said how painful a foot injury was, but the commander burst out laughing. He lifted his shirt to show us a terrible scar on his stomach and told us how he had once had to run more than a mile to an ambulance holding his guts in. He rolled his sleeve back and showed us a bullet wound to his forearm. Finally, with a grin, he showed us a bullet wound – to his foot! I felt deflated, but the meeting was still a success. He ordered a minivan to be brought to us and told us to go to the cattle station in Tell Tamer in a few days, where we would be given our own building. We returned to the hospital to start packing our stuff and celebrated with a few bottles of Pepsi. 'What shall we call ourselves?' someone asked. I recommended naming ourselves after a British *şehîd* like Kosta, but Big T said, 'We're the first medical tabur in Rojava. We need to sound professional. How about the Tactical Medical Unit?' Ryan's eyes lit up. 'The TMU,' he chorused. It was absolutely right. 'That sounds awesome!' I said. 'We're the fucking TMU!' We cheered and laughed, and in that instant, the TMU was born.

Our first operation as a unit was to head south to Ash Shaddadi, where we were directed to a front-line position ten kilometres southwest of the town. We finally reached a YPG-held hamlet about one kilometre north of a much larger ISIS-held village. With the enemy so close, we immediately came under mortar attack and, as I dived under a tank for cover, it brought back horrible memories of Tell Nasri. At least there was talk of a new operation soon and our chances of being involved were boosted when 223 tabur arrived. I waved to Servan as they parked up. Since the last time we had met, I was now the proud commander of my own tabur. OK, so it was not on a par with his, but we had our own vehicle and a noble intent. We discussed me helping to get supplies for both our taburs and he explained that there would be an operation the next day to recapture territory that had been seized by ISIS in a counter-attack a few days before. I went to see the rest of his tabur and laughed when I saw

Mario. His face, like his PKM and ammunition belts, had a thick coating of white dust and his uniform was almost crunching with filth. I went over to give him a hug and when I slapped him on the back, a cloud of dust came off him. I was more than a little envious that they had all been involved at the sharp end in Ash Shaddadi while I and my team had been at the hospital, even though I knew we had been doing good work and laying the foundations for even better work.

That night, I was woken to stand guard duty for an hour, and more memories of Tell Nasri, and the long guard duties with Kendal flooded my mind. It was a small consolation to be back in Rojava, which I loved. I even appreciated the cold, as I buried my nose and mouth into my thick Kurdish shemagh.

In the morning, there were hundreds of YPG fighters congregating in the hamlet. It promised to be a big operation, and, thankfully, Servan offered to lend us the weaponry and ammunition we needed. Soon enough, the convoy of Hiluxes roared into life and the operation started, but all that we found was a series of deserted villages. Wherever we went, ISIS had departed. Every civilian we passed had the same story. ISIS had been there the day before but when they heard we were coming, they primed their IEDs and left. The war-weary civilians happily took the YPG to where the IEDs were hidden, but they still needed clearing. We were held back a short distance while the YPG went about their work, but when a huge explosion sent a plume of smoke into the air, and the radios burst into life with reports of casualties from an IED, I stuck my foot on the gas and we roared into the heart of the village and pulled up outside a school. The guys leapt out while I turned the vehicle round and prepared to receive the wounded. One fighter's head had been blown clean off, but there was a second casualty. His brain was hanging out of his skull, he had a sucking chest wound, a broken arm and terrible lacerations to his face, body and arm, but he was still alive. Just. The guys put in a chest seal, gave him oxygen and set up a nasal tube, then got him onto the stretcher. Our vehicle was not going to be suitable, so I helped Big T and Ryan get the guy onto the back of a YPG Hilux and it sped off. We had treated our first casualty on the front line and in front of a host of Kurds and their commanders, which did our credibility a huge amount of good. The guy sadly died at hospital but at least we had given him a chance and provided some comfort and dignity in his last moments.

We made our way back to the cattle yards to reflect on what we had done and, taking our lead from what Servan's tabur had achieved, we threw ourselves into rebuilding our facility, turning it from a cowshed into a medical centre. With the help of the other guys, I had raised money through crowd-funding to renovate a military-grade ambulance and to buy more medical equipment and construction materials. We rebuilt walls, relaid tiles, put in new window panes and installed the internet, turning it into a top-notch facility. The whole team came into their own, and I was seriously impressed. We had started so well, and went to the front a few more times and trained hundreds of fighters.

More people were beginning to join us now, as word about the TMU spread, and for a few months we had a team of ten. It should have been great, but pretty soon there was a lull in the fighting. The days dragged into weeks and then months with no action. There was a high turnover of personnel, which didn't help, with people I didn't really want to join being allowed in and others who I rated being prevented from joining because of a restriction on our numbers. It all added to the frustration.

We were, nevertheless, training hard every day, from 6 a.m. until late, but the aggravation among the team grew worse and people started to push for us to go to the front – any front with fighting. They had joined us expecting to be treating combat casualties and nothing was happening. We were doing good work, handing out the IFAKs and training other taburs, but that was not enough for many of them. Morale was suffering and discipline, too. Worst of all, some of them would sneak out and come back drunk. I should have punished them, but they were all volunteers, so what sanction did I have against them? I knew that a big operation would sort out all of our problems.

Meanwhile, having ten testosterone-filled men stuck in a converted cowshed with zero action to occupy them meant that there were bound to be clashes, and I was forever putting out fires. Big T and Chris had been bickering for some time, and things came to a head after we visited the city of Qamishli, stayed over in a hotel and Big T got uncontrollably drunk on vodka at dinner. At one point, Chris poked him in the stomach as he told him he was showing us all up. A couple of days later, Big T was clearly still riled, so when Chris bought some cooking spices out of the tabur budget, Big T went crazy. I was outside of our base on the phone to my parents when I heard a roar inside. I ended my call and ran in to find Chris and Big T trying to kill each other. Big T had his hands round Chris's neck and Chris bit him on the finger, drawing blood. I was yelling at the top of my voice for them to stop and eventually managed to drag them apart. I sent Big T to stay at 223 tabur's base for the night. The rest of the team told me Big T had gone mad, so the next day, when Big T said, 'It's him or me,' I told him, 'Look! Don't put me in this position because you're not going to like the answer.' Big T was unpacified. He insisted, 'Get rid of that guy or I'm leaving,' so I said, 'Fine. You're gone.' Ryan stepped up as chief medic and did a great job, along with others. They completely reorganised our internal training, but as the general lull in the fighting continued, the team were increasingly restless. Guys were threatening to leave on a daily basis because we were not seeing any action, but when I called a meeting and asked if they wanted to go to the front, they voted to do more training! I was really struggling to keep control. Some continued to do a great job, but others seemed to go out of their way to fall out. I used to go for long walks by myself and sit for hours, breathing in the fresh air, watching the sun go down and praying to the sky for a big operation that might bind everyone together. The infighting got worse, and people were blaming me.

Around this time, Mario began to visit us from the nearby 223 tabur, complaining of headaches and a lack of energy. We gave him a drip to rehydrate him and some painkillers, and urged him to eat and drink more. He began to complain of feeling isolated in Servan's tabur, and he asked if he could come and join us. I explained that we needed medics, not fighters, but that when the tabur grew, we might be able to find room for him. I wasn't about to start poaching Servan's fighters. I thought Mario was perhaps keen to hang out in a tabur less strict than Servan's, but a German guy in my unit told me, 'You do realise that he is not just sick. He is depressed. He has all the symptoms.' I felt so sorry for Mario, but there was not much our little unit could do for him. I said, 'You must tell his commander, who may be able to change his situation.' I was sitting in our facility one day when two guys from 223 came in and asked if we had seen Mario, who had gone missing. Ten minutes later, another guy rushed in and said, 'Mario has fallen over. It looks like he's been hit on the head by something.' I told Ryan to take the medical kit down to 223's base while I went to get our ambulance ready. A matter of moments later the guy returned, panting, and said, 'He's not breathing!' As Ryan and ran to 223, I jumped in the ambulance. Internal roadworks meant I had to leave the base, drive on civilian road and re-enter at another gate to reach 223's facility. When I pulled up outside a disused barn five minutes later, one of the guys tapped on the window and informed me, 'He's dead, mate. He shot himself.' I was struck dumb. I walked with some trepidation into the barn and there was Mario, lying on his back, his head propped up against a hay bale, where the guys had tried to treat him before they had realised what had happened. If it were not for the trickle of blood from his nose, Mario could have been asleep in the hay, eyes closed, but a pistol lay nearby and what you could not easily see was the small exit wound at the back of his head. My heart sank. A fly was buzzing around the blood and I swished it away, then sat on the ground next to Mario and held his hand. It was still warm, but slowly growing cold. I felt numb.

Mario's death compounded our poor morale, and Ryan and Firat left soon after, but we had some fresh faces arrive who gave me some good advice. We really stepped up the training of taburs, and finally there was a chance of some action. A massive operation to cross the Euphrates and to capture the city of Manbij was brewing, and I told the YPG commanders how important it was for us to be involved. As it happened the TMU guys would be going, but not with me as their commander. The final straw came when someone from within the unit showed the YPG command a photo of us having a beer on the base. It was not as if I permitted regular boozing, but I was going to the commanders on a weekly basis and they would say, 'We heard that someone from your unit got drunk in town. Why did he do it?' and I would say, 'I didn't know that he *was* in town,' and they would say, '*Why* didn't you know he was in town? You're their commander!' My admiration for how the Kurdish commanders held together their taburs was immense, but, proud as I was of what we had achieved in the TMU, I did not want to carry on doing what they did.

At the end of May, I was summoned to a meeting at the academy on Mount Qarachogh. Everyone in the unit knew it was ominous. All the guys came out to say goodbye and to give me a hug or to shake my hand. I told them, 'Whatever happens, there are no hard feelings. Keep going, and I hope that the TMU is a great success.' I felt my heart sink as I drove away.

# The Road to Redemption

After all the despair in the TMU, it would take me a few days away from the unit to realise what a huge amount of good we had achieved. At least during my week at the academy I got to see my old friend Levi. I had grown fond of him, and we had kept in touch by email when he went back to the States. His presence was a reminder to me of our first year in Syria, when we were all together and Mario was still alive. We spent a good five days together, chatting or watching films on his laptop. I'd watched the Vietnam war film *We Were Soldiers* on the front line with the guys in the first year, but it was good to see it again with Levi. He was gripped by it. We shared long guard duties and remembered previous times on the front. 'Look, mate,' I said, 'what I want you to do, after this, is move to the UK and live with me and my family for a bit.' He had told me how he had studied carpentry and I told him of an idea I had come up with of building a classic Riva-style wooden speedboat. 'We could do that. It could even be a business venture,' I said. He laughed. 'Yeah, definitely. Let's do it!' he said.

My time with the commanders at the academy and with Levi helped me to come to terms with what had gone on in the TMU. If I had been frustrated, it was because I cared so much about it. I had put my heart and soul into the medical unit, and I had had so many plans for what it could become. I reflected on the hundreds of IFAKs I had sourced, that I had shipped to Iraq and smuggled over the border, and that we had distributed, and the hundreds of fighters we had trained. In doing so, we had pioneered a concept that was entirely new to the YPG but which would save many lives. I wished I had done things a little differently, but I also recognised how much other people had put into the TMU.

At the end of the week, the academy commanders agreed to send me to the front, and Levi and I sat next to each other on the bus as we shipped out. After a stop at Kobane, I was about to re-board the bus with Levi to Manbij when the Kurds stopped me and told me, 'Your note says you're going to Ain Issa.' I just had time to mouth to Levi, 'I'll catch you later,' and then he was gone. Ain Issa might have been 'on the front line', but as the bus pulled into the empty town it was like a scene from a western movie. The long dusty main street was totally deserted, and at the end was a former Assad military base that was bombed out. All that was missing was tumbleweed. A little to the south of the town, on the edge of the desert, was my position – a YPG base which consisted of a square earthen berm surrounded by trenches, with a few concrete buildings in the centre reinforced by soil and sandbags. The only way in was via a bridge that could be removed, making it a real fortress. I was, nevertheless, full of optimism; still so pleased to have had the weight of responsibility for the TMU taken off my shoulders. One of the few English speakers in the all-Kurdish tabur, Merdan, led me to the building where I would be billeted, and as we walked, I heard the whistling of mortars followed by several explosions a few hundred metres beyond the berm walls. 'What's the fighting like here?' I asked. Merdan looked at me with a little surprise. 'We haven't had any real fighting here for months,' he said. I was dismayed. While the TMU was sent to Manbij without me, it seemed like I was in a place where people were sent to be forgotten.

My only glimpses of the Manbij operation were the grainy news reports on an old TV in the mess room, and the only sign of ISIS was through binoculars, more than 800 metres away on the other side of the flat plains. It was an opportunity for me to understand the Kurds and their culture; to take time out and to reflect, which was what the commanders wanted me to do. The conditions were tough, and the weight began falling off me. In the heat of the sun, we would have to move huge sandbags to help further reinforce the fort, but there didn't seem much point. There was only flat desert between us and the ISIS positions, and we would easily spot any attempt by them to attack us across the open ground. At least, as the only foreigner, I got time to spend with Merdan, who spoke of his love for the international volunteers, having fought in Kobane alongside an American called Keith, whose hand he had held as he died from gunshot wounds. It also gave me a greater insight into the Kurds and what was important to them, and my admiration for them grew. Merdan told me: "Don't worry. I, too, have felt wrung out. What matters is the future and how you pick yourself up."

Manbij, meanwhile, was continuing to be a massive problem. For a long time, it had been called 'Little London' because of the number of British and other European ISIS fighters there, and it was a key point for ISIS supplies coming from Turkey on route for the ISIS capital at

Raqqa, so ISIS was determined to defend it at all costs. The fighting was brutal, and the casualty numbers, on both sides, were horrendous.

After two months at Ain Issa, I had had plenty of time to think. I felt I had earned the right to return to where I could help most, and the commanders agreed. 'OK, you can go to Manbij,' they told me, and they gave me a note to join my former comrade Tufan, who was now a commander of his own tabur. I gave Merdan a present of some of my belongings, including a treasured knife, and I began to pack. When I was ready to go, I saw one of the commanders wearing my knife on his belt and I asked Merdan why he had given it away. He said, 'Because he needed it.' It was typical of how unmaterialistic the Kurds were, with no sense of ownership.

My first stop was a camp near the River Euphrates south of Kobane, which was full of wounded fighters from Manbij. It looked like a First World War clearing station, with so many people limping around with missing limbs or lying heavily bandaged in rows upon rows of stretcher beds. I was cheered to hear from one of the doctors that some of the casualties had survived because they had been treated at the front with our IFAKs. I felt proud of what we had achieved.

Within a few days, I found myself on the western edge of Manbij at a forward operating base (FOB) with the ISIS positions little more than fifty metres away, constantly targeting us with mortars and sniper fire. For a week, because I had my medical kit with me and because of my history with the TMU, I was used as a combat medic, and they were bringing me casualties at all hours. As I lay with my rifle beside me on the balcony of a house, waiting for the injured to be brought to me, there were sniper shots ringing out constantly and so much noise, so many explosions, so much shouting. A shell from an ISIS 'Hellfire Cannon' exploded just a little way down the street from my position, and the terrifying blast ripped through the air, sending metal shrapnel and bits of concrete flying down the road in a huge cloud of dust. Amid the cacophony of war, I finally got confirmation about my friend Levi in a phone message, and I wished with all my heart that I hadn't. He had apparently been attached to an armoured tabur and, with another young American who had briefly been in the TMU, he had gone into a building in Manbij. Perhaps they were looking for ISIS flags as trophies. I don't know, but there was a box. The other guy was standing behind Levi when the IED went off and he was badly injured but survived. Levi was killed instantly. I buried my face in my bedding in anger and frustration. 'Fuck! Fuck! Fuck!' I was heartbroken. My poor Marine buddy. Except that I learned then that he had never been a Marine after all, however much he had wanted to follow in the footsteps of his father, who had served three tours with the US military in Vietnam. No wonder he had been so taken with *We Were Soldiers*. His mother had revealed how he had always obsessed about joining the Marine Corps, but though he trained hard for it, he was disqualified by poor eyesight, even after he had an eye operation. Far from feeling deceived, my admiration for him only increased. To me, he would always be a Marine.

I was still convinced I could do more to help in the thick of the action where the casualties were being inflicted, and I asked one of the commanders, 'Where is the fighting heaviest?' He waved a hand in the direction of the entire smoke-shrouded city. 'Everywhere,' he said, but I told him my help was most needed where Tufan's unit was, at the heart of the city, and that's where I was determined to be.

# Manbij

The Kurdish fighter looked about twenty-five but was probably still in his teens. War had aged him, or maybe that was just the haunting effect of the moonlight on his face. I looked for evidence in his eyes that he was as apprehensive as me, but his glance was too fleeting. '*Bêdeng bin*, hevals!' he whispered, as he ushered us towards the makeshift tank waiting for us at the end of the road. The order to be quiet did not need to be any more specific. We knew there were many hostile eyes watching for us from within the darkened city buildings, waiting for the opportunity to kill. Even so, in this moment of peril it felt comforting to be called heval. Friends are friends, but hevals would die for each other. I might not have been a tabur commander any more, but I felt proud to be considered a heval. The momentary feeling of comradeship was rapidly replaced by a gut-wrenching dread, which gripped me as tightly as the body armour that was pinning my sweat-drenched uniform shirt to my back in the sweltering night air. I held my rifle tighter and moved forward.

The bomb-torn street was deathly still, apart from the guttural, laboured thrum of the home-made tank's diesel engine, which I feared would surely stir every ISIS sentry in a position to rain down fire upon us. The five of us from 223 tabur wedged ourselves into the tiny compartment created by sheets of steel welded to the sides and roof of the converted digger's cab. A side door was slammed and we were entombed. The smell of diesel and exhaust fumes was nauseating and, as we lurched forwards and the tank squealed and screamed and rattled down the road, crunching stones beneath its tyre-less wheels, the noise was deafening. I put my fingers in my ears and prayed. As I'd seen only a few nights before, one well-aimed shot from an RPG and we could be incinerated in this oversized oven, but that was not my primary concern. I looked at the YPG gunner, into the small of whose back my knees were jammed, and saw that this armoured tractor had been fitted with a dushka. All I could think was, 'If he fires that weapon in this enclosed space I can kiss goodbye to my eardrums!'

The journey was mercifully short. We rumbled round the corner until we were out of the direct range of known ISIS snipers, then ground to a halt and the steel door swung open. 'Go! Go! Go!' More Kurds in the shelter of an apartment doorway were beckoning us to get under cover fast, and we stumbled out from the side of the tank and dashed for the door, expecting the crack of bullets at any moment. The narrow hallway I ran into was crammed with fighters, perhaps twenty or thirty, stretching down the corridor and up the building's stairwell, all of them panting with heat and exhaustion. I could smell the sweat and, even in the darkness, sense the unblinking tension in their eyes as we squeezed past and made our way up the stairs. The doorway was our entrance to a grim labyrinth of rat runs connecting neighbouring buildings, enabling fighters to make their way across the city as much as possible without breaking cover into the open air. This urban warren that riddled the buildings of Manbij had been created by ISIS fighters as they had defended the territory they had invaded two years before. Now Manbij was being wrested from them, piece by bloody piece, in some of the most brutal fighting this war had seen, and the battle was in its final murderous stages. Not without reason had the city been nicknamed 'the meat grinder'. The death toll on both sides had been horrendous and it was little better for the natives of Manbij still trapped in what was left of their home. ISIS's reign here may have been coming to an end, but thousands of ISIS fighters were still well dug-in and prepared to stay to the death. For nearly two months, my friends and comrades had been fighting and dying to drive them out of the city while I was exiled in Ain Issa. Now these rat runs were my route to the front line – and to personal redemption; a chance to fight side by side with my Kurdish friends once more; a chance to recapture the comradeship and camaraderie I had found when I first joined the YPG eighteen months before, but had somehow lost along the way.

The distant crump of bombs rattled window panes, and the occasional crack and rattle of automatic weapon fire somewhere outside punctured the silence as we made our stealthy way through the buildings. The air inside was thick with the smell of dust, sweat and faeces. It was sad to think that, before ISIS infested this corner of Syria with their medieval, bloodthirsty creed, these apartments had been happy homes. Families had furnished them and proudly kept them tidy; children had played in them. Now they were ruins. Broken glass, crumbled masonry and spent bullet casings crunched under my boots in the darkness as we were ushered along a maze of corridors. When we crouched to get past a window, or a blown-out wall, the moonlight revealed occasional pools of blood. I hoped it was ISIS blood, though I realised it had probably been spilled since the YPG had occupied these buildings. We pressed on through the labyrinth. Rooms that had once been kitchens, lounges and bathrooms were now just holding stations for a steady stream of Kurdish fighters, some coming, some going. All around were the whispers of other taburs hiding in the ruins. We stopped regularly to listen in silence for the enemy, lest we betray our presence to any ISIS fighters near enough to hear our footsteps. Each time we did so, I found myself holding on to the air in my lungs for fear my heavy breathing would give us away, and feeling sure my heart, pounding so loudly in my ears, would do it anyway. Resuming our progress, we stepped into a bedroom and clambered through a hole that had been smashed through the wall, only to find ourselves standing on a bed in another bedroom in the neighbouring building. Down more stairs we went, and found ourselves in another maze on a different level, then out through a further hole in the wall and we were standing on top of a garage. We scurried across it, dropped down six or eight feet into an alleyway, and then the Kurdish fighters with us gave some code words and we were let through a hole into yet another apartment block. It was totally disorientating. Suddenly, and not for the first time, my nostrils were hit by the stench of a rotting body in a bombed-out shop.

There were ten of us in our patrol: five Kurdish fighters, who were guiding us; the four international volunteers of 223 tabur; and me. It felt good to be with Servan Amriki's team. When we had met up again a couple of days before, he had spoken warmly of his admiration for what I had achieved with the TMU, even though it had not worked out how I had hoped. My admiration for Servan was immense, so to get his approval meant a hell of a lot to me. He was intelligent, articulate, calm and measured, and had quickly learned to speak Kurdish fluently. His Kurdish nom-de-guerre meant 'American Warrior', and it fitted him so well we all just knew him as Servan Amriki. Back at the cattle station in Tell Tamer, he had had fifteen or sixteen men under his command, so I was shocked when I saw how few of them there were now, including another American, William Savage, who I only knew by reputation. They'd already seen a lot more than I had of the battle for Manbij, mostly in the surrounding villages, which is why their number was so depleted and why they, like me, were moving very warily forwards, all of us praying the Kurds knew where they were going; each of us aware that with one wrong turn, we could find ourselves in an ISIS-held building, almost certainly with fatal consequences. The very thought of it had me nervously feeling for the safety catch on my AK-47. I had only the uniform I stood up in, my body armour, my medical pack on my back and my rifle, with a couple of tins of food in my pocket and a bottle of water which I was getting through fast, however hard I tried to preserve the precious liquid. In the oppressive heat, the sweat was just pouring out of me. The temperature was torturing all of us, Kurds and Westerners alike.

Making our way through the rat runs, I had Servan and two other 223 fighters immediately in front of me and William behind, but I had no idea where I was going. I was just concentrating on making as little noise as possible, painstakingly picking my footsteps in case there were ISIS fighters on the other side of the wall, making their way through their own labyrinth. The dull explosions and occasional gunshots outside were not enough to mask a clumsy footfall from an alert enemy. And then we were back in another alley, with a bigger street to cross. '*Bêdeng bin*,' came the whispered order again. '*Daîş li dawaiya rê ye!*' One of the Americans turned and gave me a wary look. 'Daesh!' he hissed. 'This is the fucking place they warned us about.' Even before we had climbed into the tank at the start of our journey, Servan had asked if there were any especially dangerous parts of the city we should worry about. The Kurds had told him about an alleyway with an ISIS position at the end where they were close enough to take a clear shot at us if they saw us. 'Looks more like a fucking highway than an alleyway,' whispered William behind me. I had to agree. I was towards the back of our single-file patrol, squeezed into a narrow alley next to a bombed-out shop, but I could see that the street, a couple of feet below us, was maybe twenty metres wide – a proper main road, with buildings the other side, one of which had been devastated by an air strike. 'Hell!' I thought. 'I'll be tossing a coin here. Heads, I make it across; tails, I'll get a bullet smashing my brains out. God, is this worth it? Do I really want to get to the front this badly?' Once more, I convinced myself I did, having come this far, but I was shitting myself as I watched the first Kurd and then the second sprint across and dive into the cover of the ruined building opposite. Every sound made my heart leap, and I cursed them as, one after another, they landed noisily on a piece of metal debris as they jumped down on to the road and then began running. 'I hate you! You'll alert ISIS. What's wrong with you?' I thought, and selfishly I wished I had been the first to make the dash across, because it's always going to be the first guys who cross before ISIS are aware; the first guys who make the noise that wakes the sniper up; and it's always the last guys who get shot. I just knew it would be me. I convinced myself. A fifth guy made it across. Then a sixth. Then a seventh, and still no shots. How many times can you keep tossing that coin and have it land on 'heads'? It had to come down 'tails' soon, didn't it? I almost *wanted* ISIS to open fire, because the apprehension seemed worse than the contact, except, of course, it wouldn't be.

Next it was the turn of the guy just in front of me. He jumped down and there was that metallic 'clang' and then, as he ran forward, he kicked a tin or something in the street. 'Bing, clink, clink', it seemed to echo, as it rolled down the road. In the quietness of the night street, it sounded deafening to me and must surely have given us away. I watched him safely disappear into the bombed building on the other side of the street, and then it was my turn. My heart was racing and I had a grim feeling of impending doom. I jumped down on to the road and found I made just as much noise as everyone else had, and then I ran. I had pictured myself sprinting as fast as I could, but now it felt like I was running through treacle. I was weighed down by my body armour, medical pack and rifle, and I knew I needed to go faster, but I couldn't. I was barely halfway across when the air seemed to explode around me. 'Snap! Snap! Snap!' went the rounds zipping past my head, so close I could almost smell them. The shockwaves were indescribable as bullets ripped the air with such violence that they sounded like deadly firecrackers, drowning out the noise of the machine gun that was pumping them out perhaps less than thirty metres away. With the echoing noise came tiny fire flashes, from where I had no idea, and my life became a blur as the air was filled with projectiles which then sparked viciously off the road beyond me. I instinctively half closed my eyes, hunched my head closer into my shoulders and ran for my life.

Sheer panic gave me more speed from somewhere, but safety was still a distance away, and my feet would just not go as fast as my head wanted them to, to get me out of there. Ten metres. Eight metres. Seven metres . . . I was still six metres from the other side, with angry rounds snapping past, when I began to stumble. Five. Four. If I went down now, I was dead. Three metres out, as I began to fall, I threw myself forward, nose-diving into a pile of bricks. If I had been at home and taken such a fall, I would have been in agony, but the cuts and bruises, the tears in my uniform and the dust and the dirt had long ago become the norm, and surging adrenaline masked my pain. I was still not safe, and I frantically scrambled up the brick pile. 'Fuck! Fuck! Fuck!' I cursed, as sheer terror kept me moving. It was only when I was safely into the shelter of the building, gasping for breath, that I felt a wave of relief wash over me. I crawled into cover and got slowly to my feet. I had made it, but now we were in contact and poor William was stuck on the other side with all sorts of rounds coming down the street. 'He's never going to make it,' I thought. 'Christ, if that were me, I don't think I'd even attempt it! It's just too dangerous.' I reckoned from the rate of fire it must be a PKM. Either that or an AK-47 on fully automatic. The latter was notoriously inaccurate. Perhaps that was why I was panting like a dog in a wrecked building and not lying dead in the middle of a Syrian street. Servan ordered me to take cover then crawled around the corner. I could hear him give covering fire with his M16 rifle, then I heard him on the radio calling for support. Another Kurdish position, somewhere, started hammering rounds from one of our own PKMs down on the ISIS position, and the enemy firing was momentarily suppressed. 'Here! Here! Amed!' our fighters urged William, using his Kurdish nom-de-guerre, and William seized the opportunity and rushed across the road. I could do nothing but watch in horror and wait for the shots as he seemed to move in slow motion, but the next second he was across the road and into the shell of the building. I walked across to him and expected to see my terror reflected in his face, but he had a huge smile. 'Jesus, man! That shot went up your arse!' he grinned. I couldn't believe it. 'Yeah, it was fucking close,' I agreed, still nursing my bruised arms. How could he be so calm? Then I remembered a story about him being previously shot in the head and carrying on. He had been lucky. It was just a scratch but it was a deep one and it bled a lot, yet he didn't even bother getting medical treatment. He just carried on fighting. He was twenty-seven, a year younger than me, and already a legend in Rojava. As I stood aghast, Servan reappeared from around the corner. 'Is everybody ready?' he asked, calmly. 'Right, let's go.'

We made our way through the building, through a hole in the wall and into the next building, and continued on our route. Two or three hours had now passed since we set off, and every road we had to cross was a fresh horror tearing me in two. It's almost impossible to imagine if you haven't been in that situation, but one part of your brain is telling you not to go on, that any minute you're going to get a bullet pulping your head like a blow from a baseball bat; and the other half of your brain is morbidly wondering what that would be like, imagining the bullet entering your face and the nothingness that would follow, forever, and urging you to risk it. We made it to a YPG staging post and paused briefly to collect supplies needed at the front. 'You carry this,' said one of the fighters in Kurdish, thrusting a twelve-pack of bottled water into my hands. 'Hell!' I thought. I wouldn't be able to carry the water and still have my rifle in my hand, which left me feeling incredibly vulnerable, but he had asked me to do it, so I swung my rifle onto my back and we moved off again, out of the safety of the buildings and onto a road. Every breath I took now was one of unmitigated terror, which only heightened when our Kurdish fighter guides came to halt in a barrage of alarmed whispers. 'Can we not just get off the bloody street and into a building? We're sitting ducks out here,' I thought. I was not the only one getting nervous. 'Fuck! They're lost. They don't know where they're going,' exclaimed William under his breath. '*Em wenda bûn!*' confirmed one of the Kurds. The chances of stumbling into an ISIS position in the maze of ruined buildings around us had suddenly soared.

We stood still, not daring to take a move in the wrong direction in the darkness. Then one of the Kurds pointed out a bombed-out shop and told us to hide in there. I crept inside, only too aware that it might have been booby-trapped by ISIS and that one foot on a pressure plate could detonate an IED which might blow my legs to tattered stumps. Other fighters also crept into the shop, which was heavy with the scent of spilled spices. The heavy steel shutters that once covered the front of the shop had been blown in and now lay on the floor covered in shattered glass. As I stood on the shutters they rocked alarmingly, and my heart almost stopped as a loud metallic clang exploded the silence and echoed around the building. The noise seemed to fill the street and shredded my nerves. 'I've got to get out of here,' I thought, with a rising sense of panic. 'OK, get ready to go,' said Servan. It seemed the Kurds had located the right route. 'Hurry,' said Servan, and the fighters in front of me rushed out of the shop, clanging their way across the steel shutters as they went, then ran across to the other side of the road. I followed, 'clang, clang', and suddenly there was a burst of gunfire which once more shattered the quiet of the street. 'Bam, bam, bam, bam!' I didn't know if it was aimed at me. It could have been from anywhere. It could have been some sleepy ISIS sentry being woken by the 'clanging' and just firing into the darkness, but I was already terrified and on heightened alert after my earlier near miss. I ran onto the pavement in front of the shop and in the darkness I missed my footing. It was only a short step down to the road, but my knee twisted horrendously and I went flying forwards, landing heavily on the pack of water, which exploded underneath me. Plastic bottles scattered over the ground and I was sprawled on my back in the street with my knee on fire. I had never felt so much pain in my life. It felt like a hot knife had sliced my kneecap in two, but the gunfire still ringing in my ears was incentive enough for me to somehow turn on to my front and get to my feet. I wasn't about to stop and gather up any spilt water bottles, but cradled the six that were left in their plastic wrapping in my arms and lunged back the way I came, half hobbling, half running. I could see people waving me on and I crashed through a doorway into the hallway of a building and landed on my back, crying out in pain because of my knee. Instantly, Kurd fighters were leaning over me. '*Gule lê ketiye, birîndar e!*' they asked, convinced I had been shot and eager to find out where. I tried to tell them that I was not wounded, but someone came up to me in the darkness to examine me, felt my uniform where it had been soaked by an exploding water bottle and thought it was blood. 'Are you shot, heval?' he, too, asked. 'No, it's my knee,' I said, fearing I had seriously damaged it, and as I looked at the person standing over me I realised it was my friend Tufan, the very commander whose unit I had been hoping to join. I hadn't seen him for months. 'Hey, Baran Amed,' he said. 'It's good to see you. You're fine,' he added, tapping me on the side of my cheek with the flat of his hand. '*Îca rabe* [Now get up]!', and he reached down with his hand to help me up. I had reached the front line.

# The Suffer Monkeys Club

It was the middle of the night but still boiling hot, and I glugged down a couple of the bottles of water without even thinking about it. I was drenched in sweat, my knee was screaming at me and my shoulders ached from the weight of my armour and medical pack. With the ever-present danger of being spotted by ISIS snipers, even within the walls of this bullet-pocked apartment block, I put on the red light of a tiny torch to negotiate what was left of the apartment building's concrete staircase and, having scrambled up a few floors, I handed the remainder of the water to some Kurdish fighters who looked to me like they hadn't had any water in a while. I suddenly felt a surge of shame for having had so much of the water and cursed myself for having lost half of it when I fell. I carried on to the fifth floor of the building, past more Kurds on the stairways, and into an apartment, my knee throbbing, my eyes gradually growing accustomed to the darkness.

The flat was all but empty of furniture, the bare concrete floor strewn with broken masonry, the glassless window frames stuffed with blankets, but standing in the middle of the kitchen, as if he was welcoming guests to his humble home, was a big, bushy-bearded American in thick glasses, armed with a large PKM. I recognised him as Jake Klipsch, who I had met briefly several months before at the academy while I was there to talk to YPG commanders about setting up my medical team. He had been there for initial training and I recalled how he had seemed a bit reserved then; a bit shy, saying that he had been in the military for a couple of years, but not telling me much else. However, he was friendly enough now. 'Hey man, how're you doin'? Who is that?' he asked me. 'It's me, Macer Gifford,' I replied. 'I'm here to help out.' Even in the darkness I could see his beard part and his white teeth revealed in a big smile. 'That's awesome, man,' he said. At that moment the guys from 223 tabur reached the apartment, and Servan took them off almost immediately to guard key positions on the perimeter of the building. 'I don't know if they'll be staying, but I will,' I told Jake, who flashed another smile. 'So, how long have you been here?' I asked. Jake seemed pleased to have an audience and keen to fill me in quickly on the situation I'd just found myself in. 'We've been here for three days and it's been absolutely fucking crazy,' he said. He explained how they had seized the position from ISIS and how, the day before, ISIS had tried to take it back. 'It was like the fucking Alamo!' he said. 'They made a pretty fucking determined effort. That's when we lost Martin,' he continued. 'Martin?' I queried. 'Yeah, Daesh were trying to storm the building from over there,' he said, with a slight nod of his head in the direction of the other side of the apartment block. 'At one point, one of the Kurds shouted out that Daesh fighters were getting in and Martin had rushed over to see. He couldn't have been by the window for more than a second or two, but it was long enough for a Daesh sniper to get a bead on him, poor fucker.' I was suddenly more aware than ever of the nearest window and whether I was in front of it. 'Yeah, man,' Jake continued. 'I was running up the stairs to take up another position and there he was, lying in the stairwell, dead. The round had gone in just below his left eye and out the back of his head. He wouldn't have known anything about it, thank the Lord.' I wanted to know more, but Jake was ready to move on. 'D'you know Jordan MacTaggart?' he asked. 'He's doing guard duty in one of the rooms down the hall.' I did know Jordan, of course, since we'd come over the border together in January, but it was immediately clear to me, from how keen Jake was for me to see Jordan again, that they had become best buddies in the time since I had last seen either of them; a friendship forged in the heat of battle. They called each other 'Suffer Monkeys'.

'Let's go see him,' urged Jake, 'but just be careful of the windows. They should be blocked up, but if the ISIS snipers see any light or any movement they'll shoot. Hey, those bastards will shoot randomly at the windows just on the off-chance we might be walking by them,' he said. I didn't need telling after hearing about Martin, but I appreciated him feeling the need to warn me. I followed Jake as we made our way through the apartment. In the darkness I could just make out evidence of ISIS's previous occupation of the building, with the torn-down black flags and the graffiti on the wall. Outside, in the distance, there were regular bursts of gunfire. None of it sounded particularly close, but knowing that this building was surrounded on three sides by ISIS-occupied positions and that there was always the threat of another ISIS attack, my nerves were jangling. Along the corridor there were three rooms, and Jordan was in one of them. He clearly recognised me. 'Where the fuck have you been?' he said, abruptly. I was a little taken aback, but I already knew what he was like.

While Jordan turned to keep his rifle trained on the street outside, Jake filled me in on more of the action they had seen in the last couple of days, and I was struck by the fact that these guys seemed utterly fearless. All they wanted to do was fight, side by side, and the more dangerous the situation, the happier they professed to be, just shrugging off danger. 'You're nothing but a Suffer Monkey,' Jordan would chide Jake. 'Hey, we're all Suffer Monkeys,' Jake would reply. I envied them their friendship. I envied them their fearlessness. I tried a weak smile to hide the fact that, frankly, I was the total opposite.

I was put in the room next to Jordan's and pulled guard duty there into the early hours of the morning. I lay there in the darkness for a couple of hours until about 6 a.m., looking as safely as I could out of the window at the street below, with instructions to shoot anything that moved down there. But nothing did. Nothing much happened at all, and an hour after dawn, having been up all night, I was exhausted. I was desperate for sleep. And then all hell broke loose. A call of '*Allahu Akbar!*' from one of the city minarets was the cue for mayhem and suddenly there were bursts of gunfire all around us. 'Shit!' I thought. 'This is it!' Some of the Kurds started lobbing grenades out of the windows at the buildings opposite. I peered out of my window but I couldn't see a thing. At least I got to fire my weapon, to show my presence, but most of the time I'm sure I was just firing at the shadows being thrown by the fast-rising sun. At one point, Jake came into the room to see how I was doing, and there was something not quite right about him. He was standing in the shadow of a wall that gave him protection from any sniper shots coming in through the windows as he spoke to me, but for a moment he stepped out of the shadow, and I could see what was odd. He was wearing a pair of ballistic sunglasses which had a tiny, perfectly round hole through the bottom of the glass on one side. 'Are they . . .' I started. 'Yeah, they're Martin's. That's where the M16 round went through,' he said, touching the hole with his finger. 'They're still good.' He gave another grin and left the room. I laid down a few more rounds in the direction I thought some of the ISIS fire was coming from, and then Tufan arrived and I was moved to the room where Jordan MacTaggart was firing out into the street. I crouched, then crawled to my post, ever mindful of the danger from the windows, and helped to guard the position for the next couple of hours, all through the firefight, watching for any attempt by ISIS to get into our building from that direction. I didn't know what was happening downstairs; how serious the ISIS attempt to get in was. I could only hope the Kurds downstairs were on their mettle. The gunfire was constant and there was no doubt we were under siege. Jordan was watching out of his window, shooting at different targets from time to time. My attention was on the building opposite, and I watched it through a small 'murder hole' that had been punched through the wall to shoot through. In between bursts of firing, Jordan explained how, on other parts of the front line, Kurdish units had been depleted by as much as 70 per cent as casualties mounted. Tufan's unit, by contrast, had lost two fighters injured by an IED when they took the building, and Martin had been killed. In a Western army, three casualties in a day in a single unit might be a significant loss, but to the YPG it was nothing. Tufan returned a short while later and I was taken off guard duty.

I crawled into another room where I curled up in the corner, just lying there, trying to sleep. The gunfire outside was constant, and the sporadic firing from our own guys echoed alarmingly around me, but it was the discomfort of my clothes, board-stiff with sweat and grime, which made sleep difficult, in spite of my exhaustion. And then a rocket hit the wall on the other side of the building and the whole room shook, showering me with dust. 'Shit!' I thought. 'If another rocket hits, then this whole side of the building could come down and I'll be sitting in the open on the fifth floor like the biggest duck on the shooting range!' I hadn't noticed it before, but when I looked across the room, I saw there was a pair of boots and a rifle just lying there, abandoned, and the boot laces and the rifle strap were drenched in clotted blood. 'Oh my God!' I thought. 'They must be Martin's!' Now that I had a chance to think about it, I remembered seeing them bring his body back when I had been on the outskirts of the city waiting to move up to the front. I had recognised him then, and the feeling of sadness that had struck me at the time washed over me again. He was Slovenian, I think. When I had been setting up the TMU, I had invited him over for some food at our base. He was a bit shy, and I didn't know a lot about him, but I didn't think he had a military background. I think he was just ideologically driven to come and help the Kurds. Now he had given his life for them. Manbij was taking a heavier toll on international volunteers than any previous battle, and more casualties proportionate to our numbers than the Kurds were taking. I wondered if I might be next, and I imagined my body being carried out like Martin Gruden's. I imagined the martyr poster they would make for me, just as they had made far too many others, and, as I lay there, my mind continued to torture me.

I must have slept sporadically for most of the rest of the morning, in spite of the gunfire still going off all around, washing over me in waves. Having dozed fitfully, I was amazed when I woke to find that Jordan MacTaggart had cooked for us. In the middle of a firefight, in this shot-up building, amidst all the crap, he had made a meal for us. He had managed to bring some tinned tomatoes with him to the front, and a bit of pasta, and he had got some water and found a little bit more dried pasta in the building, some dusty fresh tomatoes that guys had brought in in their pockets and some mouldy onions from somewhere in the apartment. He had rinsed out a couple of old pans and the guys had broken up a chest of drawers for wood to make a small fire and, by hook or by crook, he had managed to create some sort of pasta dish, spiced with some pepper he had in his pack. 'Jordan is *the* best combat cook!' announced Jake, with pride. We found a couple of spoons amid all the rubble on the floor in the kitchen, cleaned them as best we could and ate in shifts, in between guard duties. I left the others to have some first, but when it was my turn, it was like the best meal I'd ever had.

I was later moved down to the first floor of the building to guard against ISIS trying to get in, and I was positioned by a small hole in the wall, almost at ground level. Being so close to the street seemed to increase my sense of jeopardy, and my finger curled around the trigger of my rifle as I intermittently gave a quick look through the hole and, just as quickly, moved aside again, in case any sniper had a bead on the hole. I kept up this routine for a while, until there was movement and a metallic tinkling out in the street and I peered out of the hole to see who was moving out there. Instantly, my world exploded as I was thrown backwards and everything went black. 'Oh shit, I'm dead!' I thought, and though I quickly realised that I wasn't, I was blinded by dirt and grit and deafened by a muffled ringing in my ears. I desperately groped around in the dust and rubble for my water bottle to flush the dirt from my eyes, and only then was I able to feel around for my glasses. Miraculously, they were still in one piece and, putting them back on while still blinking furiously, I was slowly able to see again. I must have looked out of the hole just at the minute that a grenade detonated in the street. It had felt like every ounce of crap on the road had instantly come flying through the hole and smacked me in the face, but I was still in one piece. For the rest of the day, I kept up my guard duty without further incident.

Then just twenty-four hours after we had arrived, they told us we were leaving the building. I was shocked, and not a little alarmed at the thought of going back, and I voiced my concerns to Jake, who had come into the room to tell me they were gathering upstairs. 'I'm beginning to appreciate just how lucky you have to be to survive this,' I said. 'You can be the best trained person in the world, but if you go into a building with an IED in it, or you walk down a street that you thought had been cleared and you get shot in the head by a sniper . . . You can have all the training in the world, but you have still got to cross that street, and no amount of training is going to make you invisible to bullets!' It felt wrong to be unloading my frustration onto Jake. They had been on the front a lot longer than I had and they had been through hell, but he smiled. 'Yeah, it's shit, man,' he said. However scared I had been under attack in the building, it was clearly the thought of making our way back through the rat runs, running the gauntlet of ISIS snipers once more, that was screwing with my head now. 'If I go back on the streets I'm tossing that coin again,' I said.

Servan got to hear of my frustration and offered me the chance to stay with 223, but I had taken so long to find my friend Tufan and now he was pulling back with my new hevals, Jake and Jordan. Though my fears threatened to consume me, I decided I would risk the journey in order to follow them. I didn't know to what destination, or even whether I would reach it alive, but I was committed. 'Are we ready?' whispered Tufan in Kurdish, and my legs felt like they had suddenly turned to water. 'OK, hevals, let's move out,' he said, and once again, the night held two possible outcomes for me. Would it be heads or would it be tails?

# 'I See Dead People'

The sight and smells of death were all around me as we headed east through bombed-out villages on the edge of Manbij. At least the countryside was less claustrophobic than the nerve-shredding rat runs of the city had been. We had made it back unscathed to the forward operating base around 4 a.m., kicked down the doors of an apartment and bedded down on cushions on the floor for three or four hours. After a meagre breakfast, we were loaded onto trucks for an operation on the other side of the city. It felt good to be back among normal volunteers who just wanted to fight ISIS, not each other, and good to be back with Tufan, who was a friendly link to the feeling of camaraderie I had enjoyed in Heval Agir's tabur in my first year. Jordan and Jake were great to be with, and I could not help being impressed by them. After the weeks they had spent in Manbij, and the deaths and injuries they had witnessed, they both had a decidedly morbid sense of humour, which began to rub off on me. The journey through devastated village after devastated village took about an hour, and as we made our very careful way, in case of IEDs, the mangled remains of ISIS fighters were very much in evidence in the rubble – sometimes whole bodies; sometimes fly-covered lumps, such as a spinal column or a dismembered limb alongside the twisted metal of an AK-47. 'I see dead people,' Jordan announced, mimicking the troubled kid from the film *The Sixth Sense*. 'When do you see them?' I asked, slipping into the role of Bruce Willis's child psychologist character. 'All the time,' replied Jake, to complete the famous dialogue, and the three of us burst out laughing. It's hard, looking back, to see any humour in the situation, but it seemed funny at the time. Black situations provoke very dark humour. It was a defence mechanism against the horrors all around us, and it seemed to work.

That night, we were all divided into two groups and, while Jake and Jordan were sent with half of the tabur to do an over-watch, I was sent with around ten of the Kurds to patrol into the city. The streets were silent, but we knew the threat was there all the same. Every so often we would reach a corner and, one at a time, we would have to dash across the road to the shelter of buildings on the other side. The roads were not as wide as the one on which I was so nearly killed just a few nights before and that helped me to suppress my fear. As we patrolled, I saw two men up ahead crawling from a building that had recently been destroyed by an air strike. As my eyes adjusted to the dark, I realised they were not moving. The building, reduced to a pile of concrete rubble and twisted metal, was still smouldering, and so were the prone ISIS fighters. It looked like they had survived the initial blast and desperately tried to reach the street on hands and knees, their uniforms burning. Now they lay blackened and solidified mid-crawl. We reached another corner, and on the other side of the narrow road, a YPG fighter was beckoning us from a hole in the side of a house, urging us to keep quiet and pointing down the street to an ISIS position fifty metres away. One after another we dashed the few metres across the road and dived into the hole.

Only when the last of us was across, and we were all standing in the living room of the house, was there a burst of gunfire, and I looked back through the hole to see the earth of the road being torn up, chunks of concrete being chipped from the wall by heavy machine-gun rounds. We were led down a corridor, past other rooms, to an open courtyard. The Kurds already there were glad to see the arrival of their reinforcements.

For the next twenty-four hours we endured regular sniper fire and rocket attacks as we kept guard in the courtyard or on top of the house. The unfinished upper floor could only be accessed by an exterior staircase with a low wall, which meant we had to squat as much below the top of the wall as we could to make our way up it. To stand up would have meant instant death at the hands of an ISIS sniper. Through one of a number of small holes in the courtyard wall I looked out to a large roundabout surrounded by high-rise buildings about fifty metres away. That was the ISIS position from where the heavy machine-gun fire had greeted us on our arrival. It would only take a dozen or so ISIS fighters to make their way across the street and to lob a few grenades over the courtyard wall, I feared, and we would be fighting for our lives in a very bloody engagement. I tried to alternate the holes I looked through, for fear of a sniper getting a bead on me, but one of the Kurds who came to check I was OK kept looking out of the same hole and did not seem to understand my warnings. All of a sudden, there was the snap of a bullet, the holed breeze block he had been looking through exploded in a cloud of dust and he fell backwards. 'Oh, God! He's dead!' I thought, but a dust-covered face looked up at me in shock, and I signalled for him to move back into the shelter of the wall as three more shots blasted through the wall. The reinforced concrete pillars of the building were the only safe shelter to hide behind.

By the second evening, hunger was gnawing at my stomach. There were grapes on the vines around the courtyard but they were too bitter to eat. At least we had water. That night, another YPG tabur launched an attack on ISIS from our position, and soon the whole world around us was lit up with bright flashes as RPG rounds and hand-lobbed grenades went off. There was the constant clatter of AK and heavy machine-gun fire, and the shouts of ISIS and YPG voices added to the noise from our blaring radios. There were not enough holes in the walls of the courtyard or on the upper floor for us all to give covering fire at once, so we had to take it in turns, and all the time there was the threat of an ISIS counter-attack overrunning our position. Several times in quick succession, the walls of our compound were hit by RPGs which exploded with almighty bangs, but after a few hours, at around 4 a.m., the fighting started to die down and we were told to stand down. Clearly, whatever the YPG had attempted had not been very successful, and the next morning we were told to pull out of the position, to be replaced by another patrol.

Processed cheese and ham had rarely tasted as good as it did when we finally got some breakfast back with the rest of the tabur, but something else was about to leave a nasty taste in my mouth. I had heard rumours that Tufan was having trouble with in-fighting in the tabur and, after my nightmare with the TMU, I had every sympathy with him. The problem, as Jake and Jordan explained it to me, was that the tabur had taken too few casualties. Some of the younger fighters were accusing Tufan of being too cautious. He was a very modern, professional soldier who was not prepared to throw his men's lives away for no reason, but they saw it as some form for cowardice. It was so frustrating. I had seen him in action in my first year, putting his life on the line for his comrades. Jake and Jordan were supportive too. They thought he was the best commander they had served under. As the grumbling continued, however, the whole tabur was called to a meeting presided over by a senior commander. One after another the Kurds stood up to say how Tufan was not as aggressive as other commanders. Fighters who were not even eighteen yet were thumping their chests and saying the tabur should be pushing deeper into action. I watched Tufan's anguish until eventually he stood up and said, 'Send me away. I don't want this anymore. I resign as commander.' The senior commander was sympathetic, but he could see the infighting had gone too far, so Tufan was stood down and the tabur was disbanded, with the fighters split up and sent to reinforce other taburs that had suffered high casualty rates. Jake and Jordan invited me to join them in another tabur but Tufan was my friend. I hated to see him at such a low ebb, having had the same problems I had experienced, and I felt I should stay with him, which they understood.

I spent the next day with Tufan and the top commanders at the forward operating base, as they pored over battle plans and called in air strikes. It was just like old times, chatting with Tufan about mutual friends, some still alive but many now dead. Late in the afternoon, there were shouts outside and I ran out to meet a vehicle that had arrived with a casualty. I realised quickly he was already dead, a bullet to his body having ended his young life, but I didn't have to wait long for the next casualty, a nineteen-year-old lad who had been shot in the leg just below the knee. His comrades had used a scarf as a makeshift bandage but blood was still pouring from the wound, so I got him inside and dressed it properly. It made sense to me to set up a medical post there, and I told the Kurds to bring any further casualties to me. Back outside, there were dozens of voices, and I looked out to see maybe fifty fighters lined up in single file, ready for an operation. Jake and Jordan were among them and they shouted to me, 'Are you coming?' I told them I was caring for casualties. 'I'm needed here,' I said. 'I'll catch you later.' A senior commander was shaking the hands of every single member of the tabur in turn as they headed off into the night, and I felt a stab of regret not to be with Jake and Jordan, but another truck arrived and I helped to load the body of the dead fighter into the back. I couldn't help thinking, 'That's another *şehîd* poster that will soon be adorning lamp posts; another smiling guy in uniform whose name no one in the West will ever know.

For the next few days, I saw Tufan regularly at different positions where he was working as a staff officer, and I set up another medical post, but there were only a few casualties. The battle for Manbij was almost over, and I was acutely aware that my passport was due to expire soon. I needed to allow enough time to get back across the border and get to Erbil for a flight home before it did. Suddenly I felt very tired. I had been in Syria for seven months; it was time to go home and prepare for the next phase of the war. Tufan got me the necessary note from a senior commander and drove with me to Kobane. I knew I could make more of an impact doing media work at home than

I could joining the last days of the Manbij offensive, and my passport deadline also presented the opportunity for me to be home in time for the wedding of one of my closest friends from school. It felt like the time was right to go, to recuperate, and to get ready to return with a vengeance.

# A World Apart

With a freshly filled glass of champagne in my hand, I looked with wonder as the second of three courses of sumptuous food was placed in front of me by the liveried waiting staff. The wedding meal was a world away from the meagre diet of processed cheese, boiled pasta and chickpeas that I had been eating for months on end. Laughter echoed around the magnificently stately Oxfordshire venue and it felt like a colourful dream. Under fire on the front line, I had missed the all-round email instructing guests to wear something eccentric and I was the only one there in traditional morning suit. It didn't matter. Gaunt and hollow-cheeked as I was, the suit that had fitted me so smartly when I worked in the City now hung from me like a shroud, and I could hardly have looked more eccentric. Over a game of croquet on the beautifully manicured lawn, my friends mocked me for looking like the aged butler who had gatecrashed the wedding photos, but in every picture I had a constant grin on my face. I felt so lucky to be alive and to be surrounded by so many good friends; to be able to return to my relatively privileged life when my friends were still fighting for their homeland.

As soon as the wedding was out of the way, I threw myself once more into promoting the Kurdish cause. I spoke at more universities, appeared regularly on TV – sometimes four times a day when Syria was in the news – and carried on writing dozens of articles. I went to Belgium several times for meetings with Kurdish politicians from the Democratic Union Party (PYD), and I gave a speech at their congress in Brussels. I got the chance to go to Oslo to learn about a charity fund set up to build a Rojava parliament and gave a speech at the magnificent City Hall, where they hold the Nobel Peace Prize ceremony. I gave a speech to the Red–Green Alliance in Copenhagen, and all the while my social media following continued to grow. I was definitely making an impact.

I had been growing progressively poorer after nearly two years without a job, but I managed to sell some video footage of the fighting in Syria and some media articles, in order to earn some money for a short break. I interrupted it to return for a meeting in Germany with a policy advisor to newly elected US President, Donald Trump. The Republicans were now in power, and, with articles like those I wrote for America's conservative *National Review* explaining why America should back the Kurds, I had made a point of focusing my efforts on people who could make a difference.

Finally, I managed to take a longer break with my family. I spent my days writing articles, walking the dog on the beach, or cycling with my mother. It could hardly have been more different from the rigours of the front line, but I also took the opportunity to attend the launch of a book about my friend Mario and to meet his family. It struck me, again, how lucky I was to be travelling extensively when there were families across the world whose sons were no longer alive. In less than two years, 70 per cent of my old tabur had died. While I was determined to make the most of my good fortune, I knew that for me, the fighting was not yet finished. I was sitting with my mother watching television one day in April when a news report announced, 'YPG forces are thirty kilometres north-east of Raqqa and the battle for the capital of the Islamic State is due to begin at any time.' I felt a surge of elation. We were so close now to the physical end of the so-called ISIS caliphate. I turned to my mother and said, 'I think it's time for me to go back, because I need time to cross the border.' Things had changed with my family. They weren't exactly packing my bags for me, but they understood why I had to go and they knew there was nothing they could do to stop me. I had been on the front line just six months after the ISIS declaration of a caliphate. I had to be there for the moment it was crushed.

I messaged my Kurdish contacts that I was on my way and jumped on the next available flights to Sulaymaniyah. If I thought I would soon be joining the Raqqa operation, however, I was disappointed. There were new problems crossing the border and this time, so as not to attract the attention of the authorities with too many Westerners waiting together for the chance to travel to Syria, I was not allowed into the YPG safe house and instead had to stay in a hotel. I spent the days trying to source supplies and, as well as ordering a new AK-47 from Israel, a drone and other equipment, I spent $5000 on medicines for the hospitals in Rojava. It pushed me back into the red, but I felt they were needed, and if I didn't do it, who would? I also paid $1000 on the black market in Erbil for a new handgun. Finally I was allowed into the safe house, ready to cross into Rojava for the last time.

There were already other foreigners there and more would arrive over the coming few weeks, until there were around a dozen of us. Anna Campbell was one of the last to join us, with a friend, and they were real anarchist types, deeply socialist, highly motivated and very passionate about defeating ISIS and supporting the revolution in Rojava. They had previously been hunt saboteurs and were both environmentalists and vegetarians. I told them that they might have to change their views about eating meat if they didn't want to starve in Syria, because even if they ate absolutely everything on offer, they would still lose a lot of weight, but in the months to come they would stay true to their convictions. I had been with thrill-seeking soldiers who would scoff at people like Anna, but while the same military veterans would often pack it in after a month or two, it was the idealists who would usually stick it out, and Anna certainly fitted that mould.

The reason for the hold-up was that the Turks, who, unlike the US and the UK, viewed the YPG as a terrorist offshoot of the Kurdistan Workers' Party (PKK) they had been fighting for years, had bombed the YPG headquarters at Mount Qarachogh, killing several of my friends in the media team. One of the Kurds in the press office called me in tears to explain that he had only survived because he had been away from the mountain on a photographic assignment when the Turkish fighter jets had struck. It felt like a stab in the back, which it was. The system for getting fighters over the border had understandably been disrupted, but eventually we got the OK to make the journey. I tucked my pistol into the waistband of my trousers and threw my bergen, medical kit and spare body armour into the back of the minivan, but everything else – my new AK-47, my drone, some new body armour and thousands of vials of medicine – I gave to the Kurds to take into Syria with other supplies.

There was a nice surprise, having finally made it to the academy, when Jac turned up after the first week for a short rest and to change units. He looked so different. The fresh-faced, sleepy young lad I had known in my first year was gone. Now he had long hair and a long beard, and slung over his shoulder was a very classy-looking M16 rifle. He was still the same laid-back personality, but he sounded so much more confident. He had definitely grown up. I had not seen him often since Kosta's graveside so it was good to spend time with him and have a few laughs at the academy. And then he was gone again.

After two weeks, I was told the medical supplies I had bought, and which had gone missing with my other equipment in transit, had been found and distributed to hospitals. The drone arrived too, and I gave that to my remaining friends in the media team. None of the rest of my personal equipment had been found, however, but when I heard a week later that YPG forces were about to enter Raqqa, I told the commanders I would not wait any longer and asked them to send me to the fighting with an all-Kurdish tabur. At least I had found my old body armour that I had left in Rojava the previous year. I said my farewells to Anna and the others and, as I looked at their faces, I had no idea who I would meet again and who would die, but I knew from bitter experience that some would not make it. I also knew that, since I was the first of the group heading to Raqqa, there was every possibility it could be me.

My first stop was Kobane, just in time to attend the funerals of some of those killed in the early stages of the battle for Raqqa. Saddest of all was to visit the fresh grave of my friend Merdan from Ain Issa. As I stared at the sun-baked earth, my hatred for ISIS went up a notch, so I was delighted when I was issued with a brand new Eastern European AK-47 with a folding stock and told I could hitch a ride in a bread lorry taking supplies to Raqqa. I jumped in the front seat with my body armour on and my bergen and medical bag beside me, and we drove south for hours through the Syrian countryside. The sight of laughing, smiling crowds who waved gleefully at the glimpse of a foreigner on the first part of the journey soon gave way to scenes of burnt-out vehicles and bombed-out houses, and hundreds of forlorn-looking refugees on the roads, as we neared Raqqa. The bread lorry reached its destination and I swapped to another vehicle and was driven to a former school that was being used as a forward operating base and a mortuary by the local commanders and by American Special Forces a few kilometres outside Raqqa. I finally got a chance to speak to the commanders when I walked into their mobile communications base. 'Excuse me, hevals, but does anyone speak English?' I asked. 'I am speaking English to you now,' said one of them in a very well-educated voice. Johan was a Syriac Christian (MFS) commander from Europe and, as we got talking, we realised we had some mutual friends among the Syriacs I had met in London and Belgium. Johan translated for me as the Kurdish commanders explained that there was an all-foreigner tabur in Raqqa if I wanted to join them. 'Definitely not!' I said rather too hastily, waving my note, and we all burst out laughing. They were unsure where to send me and as they discussed the options Commander Johan said, 'Why don't you join us? We already have a couple of foreigners with us and we could really do with your help.' The more I thought about it, the more it made sense. In spite of the success of my lobbying on behalf of Rojava, I had encountered accusations at home that I was a lackey of the Kurds and that I only represented the YPG when Syria needed a multicultural solution. Here was an opportunity to join the Christian community of Northern Syria, one of the smaller communities in the region. We discussed it some more and in the end I said, 'Yes, let's do it', and the YPG commanders agreed to sign whatever note was needed for my transfer from the YPG to the MFS. Within hours, Johan's driver, Matay, had sped me to the Syriac positions on the edge of Raqqa and I had joined my new colleagues patrolling to a derelict apartment block on the front line.

# On the Enemy's Doorstep

A gentle breeze from the half-open window brushed my face, and I was dimly aware of a metallic blind flapping against the window, reflecting the morning light in intermittent flashes. 'Clack, click, clack.' If there was sunshine, there would soon be flies, and I nestled deeper into the grubby mattress on the concrete floor, clinging hard to a last few moments of precious slumber before they arrived. 'Click, click, clack,' went the blind, and then another frightening and all too familiar noise intruded my sleep: a screech, rising to a crescendo, then . . . BOOOOOOM! Glass and concrete chips showered my head and body, and pressure waves buffeted me. I leapt from my back on to my front in a panic, suddenly awake but dazed and confused. My ears rang with white noise that reached me as if through cotton wool. The blind swung limp and tattered in the glassless window, and the sunlight was now filtered through a thick fog of dust. I fumbled for my AK-47 and crawled across the debris-strewn floor towards the door. 'Keep low! Keep away from the window!' I reminded myself. Tiny chunks of masonry dug into my skin and sour dust filled my mouth as I edged on knees and elbows closer to the doorway. My head was slowly clearing as I reached the open-air corridor, only to be confronted by the smiling face of Abjar, my Syriac comrade, looking down at me where I lay prostrate in the dirt at his feet. 'Americans,

Macer,' he reassured me. I was suddenly aware not of the gunfire I had feared, but of a barrage of laughter from my Syriac Christian comrades lazing in the early morning light on the back balcony of the abandoned apartment building that had been our front-line position for the last couple of days. The blast, it appeared, had been a US air strike on the ISIS positions just fifty metres from us. I got to my feet, brushing the worst of the dust off me as nonchalantly as I could, and asked whether the usual breakfast was being served this morning. It was. I scraped the green mould off a dry piece of bread, unwrapped and applied some processed cream cheese and hurriedly put it in my mouth before the flies could land on it, then washed it down with sour-tasting black tea.

The sun was rising fast in the sky, but there seemed fewer flies than the usual swarms which plagued us every day from dawn to dusk at the position. 'Perhaps the blast has blown them away?' I thought, but clouds of them reappeared on the balcony at that very moment, like the physical manifestation of the stench that wafted from the rooms of the wrecked apartment that we used as our toilet. We were stationed in a three-storey apartment block on the residential edge of Raqqa, and our small tabur of eight Syriac Christian soldiers and three foreign fighters was enjoying a slight lull as other, mostly Kurdish, infantry units moved up to and then beyond our front-line position to engage the ISIS fighters occupying similar blocks on two and a half sides of us, 100 metres away at most. The whole of Raqqa, once a bustling city of a quarter of a million people, was now one huge war zone, infested with hordes of ISIS fighters, who had had years to fortify this place, their military capital, with countless tunnels and hidden IEDs. I swallowed the last of my tea in a bid to wash away the taste of my breakfast, but it could do nothing to nullify the smell of concrete dust, sweat and human waste that filled my nostrils. You just got used to it in this place. I wondered what the apartment block had smelled like before the war. Fresh spices at meal times, perhaps? Soaps and aftershave in the mornings, as the inhabitants had prepared themselves for their day?

The balcony on the third floor was where we foreigners slept and spent our time when not on guard duty. We would chat, listen to music or watch, awestruck, as the American A10 'Warthog' ground-attack aircraft swooped in low to pound the ISIS positions in front of us. The roar of the twin turbofan engines would announce their arrival, but it was the alien-like whirr of the nose-mounted rotary cannons spinning up to speed, followed by the deep, low 'baaarp' sound of their deadly 30-mm shells being spat out, that made the deepest impression on me. They always reminded me of the sinister noise of the Martians in a film adaptation of H. G. Wells' *The War of the Worlds*. It was a terrifying sequence, and I couldn't help but feel a twinge of pity for the ISIS fighters on the receiving end as they answered back with ambitious but useless blasts from their PKM heavy machine guns, screaming their defiance before they were smashed to pieces by a hail of projectiles. It was not as if we did not have any firepower ranged against us, however. We all knew only too well the crack of incoming rifle and machine-gun rounds and the scream of rocket-propelled grenades as ISIS fighters tried to winkle us out of our forward post, and any one of those bullets could kill us just as effectively as a 1000-pound bomb. I usually slept on the balcony, tucked in behind its wall that offered protection against ISIS snipers, but for some reason I had chosen to sleep in the ISIS-facing apartment at the front of the building the previous night. It certainly wasn't for the comfort of a proper bed. All the furniture had been thrown down the apartment block's single concrete stairwell to create a barrier to any ISIS fighters trying to infiltrate the building. It was probably because it was the only room in the entire building that still had glass in the window, offering at least some respite from the flies.

Two of the MFS soldiers who had come up to join us from the floor below sloped away to take up guard duty in the apartment on the left side of the building, the one facing the strongest ISIS positions, and moments later, the two Americans they had taken over from appeared on the balcony. 'Any word on the missing patrol?' asked Kane, resting his sniper rifle against the wall and lowering himself to a seated position on the floor. Kane Harlley was the nom-de-guerre he had chosen, and he was a constant source of fascination for the Syrians because he was both fair-haired and had tattoos covering his body and his face. Kane had been a US Marine and then served in the French Foreign Legion, so he knew his stuff, militarily. Why he chose the name Kane Harlley I have no idea. Why did any of us choose a nom-de-guerre? 'If our Special Forces guys can't reach them, I reckon they've had it,' added Kane's mate Paul, a tall, eccentric combat medic. Paul was a former iron worker from Pasadena, California, who said he, too, had joined the French Foreign Legion, before leaving them to fight in Syria. He and Kane were joined at the hip. Both had joined the TMU, though after I had left it, and we at least had that in common. The patrol Kane mentioned was an MFS platoon that had been ambushed by ISIS during an operation two nights before. They had been surrounded and had not been heard from since. A YPG column had made a vain attempt to relieve them and there was a rumour that an American Special Forces team in Humvees had also tried and failed to rescue them. After two nights without food or water or any resupply of ammunition, it was not looking good for them, and everyone was desperately worried. There were so few Christian fighters, but the MFS was determined to show that its fighters were contributing to the Syrian Democratic Forces (SDF) in the war against ISIS; that they were not just a minority group content to be protected by the YPG. They were fighting for their right to a seat at the table of any future independent government for Rojava. 'You had any luck finding the sniper?' I asked Kane. We had been targeted by one particular ISIS marksman, armed with an M16 rifle, who had come close on a couple of occasions to hitting members of our unit when they had tarried too long by a window, and Kane had made it a personal mission to locate where the sniping was coming from. 'No,' he said, 'but don't worry, I'll nail that bastard soon.'

Bursts of gunfire and occasional explosions continued all around us for the rest of the day, but there was little for us to do in our fortified apartment building apart from pull guard duty, clean our weapons, listen to music, or prepare some rudimentary food. The highlight of the day would be when cooked food arrived from the YPG post behind us, but that depended on a patrol being able to get through, and one hadn't now for two days. That was how it was, sometimes. The YPG patrol that did eventually reach us was a welcome sight as they clambered with difficulty past our stairwell barricade, bringing supplies for us before they pressed further forward to attack the ISIS positions. But the food they brought with them had sadly spoiled in the hot sunshine. At least the YPG fighters also brought with them some good news. The missing Syriac patrol had been safely rescued. Our Christian comrades beamed with joy and chattered excitedly among themselves, and I afforded myself a rueful smile as the Kurds, having completed their partial resupply of our position, shook hands with everyone, then made their way back down the stairs, ready to squeeze themselves out past our barricades and go do battle with ISIS. Apart from the commander, who was probably in his late twenties, they all looked so young. Even with the grime of war on their features, and the fluff of adolescent facial hair, they could not hide their callowness.

As the sun dipped below the horizon, the falling darkness would give them some cover for their perilous mission. It also gave us temporary relief from the flies. It was a good reason to try to get some sleep now, but first I had to venture up the single flight of stairs from the third floor to the rooftop for my stint of guard duty. It would have been suicide in daylight, but the darkness afforded me the chance to survey the war-ravaged suburb, to scan the ISIS-occupied blocks for any signs of snipers and to admire the awesome power of the US air strikes as I listened to the rumble of jets and occasional screech and blast of a missile amid the constant clatter of AK fire and muffled thuds of grenades. We had no night-vision equipment but, thankfully, nor did ISIS, at least not on this part of the front. I never wavered from my vigilance. I knew that, though another comrade was guarding the barricaded staircase, it would only take a moment's lapse in concentration on my part and ISIS fighters could swarm our building. I sat for hours at a time beneath the stars, with the cooler night air ruffling my hair, enjoying the blissful absence of flies and a much-reduced smell of sun-baked sewage.

Scanning the streets and buildings below with the PKM that we kept on the rooftop, I listened to the deep thrum of a US AC-130 Spectre gunship overhead and saw the sparks ripping through ISIS positions a split second before I heard the roar of its cannon and the whirr of its chain gun. No wonder they nicknamed it 'Spooky'. It always seemed incredible to me how, in the midst of such chaos and fear, guard duty at night brought so many moments of real serenity. When bright flashes of light were followed by the accompanying dull thump of an air strike in another part of the city, the night in our part of the city seemed particularly peaceful to me. Guard duty gave me the opportunity for many hours of quiet reflection, the chance to think about my family at home and about the dangers ahead. I was in the very place I had wanted to be since appalling images of ISIS atrocities had first filled my computer screen at home in London. Raqqa was the place where I had seen Yazidi girls being sold in cages in the marketplace; it was where I had seen pictures of women and children being butchered and young men crucified. This was the city where the railings around the Naim (Paradise) roundabout had been decorated with the severed heads of people executed by ISIS. I had always pictured one day being in Raqqa as part of the force that finally liberated the city, and now that I was here in Raqqa, I felt a calming sense of satisfaction.

It was almost a hardship when my relief arrived to take over the guard position and I had to walk downstairs to try to grab a few hours of fitful sleep before the dawn and the flies and the stink from the sun-warmed shit heralded the start of another long, slow day on the front line. Kane and Paul were sat on the balcony, and I grabbed a bottle of water and joined them. I knew from my first conversations with the Americans that both guys had experienced severe problems with the YPG commanders over what had gone on in the TMU, which was why they were now in a Christian unit, but they had apparently put their issues with the Kurds behind them, were getting on well with the Syriacs, and seemed to have not wavered from the determination to fight ISIS, which had first brought them here. There was also something caring about Kane, I thought, in spite of his warlike look and gruff manner. As well as the tattoo on his face, he had sleeve tattoos all the way up both arms, and on his hands, and when he took off his shirt, he had a huge tattoo of a Japanese warrior with a long sword which covered most of his back and sides and much of his front as well. As we spoke, he told me that he took the Japanese culture very much to heart. He said that the Samurai way of life was a huge inspiration to him and kept him calm. 'It keeps me focused and gives me a purpose,' he said. Kane, who was twenty-eight, had grown up as a virtual orphan after his mother put him into care from a young age, he said, and he had endured an extremely difficult early life in and out of different homes, raised by different families. He had joined the US Marine Corps as soon as he was old enough and had been wounded in Iraq, sent back to the US and medically discharged. He told me how he had had this really hot girlfriend but, with a big pension from the US Defence Department, he had drifted into drink and drugs and almost destroyed himself. As his health deteriorated, he realised his lifestyle was killing him and pulled himself together, got clean and joined the French Foreign Legion for a couple of years before he quit to come out to Syria to join the YPG. He must have impressed the Kurds in those first months, because he was appointed as commander of the TMU, but he had quickly found, as I had done, that it was a poisoned chalice, because the international volunteers were so unmanageable it had led to clashes with the YPG leaders.

Now, as I sat talking to him, I got the impression that, behind his rough exterior and his military efficiency, he was a restless soul, still looking for that something special in his life. My heart went out to him at the thought of his nomadic childhood, and I wished him all the best in finding whatever he was searching for. Right from my first day at this position, I had noticed there was an undeniable affection between the Syriacs and these Americans. The Syriacs loved them. The MFS had had far fewer foreigners join them than the YPG had. Usually they only got international volunteers who left the YPG. When these two Americans had been expelled by the YPG, the Syriacs had been only too glad to welcome them. A lot of the Syriacs hero-worshipped Kane in particular because he had spent years in the military and his proficiency and his professionalism were evident. They trusted him and hugged him at any opportunity. 'How about some music?' I suggested. I'd had some success playing Johnny Cash – particularly 'A Boy Named Sue' – and another favourite of mine was slowly becoming something of an anthem for us at the start of the Raqqa campaign. As we sat on the balcony, with the rat-tat-tat of automatic weapon fire in the distance, the sound of Kenny Rogers' 'The Gambler' filled our front-line balcony . . . ''Cos every hand's a winner and every hand's a loser, and the best that you can hope for is to die in your sleep . . .'

Later in the day, a very excited Kane returned to the balcony from his spell of guard duty, convinced he knew where the ISIS sniper was hiding. It was fortuitous timing, as the two Americans were due to be relieved from the position with some of the Syriacs and take a short break from the front line, as soon as a new patrol arrived. Kane pointed out the sniper's suspected lair to the Christian commander, who called in an air strike, and an hour or so later, we crept into the left-hand apartment to watch the death blow dealt, whooping with joy as the high-explosive missile was delivered with pinpoint accuracy, and the side of the building where the sniper had been spotted disappeared in a flash of burning light and a cloud of obliterated concrete. The fact that at least one human life had just been extinguished meant little to me. I felt only elation.

The arrival of the relief unit at dusk quickly put our joyful celebrations into perspective. This new batch of fighters included members of the lost patrol that had been rescued, among them a curly-haired young commander called Sofian, who looked like the actor Martin Freeman in his role as hobbit Bilbo Baggins, and who had an easy laugh in spite of the brush with death they had so recently experienced. It was good to see them, having worried about them for so long. Moreover, they brought with them freshly cooked, edible food – meat mixed with rice – that we hungrily devoured. They also brought bad news, however, of the YPG patrol which had so recently struggled to reach us with their own delivery of spoiled food. They had apparently triggered a huge IED in the stairwell of a building on their way forward and most of them had been killed. Reality ripped away our flimsy cloak of invincibility that we had worn while witnessing the successful air strike, and I knew we were all just an unlucky moment away from our own turn to meet a violent end. I had an uncomfortable sleep that night, after another uneventful guard duty.

By the time the buzzing of the flies and the brightening light of dawn stirred me where I slept on the balcony, I discovered Kane and Paul had left under cover of darkness with some of the Christians. The departure of the Americans at least gave me a chance to try to get to know my Syriac comrades better, and I moved my stuff down from the third floor onto the second floor. Time passed just as slowly, but I tried to fill the waking hours between eating, guard duty and playbacks of 'The Gambler' by talking to the Christians, hearing about their lives before the war, their suffering at the hands of ISIS and their hopes for the future. It was sobering to think that the men I was talking with might be dead within weeks. Hell, I might be dead too. I knew that hundreds more would certainly die before the self-declared Islamic State was defeated. There were many locals in the city, conscripted into the ISIS army, who would gladly give up at the first opportunity, but there were thousands of foreigners – the most ideological hard-liners – and they had the most to lose.

Back up on the third floor, in the front apartment where I had experienced my rude awakening several days before, there was a wrecked bathroom where I did my best to shower and to keep myself clean. Keeping myself and my equipment clean kept me sane. It was as I stared into the mirror that I heard a cry outside and rushed out to make a vain attempt to save the Kurdish lad who had been shot through the throat. Patrolling warily back to the apartment that evening I visualised again the tiny hole in the poor man's throat. He'd clearly been shot with an M16 round, and I knew I'd have to tell the Syriacs that either the ISIS sniper wasn't dead, or there was a new one around.

# A New Normal

Sofian leaned against the wreckage of a home-made YPG tank at the side of the rubble-strewn road. 'Are you ready, Macer?' he asked, but before I could answer, he had sprinted to the other side of the street and into the shelter of a bombed-out shop. A volley of ISIS rounds instantly tore up the ground he had dashed across just a split second before. 'Fuck!' Now I had a dilemma. Should I follow, knowing that an enemy sniper was waiting for me to do just that, or wait? And how long would I need to wait before the gunman decided that no one else was coming? If I waited too long, I risked being blown apart by one of the mortars that regularly rained down on us or spotted by the ISIS drones, which were also an everyday threat. Three of our number in the *noctas* (bases) had already been injured by drone-dropped bombs, and I myself had known the terror of being targeted by a drone, though mercifully I had escaped injury. I took up a sprinting position, then paused. This was a decision that could cost me my life.

We had left the apartment block after eleven days of holding the line and, in early July, pushed further into the Western side of the city. Our new nocta was in a two-storey building that dominated the poor district of mostly single-storey dwellings. The war-devastated neighbourhood was totally abandoned by civilians, and ISIS fighters would regularly launch attacks against us through this rocket-scarred wasteland. Whether they were meant to be suicide attacks or not, they usually ended badly for the terrorists, picked off by us or by the US Apache helicopters and Spectre gunships, and their bodies littered the pockmarked streets. Sofian and I would often take our rifles into this perilous no man's land and visit other noctas along the front, darting between the deserted buildings, running the gauntlet of ISIS snipers and taking shots of our own when we could.

Now my route was very much in someone's sights, and my heart was racing. It was so different to the hours of tedium when I would sit in the shade of our nocta's courtyard and lose myself in one of my downloaded books, barely noticing the missile strikes on buildings close to us or the showers of debris from the nearby air strikes that had become my new normality. Bombs and bullets would be going off in the background for real as I visited war zones with Wilbur Smith, relived George Orwell's *Homage to Catalonia* or pursued adventures with Dan Brown. Beneath the stars at night, I explored the universe with Stephen Hawking or *The Hitchhiker's Guide to The Galaxy*, or read up on the life of Byron. At other times I would watch videos posted by my family on our WhatsApp group. I would watch them over and over again, or close my eyes and just listen, pressing 'repeat', 'repeat', 'repeat' on my phone. It was not like I was in any kind of emotional turmoil, but I got comfort from listening to my mum's voice, or my dad's, because life in Raqqa was difficult. It was boring, or terrifying, and I was homesick, but I knew it was where I needed to be.

Three minutes had passed since Sofian's dash and now he was urging me to follow. I would be gambling again, just as I had in Manbij, only this time I would be tossing the coin in Raqqa, in the heart of ISIS territory. I took a deep breath, launched myself across the street and was sharing Sofian's shelter before the sniper's bullets belatedly filled the street, and we both laughed and continued on our risky way. It was so good to spend time with Sofian.

By the middle of August, we had been under attack in the nocta for six weeks, but our chance to go on the offensive was coming. Just before it did, we were joined by my friend Jake. He had sent me a couple of messages from time to time over the previous months, saying that he was coming back to Syria and that he wanted to hook up with me, and I was delighted. He had impressed me so much in Manbij that I felt like I had to have him with me in Raqqa. He was brave, fearless, well-trained, funny and a good guy. I was really looking forward to seeing him, and then he arrived – and I was shocked. I was sat in the darkness on guard duty with Kane when I heard a commotion. Jake came on to the roof and the first thing that struck me was that he was obese! He had put on so much weight that he looked terrible, though obviously I didn't say so. 'Hey, how are you doing?' I said, and I gave him a hug. 'Man, it's been a fucking job to reach you,' he grumbled. 'I've been stuck for weeks in a YPG tabur outside of Raqqa doing absolutely fucking nothing. Never mind that I had the permissions to join the MFS.' Jake was clearly not a fan of the YPG note system. The profanities and the attitude were just as I remembered, but physically Jake was so different, and it was soon apparent that he was not the same man that I had last seen in Manbij. As he told me what had happened there, it became clear why. 'Man, it was shit,' he said with a deep sadness in his eyes. 'We were patrolling deeper into the city, half of the tabur on one side of the road and half on the other, when one of the guys triggered a massive fucking IED on their side. Jordan was lucky but several of the guys were killed, and immediately we came under a shit load of fire from a big ISIS force further up the fucking street. Jordan could see I had the better fire arcs and he tried . . .' Jake swallowed hard before he could continue, 'he tried to cross the road to where I was. I mean he was so fucking close, man.' Jake fixed me with a mournful stare. 'The round went through his side and straight through his heart. He was fucking dead before he hit the ground.' For the next twenty-four hours, pinned down by ISIS fire, Jake had to stay with his best mate's body at his feet until he could carry Jordan out of there. It didn't help that he had to watch as another international volunteer, injured by the IED, slowly died during the night. 'And you know what?' he asked. 'A couple of days later I was on fucking guard duty on top of a roof when they attacked again and one of the ISIS bastards got lucky with a grenade.' He suffered a head and eye injury from grenade shrapnel, and though he eventually got back to the United States, he told me he had been drinking heavily since. It had clearly taken a toll. At least now he was back in Syria, and it was good to have him at my side. 'You've timed it well, mate. We've had weeks of holding the line, suffering casualties, but now it's our turn to attack,' I told him.

# Hidden Killers

It was broad daylight, and I felt desperately exposed by this rare departure from normal procedures as we patrolled forward some 200 metres through the quiet streets of Raqqa. The thirty-strong YPG tabur from Afrin we were to meet up with had apparently secured the area a few hours before. Yet it still seemed risky to be out in the open this close to ISIS positions. The sun was high in the sky and the temperature was already stifling, but the handful of Kurds with us behaved as if there were no danger, so we tried to hide our own anxiety. Kane, Abjar and I had been chosen by the Syriacs to represent them in a small YPG tabur for this operation. Jake, because he had just joined our unit, was back with Sofian and the rest of the Syriacs at our new nocta, a high-rise apartment block some 400 metres forward of our two-storey nocta in the western suburb.

When we reached the Afrin tabur, they were resting up, but we were told we would be leapfrogging beyond them, deep into ISIS territory. As our Syriac units had been static for so long in the west, we had already been left behind by the YPG taburs taking ISIS territory, and I was shocked at the extreme damage I could see on this, our first venture into this part of the city. Even for Raqqa, it was clear there had been very heavy fighting, with apartment buildings all but destroyed by air strikes, houses gutted by fire and homes torn apart by grenades.

A Humvee arrived and, with some trepidation, we climbed in and were driven through the bombed-out streets until we came to an abrupt halt outside another apartment building, where a couple more Kurds waved frantically at us to join them. Just as I dashed inside, there was an almighty bang from the hallway of the apartment block opposite. 'Mortar?' I asked, as debris rained down in the street and the acrid stench of smoke filled my nostrils. 'No, an IED,' said Kane. 'They're everywhere. Don't touch anything you don't need to,' he said, as if I needed telling. Inside, with other YPG fighters, were a couple of Italians who had helped to seize control of the block from ISIS the night before, and they were glad to see the arrival of their replacements. As Kane and I sat with them for some food and spoke to the tabur commander about the situation we were in, we were joined by a really bubbly Kurd who kept coming up to me to take photographs, laughing and joking with us. He was a really likeable guy but totally off the wall. When he and a couple of other Kurds went off a little later to clear the apartment block opposite, they were not gone long before the joker returned, brandishing an ISIS flag. 'You should be careful. If you go looking for stuff like that you gonna find an IED,' one of the Italians told him. The joker laughed. 'You think I'm going to şehîd here?' he said. 'Hah!' and his cheeky smile reminded me of my poor friend Kendal.

As the afternoon shadows began to lengthen, he and others went back to the apartment block opposite, and I got my head down in case we were needed for an operation that evening. I had barely got to sleep when there was a tremendous explosion, followed by a scream of pain. I jumped to my feet, grabbed my rifle and medical bag, and started to run down the stairs of our apartment to see what was going on. Smoke was billowing from the building on the other side of the street. 'I've got to get across there,' I thought, then paused at the realisation that there could be snipers training their rifles on the street and I was about to run into a block where there had already been two explosions. Out of the swirling dust I could see the joker on the balcony of the other building, gasping for air, his face covered in blood, and I knew I had to go. The street was now full of smoke, which at least gave me some cover, and I ran across and scrambled up the concrete staircase, over heaps of rubble, to reach the first floor, where I saw the guy, who had a terrible head wound. His eye was gone and his face was covered in thick blood, which was dripping off his chin. His uniform was ripped and bloody, and he was peppered with shrapnel all over his arms, legs and face, and he was crying out for me to help him. At least he was walking. Behind him was another injured Kurd, and I checked them both. There was no heavy arterial bleeding and they had all their limbs. The second guy had a nasty cut to the side of his face, but it was the joker who was in a worse state. I grabbed him and started helping him down the stairs as he began to stiffen and sway with shock. In the end, I had to pick him up and carry him down the stairs, and half-carry him across the road, as the other guy held on to my shoulder for guidance and support.

Kane was already waiting for us and we both set to work treating their wounds. We did all we could to patch them up, but they needed further treatment behind the lines and, fortunately, within twenty minutes, a Humvee arrived to evacuate them. There was precious little time to mull over their carelessness before we were ordered to move out.

Abjar, Kane and I, and four Kurds, ran in single file down the street to yet another apartment block, where five more Kurds were waiting for us, and together we all went out the back door and began patrolling cautiously through neighbouring buildings. This was certainly ISIS territory, so my heart was thumping as we covered windows and doorframes, where a sniper might be lurking. There were so many of them, and all the time we knew that the doors we were passing through could be rigged with IEDs. We went through a back garden into the courtyard of another building and into the living room of yet another, before crossing a further street and going into another apartment complex, where we were told to set up a base for a tense night of guard duty. As we fired at the ISIS positions through holes punched by earlier dushka rounds, a direct hit from an ISIS RPG blew another hole in the wall, filling the room with flying debris, seconds after Kane had left that very spot to get a drink of water.

The next morning, as another tabur gave us covering fire from the same 'murder holes', we were on the move again. We ran through the streets, leapfrogging other YPG units which then leapfrogged us as, together, we advanced to contact with ISIS. Intense incoming fire was whistling over my head as we dashed across the open ground. I was glad we had the ability to call in air strikes, which annihilated the Islamic State positions before we ran forward once more to occupy the next set of buildings, punching deep into enemy territory.

The ISIS counter-attack, when it came, was determined and vicious, but luck was on our side. I was on guard duty in the middle of the night when the concrete floor shook with the sound of grenades – in the building immediately in front of us. The jihadists had misjudged where we were. They were too close for us to call in an air strike so the Kurds decided to counter-attack themselves, while we gave covering fire. No sooner had the YPG fighters entered the building than we had to stop firing for fear of hitting our own guys, and all we could do was listen to the sounds of a terrible firefight going on inside. We had an agonising wait before, eventually, the Kurds emerged, dragging the bodies of two dead terrorists, and reported that the rest of the ISIS fighters had fled.

From our watching position, it felt surreal to be sitting in the heart of Raqqa, with smoke plumes all around, with the constant clatter of gunfire and occasional explosions, and to think, 'We're actually taking ground off ISIS, who are falling back.' I was shaken from my reverie by a horrific, guttural roar and the sound of crunching gears as a suicide vehicle emerged from a building just a couple of hundred metres away. There was something truly heart-stopping about the sight of the crudely adapted suicide trucks, with sheets of steel welded to them to protect the driver long enough for him or her to reach their target with enough explosives to rip our building – and us – to shreds. I held my breath for a moment, but the truck had not gone far before it was blown to pieces. I actually saw the white flash of the US missile in the second before it struck home. That sort of thing was happening all around the city. You could watch Raqqa stretching all around you, see the various battles going on and, every so often, see the remains of a vehicle go spinning up into the air or a building dissolve as it was hit by an air strike, and a second or so later you would hear the vast explosion.

Under the cover of darkness, I spent several hours with a sniper rifle, moving around, looking for ISIS positions through holes in the walls of our building, but most of the time I saw nothing. Maybe I didn't have the patience, or the talent, but there were so many windows and so many places for ISIS to shoot from. I certainly had no evidence that I ever hit anyone.

Finally, we were relieved from the operation, but, with other taburs, we had advanced more than a kilometre into ISIS territory and liberated an entire district. More units were sweeping round and pushing ISIS out of other districts using the shock of frequent, brutal infantry attacks together with air strikes to hit ISIS command posts and any reinforcements they sent to try to bolster positions. ISIS was really on the back foot now, and SDF units were pushing further and further into the city. We would be back in action very soon, but not before we got a chance for a couple of days' rest away from the front line.

It felt good to dive into the cold, crystal-clear waters of Raqqa's canals, washing away the dust and the grime of conflict, for a short while at least, much to the amusement of local kids and the alarm of passing YPJ units, who saw us standing dripping in our underwear beside the concrete watercourses. With time to think, I couldn't help but reflect on how fantastic it was, having arrived in Syria when the YPG was such a small group on the fringe of Syria, battling for survival, that I was now alongside 10,000 SDF fighters with US support, in the capital of the so-called Islamic State, closing in on the cornered terrorists.

Jake had been disappointed to miss out on the previous operation and insisted to the Syriac commanders that unless he got to fight soon, he would switch to a YPG tabur. I knew where he was coming from. After our previous two years, we were both YPG at heart. There had been a few occasions over the previous months where I had wanted to leave the MFS for no other reason than I missed the YPG's culture, but I had made a commitment to liberate Raqqa alongside the Christians, and I was determined to see it through. Jake was more ambivalent, but with August turning to September, and no let-up in operations, he didn't need to worry. We were soon ordered to pack our things and to help Sofian and the rest of our Syriac unit move deeper into the city.

The commanders sent a Humvee and two Toyota trucks, but since there were twenty-five heavily-armed MFS fighters with a significant amount of equipment and food, we had to pile on to the vehicles and hold on to each other as we bounced over Raqqa's debris-filled roads, the Humvee's machine gunner anxiously revolving in his turret and scanning the windows and doorways of passing buildings for any sign of ambush. When we arrived at the block which would be our next nocta, we all jumped out to unload the kit and to patrol to a large, heavily damaged apartment complex and naturally fell into two groups, one led by Abjar, the other by another good Syriac platoon commander, Bennie.

There were holes smashed through walls, grenade-scarred corridors, and in one apartment there was a dark red puddle of clotted blood. Every few seconds, the thump of a nearby explosion would disturb the concrete and plaster dust that lay everywhere, and it didn't take long before we were all coated in a fine white powder. More ominously, there were regular bursts of gunfire around us. It was worse when we left the building and went out into the open street. Entire buildings had collapsed and spilled their contents all over the roads. We had to climb through one of the ground-floor windows to access the next building and make our way up several staircases filled with the furniture that previous YPG units had thrown there to prevent ISIS creeping up on them. Nearby explosions had caused huge cracks in the walls, which looked close to collapse. Staggering under the weight of our weapons, ammunition and supplies, we climbed over the various barricades. Poor George, one of the smaller Syriacs, had been left carrying the PKM and about 400 rounds of ammunition. I stuck behind him the whole way and guided him over the rougher patches. With a lot of effort, we got to the third floor and put the gear down.

While others picked over the rancid bedding and poked through moulding boxes of old food from the building's previous occupants, I went upstairs to explore further. I didn't get far. The floor above was in a terrible state. Most of the external walls had been blown in and there was a forest of pillars and rubble. I crept around what was left of the ruined apartments, ever mindful to stay away from the windows or missing walls. At least I was comforted to see numerous piles of human shit. It meant there was less chance of any IEDs. Beyond the apartment block, just 100 metres ahead, lay a huge brown-field site, which would have been ripe for redevelopment before the war, and in the centre was a modern secondary school, which had been flattened by several air strikes but which still had plenty of places for ISIS to hide.

After an hour of kicking around the new nocta and listening to the heavy fighting in the south, Jake and I were called back to spend the night at the YPG forward operating base because, apparently, an operation was planned for the following morning on another part of the front, and the senior commander of the Afrin taburs, Heval Sipan, had requested we join them. I was glad of the opportunity to use Sipan's internet and to message mum, because I had not managed to contact her in a while. I gave her a suitably up-beat update, emphasising the progress we were making, glossing over the dangers, highlighting the ISIS retreat and hiding from her any mention of the numerous IEDs. She was clearly relieved to hear from me and, though I could sense the concern in her messages, I was glad to have been able to make contact.

The following day, Jake and I were sitting with Sipan, waiting for transport to take us to the operation, when we were disturbed by the roar of an engine and the screech of brakes. Matay came running into the room. 'Get your things, we've got to go!' he told me in his perfect English. 'What's going on?' I said. 'There's been an explosion. Two guys have been injured,' he said, grabbing my medical bag for me and pointing to my body armour. 'You'll need that.' I leapt to my feet, threw on my armour, grabbed my rifle and followed Matay out of the door.

Before long we were roaring down the main road to the Raqqa front lines. In the distance, among the tomb-stoned buildings, was a pall of black smoke. I could hear the distant thump of mortars and I was more than a little alarmed that we were in a standard unarmoured Hilux. I was keen to ask Matay more questions, but he was gabbling into his radio and listening intently to the squawk of noise coming back. Suddenly, he stopped and turned to me. 'It's George and Hiro. They've been hit by an IED.' I didn't know Hiro, but George was such a lovely kid. I suddenly felt the huge weight of responsibility that would be on me if I was the only one in a position to save them. If, indeed, they could be saved. 'Fuck, I hope so,' I thought.

We arrived at the first set of buildings that led to the new nocta and, with my heart pounding, I threw open the car door and began to run inside. The first room we reached was covered in blood, but there was no sign of the casualties. 'Where are they?' I asked Matay, as he came running in behind me. We followed the blood trail but soon got lost in the maze of corridors, smashed walls and damaged rooms. I forced myself to stay calm as we retraced our steps. We were losing precious minutes and, from the amount of blood I'd seen, the guys didn't have long. There was also a huge risk that we could trigger an IED ourselves. The acrid smell of burning metal still hung in the air from the blast and I suddenly pictured twenty-year-old George's impish grin and thought of his childish humour. 'Shit! We've got to find them,' I said. By the time we found the right way, Matay's radio was squawking again, and he put up his hand to stop me. 'We're too late. They've already been taken to the hospital,' he said. 'What the fuck does that mean? Are they OK?' I asked, but I would find out soon enough. It seemed the guys had been patrolling back to pick up more food supplies but had taken a shortcut and set off a massive IED. Hiro, an Arab lad whose real name was Mohammed, had lost his leg, and George, bleeding heavily from a head wound, had run back to the unit to get help. The guys had moved quickly to carry Hiro to a nearby YPG position for evacuation to hospital, but he had bled out on route and was dead before they could reach further help. He had only been on the front line for a few days.

I sat for a moment and felt distraught. It was clear that Jake and I weren't going to make the operation we had been due to join. Bennie's unit was now two men short and we were needed at the Syriac nocta to make up the numbers. Matay and I immediately returned to Jake, and while Matay drove off to see George, Jake and I were left to return to the front in the next available Humvee. When we arrived back at Bennie's position, it became clear that the unit's morale was at rock bottom. Not only were both lads hugely popular, but Hiro's cousin was in our unit, and though he was not refused permission to accompany the body home to their family, he was told he would have to wait until reinforcements arrived. The next couple of days were heartbreaking, listening to the lad's constant sobbing.

To make matters worse, ISIS must have been aware we were in the building, because the amount of sniper fire coming through the windows from the direction of the flattened secondary school was extraordinary. It wasn't long before the radios crackled with messages between the commanders and we were told to expect an air strike. I waited for a lull in the fighting before creeping up one of the stairwells to watch. Sure enough, there was the 'Whoosh!' then a terrific blast, but instantly from the smoke came another burst of ISIS gunfire. 'They must have a tunnel,' yelled Jake. Bennie warned us there would be another, bigger air strike, and I took shelter in the stairwell. Moments later, there was a roar followed by a massive explosion. My eardrums ballooned and the building began to fall around me. I cried out in shock as lumps of rubble and plaster and dust covered me, and Jake called out, 'Macer? Are you OK?' I staggered, coughing and spluttering down the stairs and told him, 'It's OK, mate.

I'm fine,' as I spat out a paste of dust and saliva. Around us, MFS fighters where whooping with glee, and I looked out to see the school had completely gone, to be replaced by a mushroom cloud several hundred metres high. ISIS positions around the edge of the site began firing in our direction, but they were too far away to bother us and we just laughed. By then, the sun had gone down, and we prepared our rotten, bedbug-infested mattresses and lay down in our filthy clothes, buzzed by mosquitoes. I tossed and turned for hours before I fell into an exhausted sleep.

Around 1 a.m. I was awake again, and went back to my lookout position to check all was well. The smoke from the air strike hadn't dispersed but hung at ground level like a fog, and the ruins of the school, lit up by the moonlight, poked through like mountains piercing the clouds. In the silence, and with the dark haunting ruins of Raqqa stretching off into the distance, it was an image of terrible beauty that only war could create.

# The Heroes of Aleppo

There was barely a half light, and I was still drowsy with sleep when Matay arrived at 6 a.m. to collect me and Jake. He stood outside the building and shouted for us to hurry up. The YPG was attacking the ISIS strongholds at the heart of the city from which we had received so much fire the previous day, and Abjar was going to lead us on the operation, he said. I grabbed my AK and medical bag and brought a small backpack with tins of food, two small water bottles and forty extra rounds of ammo. Altogether, with my body armour and six magazines, it was a heavy load, but it was nothing on Jake. He was weighed down by his PKM, 600 rounds of ammo, his folding-stock AK-47 with four mags and extra grenades. He also had a small backpack with a metal hammer dangling off it – a useful tool for smashing murder holes through walls. He was bristling with weaponry and, with his size, he looked like a walking tank. I had no doubt that if I was wounded he would comfortably be able to carry me as well, but if the roles were reversed and I had to carry him out, it would be the end of me. Or, more likely, of him.

We met up with Abjar and a Humvee sped us to a staging area in the city where twenty Kurds were hanging around, sullen and unwelcoming. The plan appeared to be to flank the position we had attacked the day before, to hit ISIS reinforcements from the rear. It was a clever tactic and the same thing was happening with taburs on the other side of the city as we punched into ISIS territory. As we waited, the sun was getting hotter and my kit was heavy, so I found some shade for a sit-down and was soon followed by some of the YPG fighters who thought it was a good idea. We waited for more than an hour, which gave us time to make friends and talk. There were Kurds and Arabs from all over Northern Syria. We sat, shared water, smoked cigarettes and watched the Humvees roaring back and forth with other taburs until at last we were called forward.

The level of destruction in this part of the city was almost total. Entire buildings had been brought down and the rancid stench of rotting bodies wafted out from under the rubble. 'I smell dead people,' grunted Jake, sadly referencing our time with Jordan in Manbij. 'They got what they deserved. Fuck 'em! I hope they heard it coming,' I replied.

We were finally off-loaded in a street with apartment blocks on either side, and as I leapt off the vehicle I was shocked by the sight of an unexploded ISIS rocket embedded in the tarmac up to the tail fin. Our Humvee could only have missed it by inches, and I couldn't wait to get away from it. The Kurds already at the position were busy clearing the buildings of any possible ISIS fighters or IEDs, and there was a steady thump of home-made YPG bombs as the fighters lit the fuses and tossed them into every room. Just a few streets away, one of our taburs was at that moment engaged in a fierce firefight with ISIS. Jake and I had just stepped into the doorway of an apartment block when there was a massive blast from an IED inside which sent us both staggering back into the street, showered with dust and concrete chippings. 'Jesus! That could have killed both of us,' I said. Jake simply lit up another cigarette. 'Yes. Yes, it could've,' he said before we went back into the smoke-filled hallway. Hidden killers were all around us, from the snipers to the mortars to the IEDs hidden in doorframes, and we had to be permanently on our guard, never knowing what was coming next. We did little but hold our position for the rest of the day, but we did take one casualty among the YPJ fighters clearing buildings on the same street as us. I heard the explosion followed by calls for help, but when I ran outside, she had already been loaded into a Humvee and all I got to see was her agonised face as she was driven past.

The only good thing about killing time was the opportunity to get to know the small tabur stationed with us. They were led by a twenty-two-year-old guy called Öcalan. I was on guard duty, sat on an old sofa on the second floor, looking out of one of the windows, when he introduced himself and, as per usual, my terrible Kurdish left me struggling, but we managed. It turned out his unit had waited in the road with us for the Humvees to come. Öcalan soon chilled, however, and I had him and his team laughing as the hours passed. They were all from Afrin and most had fought in Aleppo. We struck up the sort of instant friendship that only youth and war can produce, and Jake, Abjar and I insisted to the local commanders that we wanted to be in Öcalan's tabur. We soon got our way, and I felt a tinge of pride to be attached to an Afrin tabur – the heroes of Aleppo who had defended their community from both the Islamist rebels of the Al-Nusra Front and ISIS.

The next day, we patrolled as a unit to a half-built apartment block some fifty metres north. There were signs on the third floor of where ISIS had set up an ambush, with murder holes and reinforced firing points facing the direction they had presumed we would be assaulting from. I was hugely thankful that they had fled the position before we had indeed approached, otherwise we might have been slaughtered. We spent the rest of the day holding the building, and Jake and I passed the time by shooting at suspected Daesh sniper positions with the PKM. We also got a chance to know more about our tabur comrades. Öcalan seemed wise beyond his years. Calm and collected, you could tell he loved his men and that they loved him too. There was quiet Shaheen, an incredibly sweet guy who was reserved and shy most of the time but who lit up when you spoke to him. Then there was Demhat, a big guy who carried the unit's PKM. He, too, was shy around us foreigners, but he loved a selfie, and my phone quickly began to fill up with laughing images of us all together. Not only were they a very close-knit team, but they were also well-trained. They took their guard duty seriously and they briefed us regularly on what was going on around us. There was also always someone ready to sort food and produce chai. As we sat together later in the afternoon, sharing small plates of rice and beans, Öcalan pointed to the plates, the cold bottles of water in buckets and the thick blankets that we were sitting on, and, with a mouth full of beans, he said, 'This is living!' I knew what he meant. All he needed to be happy was a rifle, a square meal and the chance to fight. I gestured with a sweep of my hand at all of us sitting there. 'Hevals,' I said and Öcalan smiled. 'Yes,' he said, 'all of us are hevals.' I don't think the word had ever meant more to me.

★

I drew the short straw that night, assigned a 2 a.m. guard duty. I finally settled down on an old mattress, but barely an hour had passed before I realised something was up. I checked my watch and I could see it was 10 p.m. There was constant chatter on the radios in the next room, and I could hear the heavy footfalls of dozens of fighters coming in and out of the house. Before I could investigate, the door swung open and Öcalan ordered us all up. We were needed for a night operation into ISIS territory. I grabbed my kit and could feel the familiar pre-fight adrenaline begin to surge through my body. We climbed into a waiting Humvee and drove through the darkness. The driver couldn't use his headlights for fear of making us a target for ISIS so was going by memory alone, and he couldn't afford to slow down and risk a well-placed RPG hitting us and burning us all to death in the cab, so it was a nerve-wracking ride.

We reached our destination and got out. It was deathly quiet when the Humvee engine was cut. I followed Öcalan and the rest of the guys to a large house, where there was the familiar sound of furniture and bricks being moved from a barricade on the other side of the gate before the occupants ushered us in. As we made our way deeper into the building, it was clear there was more than one tabur there, and even in the pitch black darkness I could sense people everywhere. They were on the stairs, in the hallway and in the corridors, and the sounds of whispered conversations were coming from every room we passed. It seemed it had been the very smart home of some wealthy people, and on the third floor there was a huge apartment with a living room being used as a temporary command centre. Huge picture windows were hidden behind thick curtains and furniture that had been piled up as protection against snipers and explosions, and the only light was the blue-green glare from computer screens that illuminated the faces of the commanders poring over them. The hours ticked by until eventually it was our turn. 'You ready?' asked Abjar, as I threw on my body armour. 'Ready and happy,' I said. Next to Abjar was Öcalan, not sure of what we were saying but watching us chatting with a grin on his face nonetheless. 'We attack?' was all I could manage in Kurdish. 'Yeah, we attack,' said Öcalan, and he clapped me on the shoulder and went to check on the rest of his unit. Soon enough he led us out into the street. I checked my watch and it was 2 a.m. Öcalan went along the line and counted us off. I felt a spike of admiration for the guy. He was so relaxed in the face of danger. He gave us a brief pep talk in Kurdish, which Abjar translated for me. It was simple: 'Move quietly. If we get contacted, give heavy return fire and seek cover. Above all, listen to my commands and stick together.' With that, Öcalan gave a wave of his hand and we moved off silently into the night.

# Hell on Earth

The night air was cool on my face, but my heart was racing as I listened to the occasional clatter of AK fire in the distance and dreaded, at any moment, a deadly burst closer to hand. Silver moonlight illuminated some of the ground ahead of us as we made our stealthy way through the streets, but it did nothing to penetrate the ominous darkness which shrouded countless windows and doorways in the towering buildings around us. I was grateful to know that Jake and his heavy machine gun were behind us in support. He had lumbered off, panting and wheezing, to take an overview position in a building with a clear sight of the road. Never mind his lack of fitness, he had the accuracy of a sniper and a weapon that could smash through walls, so if ISIS were to ambush us, he could hopefully provide us with lifesaving support. I was one of the last guys in the patrol. Following a few feet behind me was Shaheen. He kept his rifle up and circled around to watch in every direction for signs of danger. A few metres ahead of me was Demhat, and in front of us all was Öcalan. Our mission, I would gather, was to try to seize a key building 150 metres ahead of us, at the end of the street, control of which would cut the road link between the last two ISIS strongholds, at the city's main hospital and the sports stadium. Success would end the jihadists' ability to reinforce each other from either position, finishing the conventional battle and heralding the endgame of a siege situation. Failure would likely mean our deaths.

After fifty metres walking silently in the dark, the road split. If we were to fork right, it would lead us directly to the hospital and into the teeth of the enemy. Instead, we picked up the pace as we continued straight on. I could feel the comforting weight of body armour and magazines sliding up and down on my chest as I ran, but somehow it made my unprotected areas feel more vulnerable. The new stretch of road to our target was only about 100 metres long. There was a succession of three- and four-storey townhouses on the left-hand side, and on the right was a two-storey house next to a substantial five-storey block under construction, after which there was another half-built two-storey house. At the end of the road was the T-junction that was our objective, with a road leading left to the stadium and right to the hospital. My hands tightened on my rifle, and I checked again that my safety catch was off before I lifted my weapon and scanned the multitude of possible hiding places. I wanted to get into cover as soon as possible.

I was comforted to see YPG fighters from another unit at the end of the road talking to two shirtless old men. It was apparent that the old boys had been forced to strip by the Kurds to check they were not suicide bombers. Now they were putting their shirts back on while engaging the YPG fighters in a heated discussion. Öcalan was the first of our patrol to reach them and began talking to the old men in Arabic, while the rest of the unit bunched up around him and I stood away from the group to keep guard. I was glad to see a few Kurdish faces at the window of one of the houses on the left-hand side of the street. At least we weren't alone and they were ready, like Jake, to give us covering fire. Öcalan was listening patiently as one of the old men gestured vigorously towards the buildings on the other side of the road that ran between the stadium and the hospital, but other members of the unit were adding their own views. Though they were arguing in hushed tones, it alarmed me how much their voices seemed to carry on the still night air. 'What's going on?' I whispered to Abjar, as I pulled on his arm. 'The old man says his family is on the other side of the road. They're trapped in those houses and he wants us to rescue them,' Abjar explained. I wasn't happy. 'I've got a bad feeling about this. We need to get off this fucking road,' I said. With a few expletives of his own to silence the arguments of dissenting team members, Öcalan gave the order for us to follow the old man. While others muttered that it was not part of the mission, Demhat dutifully began to follow. I turned to look at the rest of the group, still not moving. 'Fuck it,' I thought. 'Öcalan is my commander,' and I fell in behind Demhat. As the three of us began to cross the road, I was just glad that we would soon be in the safe shelter of the buildings on the other side.

Bam! Bam! Bam! Bam! An explosion of noise suddenly distorted the air, and sparks were flying off the road at my feet and off the buildings around me. The next few seconds seemed to happen in slow motion. Panic-stricken, I spun around so violently to escape the deadly hail of heavy machine-gun bullets that I lost my balance and began to fall. Mercifully, I managed two giant steps before my momentum had me sprawling nose-first onto the tarmac, my backpack somersaulting over my head and my glasses flying off my face. My rifle was the only thing my instincts told me to hold on to, and all the while there was the terrible SNAP and CRACK of bullets ripping past me. In an instant, I was back on my feet and scrambling the last few metres off the road. The patrol had scattered in confusion, with half the unit seeking shelter in a nearby house while the other half gave covering fire. I put my rifle to my shoulder and fired down the road. As I couldn't see anything, it was more to make the enemy keep their heads down than anything else. Without my glasses I was in a world of trouble. I stopped shooting and decided to run to the other corner of the street, to see if I could get a safer firing position, but halfway across I could hear the commander of the other unit calling me to join the rest of my patrol. I quickly changed direction and ran towards a house, where I could just about make out YPG fighters manning firing positions in the upper windows, but there was another burst of gunfire from behind me and, with rounds now striking the building I was running towards, I swerved again and ran straight into a small shop next door. 'Fuck!' I thought. There was no way I could have got to the house in time, but being stuck in the shop, isolated from my comrades, was far from ideal. On top of that, it was dawning on me that the ISIS fire was coming from both directions. It seemed apparent that enemy fighters were coming from the hospital to support their fellow jihadists who had ambushed us from the direction of the stadium. We were firmly stuck in the middle of the two largest concentrations of ISIS fighters in Raqqa.

As my eyes adjusted to the gloom of the shop, I threw up my rifle again when I saw movement in the darkness. To my surprise, it was the other old man staggering towards me. He seemed terrified and started shouting something in

Arabic. I reached out with my left hand, seized his shoulder and pushed him towards the back wall. 'No problem, no problem,' I said firmly in Arabic. It had been this old bastard's friend who had led us into the road. Thankfully he didn't look much of a threat himself, and his loose fitting *thawb* didn't appear to be hiding anything. I took a step back and aggressively told him to stay put. This calmed him a bit, and meant that I was able to turn my attention back to the road. I was happy to see a YPG fighter from the other unit join me in the shop. He ran in holding an RPG launcher and immediately began prepping it to fire. Even without my glasses, I recognised him from another of the Afrin units we had met just a few days before. Knowing I wasn't alone meant I could focus on getting my contact lenses into my eyes. I had a pair ready in my pocket and it took only a few seconds before I could see clearly again. I waited for a moment, panting hard and listening to the gunfight going on around me. The shop was empty except for a mess of tangled metal shelves. My boots crunched on broken glass and I noticed a liquid on the floor. Every time my chest swelled to suck in more air, it came up hard against my immoveable body armour and it felt like I was being suffocated. As I went to loosen my collar, a pain shot down my arm. My shoulder was killing me. The fall had not only skinned my elbow but nearly wrenched my arm out of its socket. I could hear Abjar calling me from next door. On one side, I had comrades from my patrol sheltering in a house; on the other side – the house on the corner – was the YPG patrol we were supposed to have leapfrogged, and I couldn't reach either. BANG! The lone YPG fighter with me had stepped back into the doorway of the shop and fired an RPG. The rocket's back-thrust blasted into the room, kicking up all the dust in the shop and making my ears scream in protest, and I staggered backwards, stunned. The old man let out another wail and hobbled back towards the door. I recovered myself and grabbed him again by the shoulder. I couldn't have him running around in the street by himself – ISIS would gun him down the instant they saw him. The YPG fighter, still at the door, called out in Kurdish and pointed at something across the road. I quickly gathered that the RPG had found a target and the ISIS firing outside had stopped, so if there was ever a time to make a move it had to be now. 'Go, go, go!' I shouted in Kurdish. The YPG fighter bolted out of the door and I seized the old man by his wrist and dragged him outside.

Thankfully there was only about five metres of pavement before we were through a gate leading into the other property, and we ran into the welcoming arms of the hevals who held the gate and slapped me on the back as I ran past. This was a much safer position. The house had a five-feet-high wall in front of the property and a thin paved veranda between the wall and the house. It was half-decent cover and gave us a better view of the street than the windows above, which were a magnet for enemy fire. To try to get an idea of my surroundings, I walked straight into one of the front rooms and was immediately confronted by a huge ISIS flag on the back wall. Next to the flag was a door leading further into the property. The rest of the room was trashed, with a large dusty armchair in the corner covered in books. I called the old man in and told him to sit tight. I then went over to see Abjar, who was standing guard at the wall. Before I could say anything, Abjar turned around and I could see his face twisted with grief. 'Öcalan is dead!' he said. The words jarred in my head. 'What? He can't be!' I said. 'He was right in front of me. Where is he?' Abjar was struggling to hold it together and his voice was high-pitched. 'In the road,' he said. 'They shot him. He's şehîd! Öcalan is şehîd!' There was a burst of gunfire above us as one of the hevals blasted out of a window and we both ducked slightly. 'Where is he?' I asked again. 'Look!' Abjar said, and he took my arm and pointed to the gate. I took cover by one of the concrete posts and carefully peered around the corner. It was just twenty metres back to the road where we had attempted to cross just minutes before. Öcalan was sprawled out in the middle of the street. His arms were thrown outwards and his head was back. The light of the moon was on his face and even at that distance it was clear he was dead. I ducked back inside. 'God damn it! What a fucking mess!'

BANG! There was a huge explosion out on the street. Someone had either thrown a grenade, or a landmine had been triggered somewhere. I looked back at Abjar and was about to say something when his eyes narrowed as he looked at my spare rounds. 'You've been shot!' he said. I looked down and saw a ragged gash in one of my magazine holders. I reached down and pulled it open. The magazine inside was almost ripped in half. I took the mag out and saw the jagged hole where a bullet had gone straight through. The spring inside was destroyed, and without the tension in the magazine, the bullets just rattled around uselessly. I pushed the ruined mag back into my rigging. I was one lucky SOB. The bullet had clearly come in at an angle and punched straight through without hitting my body armour or, more importantly, me. Another four inches and it might have missed my armoured plate and come under my armpit. It could so easily have been my body lying in the road next to Öcalan.

Abjar turned and started talking to the commander of the other unit while Shaheen spoke rapidly into a radio, clearly updating more senior YPG commanders on what was happening. Not knowing what to do, I walked the length of the front wall and found a spot to pull guard duty. For the next few minutes, I kept watch of the buildings on the other side of the road. The firing had died down and it had gone eerily quiet. I felt a tap on my shoulder and Abjar whispered into my ear. 'Get ready, we're going to get Öcalan's body.' I was bemused. 'Why?' I asked. 'If he's dead then what's the point in risking it?' Abjar had got it together again and was fully in control of his emotions. 'He's still got his radio! If Daesh get it, then they will know our radio frequencies. They'll be able to listen to us talking,' he said, and I could see he was right. My mind raced to come up with a plan. 'Why don't we call in an air strike?' I said. 'When the smoke fills the road, we'll run out and drag him back?' Abjar shook his head. 'The Americans can't provide air cover tonight. We have to wait until tomorrow. Daesh are moving into positions around us. If we're going, we have to go now,' he said. 'Fuck!' Everything had gone from bad to worse. If we had no air cover, then we were in a horribly vulnerable position. ISIS knew they had hit us hard and that we were out on a limb, surrounded on all sides. They would expect us to call in air strikes and when they realised nothing was coming, they would surely attempt to overrun us. No doubt the reason they were so quiet was because they were already moving into position and hiding from air strikes they didn't yet know weren't available.

The commander of the other unit was the first to venture out, and from my position at the wall I watched him move cautiously into the gateway and then, when nothing happened, slowly into the road. His rifle was up and ready to fire, but it was quiet.

Shaheen and a second fighter from the other platoon followed the commander onto the road, and when Abjar joined them, I was compelled to go as well. If they were willing to risk their lives, then there was no way I was going to sit back and watch. It felt terrible to be back on the road where, I now knew, I had come so close to death. I stuck to the pavement on the left-hand side of the road and I had my rifle raised. I scanned the dark buildings around me, expecting at any moment for hell to be unleashed. To my right, in the middle of the road, with their rifles slung on their backs and their hands ready, were Shaheen and the fighter from the other unit. Abjar was to the right of them, giving good cover at a different angle. As we advanced the short distance back to the T-junction, I suddenly realised the full extent of the ambush and was horrified to see that it wasn't just Öcalan's body illuminated by the moonlight but that there were *two* bodies lying in the road! 'Heval Demhat!' Abjar exclaimed. There was a rapid conversation in Kurdish and the new information was shouted back to the commander. I could see Demhat's PKM at his feet where he lay on his back. His head was turned away from me and was almost looking in the direction of Öcalan's body just a few metres away. I forced my eyes away and back to the dark buildings around us. In the confusion of the ambush, we had missed Demhat, and we were now confronted with two casualties instead of one. It was a crushing blow. I stopped at the corner and indicated to the guys that I was ready. Abjar had a better angle down the road, where much of the firing had been coming from. He fired his rifle a few times but nothing came back. 'Go!' he said to the others, and I felt a sudden surge of respect for the two Kurdish lads in the middle who were expected to run out and seize Demhat and Öcalan's bodies. It was clear the road was a death trap, and I could see they were nervous. The guys ran out and were a few feet from Demhat when Abjar suddenly fired another shot. The bang from his AK was shockingly loud and the guys staggered back off the road in a panic. There were a few whispered obscenities and Abjar told them to get back out – he had only fired to make ISIS keep their heads down. The lads crouched, and were about to run back into the road when something wonderful happened. Demhat lifted his head off the ground, turned, and looked at me. Just moments before, he was either unconscious or unaware that we were coming for him. Abjar's shot had clearly roused him. 'He's alive!' I cried out in English. 'Go, go, go!' The two guys ran back and seized Demhat's legs and shoulders. I scanned the buildings for any sign of ISIS movement. Seeing nothing and with the lads struggling in the road, I had no choice but to run out and join them. I was surprised at how unfazed I was about going back out there. Finding Demhat alive had given me a renewed confidence and purpose, but it also gave me a tinge of shame. I felt disbelief that we had been so focused on Öcalan that we hadn't noticed Demhat missing. We couldn't miss him now.

Demhat was so damn heavy that my shoulder was in agony as we struggled to lift him. We staggered back towards the safety of the house and, as we arrived at the gate, there was a sudden burst of gunfire behind us. I half ducked and glanced back. I could see dust and sparks being kicked up around Öcalan's body, but it took me a second to realise what was happening. 'They're shooting Öcalan,' said Abjar. 'Get inside, now!' I felt a surge of anger. 'Those fucking animals!' I shouted in frustration. One of the ISIS fighters must have seen us carry Demhat off the road and they were now making sure Öcalan was dead. We hurried into the courtyard in front of the house and set Demhat down on his back. I cut off his magazine holder and ripped open his shirt. His skin looked pale in the moonlight, head was raised as he watched me, and it was clear he was now fully conscious. 'Where is he hit?' I said to the crowd around me. A couple of the YPG fighters from upstairs had come down and were keen to help. 'Talk to me someone,' I said, as I searched his front. 'He said his back,' Abjar replied. I turned Demhat over and lifted his shirt. High up on his back – in line with his shoulder blades – were an entry and an exit wound. The bullet had passed straight through him at an angle. About an inch to the right and it would have missed him altogether, but he hadn't been as lucky as I had. I could see that the bullet had certainly gone through his spine, and it was possible that both lung cavities had been penetrated. The entry wound was the size of a five-pence piece and the exit was the size of a two-pence piece. It was a ghastly sight. I listened for the grotesque sound of a sucking chest wound but found nothing. I still put a chest seal on both the entry and exit wounds.

I was concerned that blood and liquid might leak into his chest, though I now thought the bullet might have only clipped his lung cavities. Hopefully only a small amount of blood or air was getting in. Either way, he had to get to hospital quickly. Apart from applying the chest seals and giving pain relief, there was nothing more that I could do.

With Abjar translating, I begged the commander to allow me to carry Demhat out. 'It's too dangerous,' the commander told me. 'We're surrounded. You won't get fifty metres down the road before you are shot,' he said. But the road outside appeared quiet. If there was a chance to go, then it had to be now. I offered to give them my ammunition and even my body armour. I would go alone, with Demhat on my back and with an AK in my hands. Speed was key. If the hevals were warned that I would be running around the corner, then they could get a Humvee ready for evacuation. We were just a few hundred metres away from a reasonably safe area, I reasoned. The commander spoke rapidly into his radio. I could see that he was in turmoil. He wanted to let me go but couldn't risk me getting shot as well. Finally, his concern for Demhat changed his mind. 'OK, you can go,' he said. I didn't need any further encouragement. I pulled my body armour over my head and tossed my backpack to Abjar. 'I need help guys,' I said, and I bent my knees while the others lifted Demhat onto my back. He was an enormous dead weight, but thankfully his arms had some strength left in them, as I felt them tighten around my neck. Even so, he kept slipping off my back, which meant that I had to lean forward quite a lot. Eventually I was ready.

'ALLAHU AKBAR!' came a cry from outside, then WHOOSH! . . . BANG! Everyone dived for cover as an RPG struck the outside wall, sending a cloud of debris and dust over us. The explosion was the signal for a huge amount of gunfire from multiple ISIS positions around us, including the buildings directly on the other side of our street. Our guys scattered. Some returned fire at the wall while others ran upstairs to find firing positions in the house. As soon as I heard the explosion, I knew my chance to get Demhat out had gone, and with a little help I laid him back down on the ground. The bullets were flying over the small wall at the front and striking inside the house. Fearing for Demhat's safety, I dragged him into the front room with the old man. I then took a few minutes to make him comfortable. I put him on an old mattress and found a blanket to keep him warm, gave him pain relief and then reassured him that everything would be OK. He held my eye and nodded bravely. He clearly had a lot of faith in me, which I was desperate to repay.

With the patient secure, I ran back outside to join the others. There was now an intense gunfight going on between the YPG and the Islamic State fighters. You couldn't move without crouching down below the trajectory of the incoming rounds, and I ran to the low wall and glanced over. I could see the windows and corners targeted by the others, and at first I simply joined in and began shooting the same places. After fifteen rounds or so, I noticed a muzzle flash from a window on the ground floor of a building thirty metres from us. I immediately put a few rounds straight through the window and then dropped down into cover. I pulled out my magazine to check how many rounds I had left, and I was glad to see the golden gleam of fresh rounds at the top. I clicked the magazine back in and was rising to my feet, so I could shoot at the same window again, when suddenly, WHOOSH! . . . BANG! I ducked as an RPG exploded ten metres to my right. I wasn't sure what it hit, but thankfully the wall protected me. Seconds later, as I was rising again to start firing, there was another loud BANG! Another RPG had hit exactly the same place. Dust flew everywhere and there was the pattering sound of rocks falling back to earth. '*ALLAHU AKBAR!*' screamed a voice on the other side of the road. Immediately the YPG shouted back their defiance – '*BIJI SEROK APO!*' – yelled one of the Kurds, and a burst of gunfire from a window upstairs sprayed the ISIS position. 'AFRIN!' shouted another Kurd upstairs. There was a further loud BANG! and a Kurdish RPG struck the enemy building on the corner of the street. Rubble and dust spewed out on to the road. I leapt up and fired back at the window where I'd seen that muzzle flash. Fearing I was drawing too much attention, I swiftly changed position and went over to the gate. '*ALLAHU AKBAR!*' Yet another fanatical scream was followed by a long burst of PKM fire, which struck our building somewhere above my head. Chips of mortar and brickwork fell around me. I rose to my feet and emptied the rest of my magazine into the building across the street.

I then ducked back down to reload. I stuffed the empty magazine into a pouch, pulled out a fresh one and clipped it into place. I cocked the rifle and was about to stand to shoot when I was tapped on the back by Abjar. He had been upstairs, firing from one of the windows and had come down because he had found the unit's bag of explosives. He pulled out one of the home-made bombs and straightened out the fuse. The next moment, he ran out of the gate and threw the bomb over a wall on the other side of the street. BOOM! The explosion was deafening, and lumps of concrete from the blast peppered our building. There was a stunned silence followed by cheers from the Kurds for Abjar's efforts. Above us, a YPG fighter fired another RPG from the upper windows of our house. This was followed by a burst of gunfire from the Kurds. Abjar ran back onto the road and tossed another grenade. Every time he did this he exposed himself to fire from pretty much every ISIS position around us, but, through luck and incredible bravery, he not only survived but was also helping to drive the Islamic State fighters from the building closest to us.

With a noticeable decrease in the fire coming from ISIS, I took the opportunity to check on Demhat. He was lying on his back, staring at the ceiling. I took his wrist to check his heart rate and, to make it easier for myself, held his hand while I searched for his pulse. His hand was cold, and I squeezed it gently to try to warm it. The loud thumping of my own heart and the odd explosion outside made counting Demhat's pulse impossible. I would search, find it, attempt to count the beats and then lose it again. Then I realised that Demhat was gently squeezing and caressing my hand. He seemed to be deriving genuine strength and comfort from this simple act of compassion, but there lay my big deception. I wanted to give off a calm assurance, but the placebo effect of my fussing and pulse-checking masked the fact that there was nothing more I could do for him. I could hear a gargling in his lungs, and he was complaining of not being able to breathe properly. I knew his chest was filling with blood, his lungs were collapsing and he needed a chest drain. As this was not something I could do, what he really needed was a hospital, but we were 300 metres into ISIS territory, which meant that we might as well have been on the moon. I turned to see the commander walking past me; he stopped and asked if

Demhat could live twenty-four hours. I said that he'd be lucky to live forty-five minutes. The commander rubbed his face with one hand. His face was grey with dust and lined with worry. In that case, he explained, Demhat was going to die. There were no air strikes and no reinforcement coming for us. We were completely surrounded, with no water and no chance of a resupply of ammunition. There was no guarantee any of us would survive the night. With that, the commander left the room, but not before he tore the ISIS flag off the back wall and threw it in the dirt.

# Too Close to Call

I gave up searching for Demhat's pulse and sat holding his hand while the world around us was falling apart. A few minutes passed as I sat comforting Demhat, before the sound of a commotion outside forced me to leave him and rejoin the others. I ducked through the door, took cover behind the wall and looked over to the gate to see Abjar stripping a PKM. 'Where did you get that?' I asked. He was so focused on meticulously checking his new weapon that he barely looked up. 'It's Demhat's. We forgot it on the road,' he replied. I couldn't believe it. 'You ran out in this firefight to get that? Are you fucking crazy?' I asked. He just looked up and grinned. Abjar took the weapon to the top floor of the house while I stayed to pull guard duty with Shaheen, next to the gate. As if in protest at Abjar's retrieval of the PKM under their noses, the ISIS shooting had intensified. In response, every time the YPG above me fired an RPG or a long burst of the PKM, they cheered or shouted a Kurdish war cry, and I shouted as loudly as the rest of them! '*Biji Rojava!*' I screamed, then grinned at the absurdity of an Englishman yelling Kurdish battle cries in Raqqa. A few minutes passed before I heard my name being called by Demhat. I ran inside and took hold of his hand. He was deteriorating badly. He was feeling sick, and I gently rolled him onto his side so he could throw up. When he rolled back, I noticed a trickle of pink liquid coming out of his nose. I found a rag to clean up the mess. I then got a wet wipe from my bag to clean his face. I'm not even remotely religious, but I prayed desperately for help.

I had no way of knowing the extent of the growing crisis around me, but we were not the only position in contact. Just a few hundred metres away, Jake and the one Kurd with him were also fighting for their lives. ISIS fighters had come up from the hospital and had managed to battle right up to their building. Jake was on the second floor of an apartment complex while ISIS fighters were in the building opposite and on the floor below. They were throwing grenades through Jake's window, to try to flush him and the other heval out. While ISIS explosives blew up around them, Jake was taking cover wherever he could. He also had the added jeopardy of having to defend the stairwell, to prevent ISIS fighters from coming up. The only way he could do this was to go full Rambo and fire his PKM from the hip, spraying dozens of rounds down the stairs. He would then follow this up with his own grenades.

About ten kilometres outside of Raqqa, at the US Special Forces base, MFS and YPG commanders were staring nervously at live drone feeds. They could see dozens of ISIS fighters moving between buildings and slowly surrounding our positions while there were no available fighter jets in the air to help us. US planes had been bombing all day, and now other coalition partners had taken over for the night; French and British planes over Raqqa had either already dropped their payloads or had retired for the evening for lack of fuel. There were still hours to go before US planes were due back. BOOM! I ducked as another huge explosion sent debris and smoke out onto the road from the building next door. More shouts of '*ALLAHU AKBAR!*' were evidence of the increasingly ferocious ISIS effort to overrun the position being held by the few YPG fighters who we had been supposed to leapfrog earlier in the evening. The jihadists were throwing large explosives through the ground-floor windows. They had also taken a tall building a little further down the street, towards the stadium, and were using their height advantage, with RPGs and snipers, to drive the YPG defenders off the roof and away from top windows. Without being able to properly defend their building, the Kurds were struggling to stop ISIS fighters getting into the basement and onto the ground floor. They had pushed refrigerators, old beds and furniture against the doors and windows in a desperate bid to hold them back.

There was no way we could go to support them. We still had ISIS fighters just ten metres away on the other side of our street. I kept a constant guard in case an enemy fighter did 'an Abjar' and ran across the road hurling bombs. I could see muzzle flashes from half a dozen buildings and houses, and it was clear ISIS were moving around with growing confidence, emboldened by our lack of air support. 'Baran!' I could hear my Kurdish name being called by Demhat. 'I am here, heval,' I said, as I ducked through the door. 'I can't breathe. Help me,' he gasped in Kurdish. 'It's OK, heval. I'm here. Relax, we're going to get you out,' I said, getting one of the YPG fighters to translate for me. Demhat moaned angrily. He muttered in Kurdish and shifted uncomfortably in his bed. I reached out and put my hand on his shoulder. In broken Kurdish and English I hushed and tried to calm him. It worked for a while but he was getting more distressed.

'Heval?' I felt a tap on my shoulder. It was a fighter from the other unit. He said something in Kurdish and pointed to his head. I took him to the back of the room and switched on my little torch to take a closer look. He was wearing a dirty bandana around his head and there was a large patch of dried blood over his eye. I removed it gently to see a huge bump above his eyebrow and a thin but deep cut oozing blood. I gently tilted his head back to get a closer look and he grimaced with pain. He tried to explain in Kurdish, which I didn't understand, but thankfully Abjar was walking past and I called him over to translate. 'He says he got it when we were ambushed. He fell on the ground and has a terrible pain in his head.' 'He banged his head?' I asked. 'I think so,' shrugged Abjar. The guy wasn't in a good way and was complaining that he couldn't see properly out of his eye and that he was dizzy. I presumed he had concussion of some sort. I bandaged his head properly and got him to sit down on another mattress, but within a couple of minutes he had passed out and was unresponsive. He was breathing normally and his heart rate was fine, but he wouldn't wake up. I placed him in the recovery position and left him.

The firing outside hadn't let up and we were down another man. BANG! There was yet another explosion and the sound of falling masonry. I ran out of the room with my AK up and was confronted by Shaheen covered with dust. An ISIS grenade had been thrown and had landed in the gate. The explosion had brought down the top of the concrete gate post and a lump of stone from the front of our house. 'Goddamit,' I thought. That was the closest grenade they'd thrown; another foot inside the gate and Shaheen would be dead. I stuck my rifle over the wall and sent a stream of bullets into the house across the road.

'Baran!' I heard my name being called again and I ran back inside to see Demhat. I spent a few minutes fussing over his injuries and tucking his blanket closer around him. I also checked on my other patient, who managed to groan loudly as I felt for his pulse, and he finally woke and nodded that he was OK. There was another burst of gunfire outside, and I rushed back to the wall to make sure the street was clear. Over the next twenty minutes, I ran back and forth between the wall outside and the two patients inside the front room until finally the firing was dying down. I checked my watch and saw that it was approaching 5 a.m. Dawn was breaking, and the first glimmers of light were shining through the smoke that hung about us like a haze.

The YPG next door had put up a heroic resistance and had managed to fight off the ISIS attackers, even when some had got inside their building. They fought room to room, eventually killing several jihadists and driving the rest away. 'Heval Baran!' I heard my name being called, but Shaheen had been called away and I was the only one at the wall. If I left the gate it would be completely unguarded. 'One minute, heval!' I called back in Kurdish. I had to wait for Shaheen or Abjar to come back and take my place. We had barred the gate the best we could but it was badly damaged. A well-placed kick would have it flying inward, and allowing Jihadists into our building would mean death for us all. I heard a tinkling sound of metal outside and fired a long burst from my AK, ducked down, moved position and kept watch for a response. Nothing happened. I could hear Demhat groaning loudly in the next room but I ignored him and kept watching. I was exhausted. It wouldn't have surprised me if I had been hearing things.

I waited for another five or ten minutes before Shaheen came back clutching the radio, then gave him a moment to see if he was happy before I motioned that I needed to go. He nodded and waved me away. I crouched down and ran quickly into the front room.

It took a moment for my eyes to adjust to the gloom. Demhat had rolled off his bed and was now lying on his side on the concrete. 'Shit, Demhat, are you OK?' I asked, but there was no response. I ran over and rolled him on to his back. He was unconscious. His breathing was ragged and his body was cold. The other casualty raised himself up and looked over in surprise. I caught his eye and told him to get Abjar. They arrived back a few minutes later. 'What's going on?' demanded Abjar. 'Demhat's dying. He needs to go now!' I said. Abjar began to shake his head, but before he could say anything, I interrupted him. 'I'm telling you Abjar, he has to go NOW. He will be dead in the next hour.' Abjar's look told me he understood but there was nothing he could do. 'There's no way,' he said. 'The air support will come soon, but we can't leave this position until tonight.' I felt gutted. I placed Demhat's head in my lap and tilted it back slightly to aid his breathing, and I stayed like that until the end, talking to him and dabbing his forehead with a wet cloth. After twenty minutes or so, his breathing slowed and then stopped. I placed my hand on his chest and a few moments later, I felt his heart's last beat. I was horrified to now be holding Demhat's corpse. I had been with him for days, talking, laughing and smoking. I had watched him bravely endure his injuries, and I had held his hand to comfort him in his last minutes. To now find myself holding his dead body was heartbreaking. I gently placed Demhat's head back onto the mattress and pulled the blanket over his head, then I went outside to get a breath of fresh air. As I walked out, Shaheen looked at me and asked after Demhat. I simply shook my head and muttered, '*şehîd*'. I sat on the ground, leant against the wall and put my head in my hands. Shaheen turned away and carried on keeping guard. It took me a few minutes to realise he was hiding the fact that tears were falling down his dusty face. After losing Öcalan, risking our lives and bringing back Demhat had been a much-needed morale boost. Watching Demhat deteriorate and then die as well, was a bitter blow. The sun was now rising over Raqqa, but the day wasn't going to bring us much relief. In fact, we would be lucky to survive.

An hour after Demhat died, the fighters from the other house ran over to join us. They had nearly been overrun in the night and had survived so many grenades and RPGs that their building was in danger of collapse. Now the morning brought fresh challenges. I felt sure ISIS would think of more innovative ways to attack us. By pooling our resources and coming together, we were giving ourselves the best chance of survival, but there were only five of them and they were nearly out of ammunition. They had performed heroically and had given ISIS a bloody nose. Dead ISIS fighters were lying in their stairwell as testament to their resistance.

Still, things weren't looking good. We had suffered the morale blow of losing our commander and PKM gunner; we had no way of resupplying our food, water or ammunition; and all of us – in both units – were already suffering badly from exhaustion and dehydration. I had brought two bottles of water, but between all of us it only lasted a few hours. At first light I pulled out the few tins of sardines that I had in my bag. It was my emergency stash, and although it meant only a few bites each, it was a welcome boost. I noticed Shaheen replenishing the teams' magazines with whatever spare rounds he could find. He had an upturned cap half-full of bullets and next to him was a pile of empty mags that he had been asked to fill. Every time a mag was ready, he piled it neatly next to the wall, ready to dish out to the whole unit. I had a few reserve boxes myself and was able to tip an extra forty rounds into the hat. I fetched the magazines that I had cut from Demhat's body and put them on the completed pile. I then pulled out my magazine that had stopped a bullet the night before and, since the spring was gone, I simply poured the rounds out into the cap. I tossed the ruined mag and replaced it with one of Demhat's. If we had another nasty encounter with ISIS that lasted more than a few hours, we were going to run out of ammunition. We had been informed by the commanders at the American base that we were completely surrounded. Before our last rounds were spent, we would have to try to retreat. That would mean battling our way back to our lines during daylight hours, which was not something I wanted to do.

After an hour of pulling guard duty and with no movement from ISIS, I went to rest for a few minutes in the front room. I sat next Demhat's body and pulled back the blanket. He looked peaceful. I felt horribly guilty that in his last moments he had called out to me and I had been too busy to attend to him. Finding him off his bed and close to death had made me feel like I had failed him. I suddenly had the idea to try to dignify his body, so I took a wet wipe and cleaned his dusty face. His uniform shirt was ripped open and his chest still bare, so I pulled the shirt together and zipped it up. I wanted to fold his arms and place his hands on his chest, in the same way I'd seen bodies placed in the movies, but when I took his arms and pulled them into place, they simply sprang apart again and went back to his sides. Shocked by his rigor mortis, I hurriedly wrapped the blanket around him. I looked up and realised I was being watched by the old man. I had forgotten about him sitting alone in the corner of the room. He quickly looked away when I caught his eye, and I wondered what he was thinking. He knew that I was a foreigner, that Abjar and I were in the MFS and that we were battling alongside the YPG. He must have imagined this day for a long time. It was the day he was able to leave the so-called Islamic State and find his family – if he survived, that was. I made an effort to talk to him and he said he had been a court judge in Raqqa before ISIS took over. His family had all fled to Turkey and he was going to follow them as soon as he could. I shared some of our food with him and told him that I hoped he would see his family again.

A few hours passed and things were still quiet, but the heat of the sun and the renewed threat of snipers forced us to pull back into the house. There were several entrances to the building, but as long as we had someone on guard at all times, then the building was relatively secure. I got the old man a pillow and told him to sit in the safety of the hall, in the centre of the house. The fighter with the head injury called me over and asked me to help him move Demhat's body. I put my hands under Demhat's armpits and lifted his torso off the ground. He was unbelievably heavy. I staggered with him to one of the rooms in the back and laid him on a mattress on the floor. Shaheen saw the care with which I laid the body down and made a point of thanking me for treating Demhat. After taking my head firmly in his hands, he gently kissed both my cheeks.

Keeping busy helped, but I was very uneasy. Why weren't the Islamic State attacking? They must have known by then that we didn't have the ability to call in air strikes. Another thirty minutes had passed when I next checked my watch. It was 10 a.m., and I hadn't heard a shot from ISIS in at least a few hours. That wasn't to say they weren't preparing. There was definite movement. I could hear the dull thumping noise of metal on concrete coming from across the street and next door; ISIS were clearly smashing firing holes in the buildings around us. I found a dirty mattress and placed it opposite the door that led outside. I lay down and pointed my rifle at the door. I was ready to shoot anyone coming through. I don't know how long I stayed like that. My eyelids were heavy and I was dizzy with fatigue. On the floor around me, the old man and a few of the Kurds from next door had curled up and fallen asleep. To help keep myself awake, I chatted with Shaheen in broken English and Kurdish. I liked him a lot, and he clearly thought the world of me and Abjar. I turned on my bed and was trying to ask him if he had any brothers or sisters, when suddenly his face froze and he raised his hand to silence me. In an instant I heard it too. It was the mechanical roar of an engine.

'What is that?' I asked, getting quickly to my feet. I stood at the door to the front room, cocked my head and listened again. Sure enough, I heard the roar of an engine and then the squeal of tyres. 'It's a vehicle!' I walked

a few feet into the room and raised my rifle towards
the door. I was concerned that this was the beginning
of a fresh attack. I heard again the squeal of tyres and
the shifting of gears. It was the unmistakable sound of a
vehicle going around corners and coming in our direction
at speed. With horror, I suddenly realised what we were
dealing with. 'SUICIDE VEHICLE!' I yelled at the top
of my voice, then I turned and ran back into the hall.
The old man and the hevals jumped to their feet in shock.
'Quick, get to the back room!' I shouted. I then kicked
open the door and got out of the way as everyone else
piled through. I turned around to look for Shaheen, but
just at that moment, the world exploded. BOOOOOM!
I was suddenly on the floor, unable to breathe because
all the air had been sucked from my lungs. I gasped with
shock and struggled to remain conscious as dust swirled
in a thick cloud around me. In the same instant came a
dreadful ringing in my ears. My head was pounding, and
I stayed on my hands and knees for a moment, waiting
for the tinnitus to end and for the world to stop spinning.
A few seconds passed, and I could hear muffled voices
around me. A shadow ran past me into the front room
and moments later, someone grabbed me by the shoulder.
I turned around to see Shaheen. He said something to me
and tried to lift me to my feet. I pulled back and shook
my head. 'I can't hear anything,' I said, my own voice
muffled in my ears. There was a noise inside my head
that wouldn't let up. Shaheen pointed to the front room,
shouted something and ran off. I staggered to my feet and
picked up my rifle, which had been lying next to me
on the floor. 'What's going on?!' I called out. 'Is Daesh
coming?' I flicked off the safety catch of my AK and, with

my ears still ringing, staggered towards the front door. I got halfway there before I heard a shot ring out. 'Shit!' I thought. This had to be the beginning of another attack!

I blinked as I emerged into the light and saw that the hevals had spread out along the wall. I rushed to join them. I looked up and saw a mushroom cloud filling the sky above and to the right of me. It hadn't been a direct hit! The suicide vehicle must have hit the building next door. The dumb bastard had got the wrong house! 'Thank fuck for that,' I thought. If it had been a direct hit, then the whole unit would be dead. It was damn close, but it had been blind luck and the confusion of battle that had saved us. My hearing started to improve and I became aware of another fanatical bastard screaming '*ALLAHU AKBAR!*' somewhere out in front of us. Another gunshot was fired, and I realised the shooting was coming from one of our windows. There was nothing yet from ISIS.

The unit commander called us back into the building and told us to get back into our previous formation. It was too dangerous to be outside; we were just going to defend the entrances of the bottom floor. I pulled back and prepped my gear. I made sure my rifle was clean; that I had a full mag; and that all the ring pulls on my grenades were loose and everything was ready to go. I didn't feel tired anymore as I laid down again and pointed my rifle at the door. 'I'm ready you bastards,' I muttered, 'I'm ready.' There was the sound of gunfire but it was in the distance. I shuffled nervously on my mattress and gripped my rifle with sweaty hands. ISIS had been smart enough to try to soften us up with a huge suicide vehicle. All they needed to do now was follow it up with an infantry attack. I kept my iron sight on the door and prepared myself for the worst.

My tortured eardrums hadn't yet returned to normal and I had throbbing pain deep inside my ear, so I did a double take when I realised I could hear a rumbling noise that only seemed to be growing louder and louder. 'Jesus!' I thought. 'I'm not imagining *that*!' The rumbling became a demonic roar, then there was the whoosh of an incoming missile followed by another terrible BOOOOM! Once again, my eardrums were in agony and the air was full of dust, but as I got to my feet, I could hear the YPG throughout the building cheering their approval. Finally, the US air force had arrived! I felt a weight lift off my shoulders and couldn't help but let out an excited 'Whoop!' myself. It had been a close one. Judging by the pain in my ears and the shockwave, I reckoned it had been within 100 metres.

WHOOOOOOSH . . . BOOOM! There was a second terrible explosion that sent another shockwave smashing through our building. A couple of hevals had strayed out into the front room, to look at the huge mushroom cloud from the first air strike, and only just had time to whirl around in shock and dart back to safety. Three more huge explosions followed in quick succession. My enthusiasm for the American intervention began to wane as the pounding in my head intensified. The US jets were blitzing the buildings around us, which was great if it eliminated the ISIS threat, but it was too damn close for comfort. We waited patiently for the mayhem to finish, and I reached out to calm the old man, who was getting hysterical. After the fifth air strike everything appeared to calm down.

We waited, and the minutes slowly turned into hours. Abjar came down from upstairs and told us that the commanders had been on the radio. Our orders were to stay until darkness, when another tabur was going to come to replace us. The pounding in my head wasn't just from my tortured ears. I was so damn thirsty. The dust from the air strikes had coated the back of my throat; I had no saliva left in my mouth and it was hard to swallow. We all collapsed back on the floor and took it in turns to stand guard. Another hour passed before we were warned to get ready for another fight. The radio was reporting enemy movement and we were told ISIS fighters were running back into the buildings around us. The jihadists knew the closer they got to us, the safer they were from air strikes. The Americans weren't crazy enough to drop bombs on their own guys, we hoped! The Islamic State commanders must also have been hoping that the US jets would once again not be there to protect us after nightfall, which would be when they would try to overrun us. For now, they were just getting into position.

A few minutes later, another message was sent down to us. The Americans were going to hit the large apartment building on the other side of the street. They had been watching live drone feeds, and the reason we had faced so many ISIS fighters was that they had a tunnel which came out just a few dozen metres from our position. If the Americans were going to conduct an air strike within fifty metres of us, then they must have judged that the threat was serious enough to take the risk; that if they didn't throw the dice, we were likely to be overwhelmed and killed anyway. I felt the hairs on the back of my neck stand up. I was nervous. Very, very nervous. I could hear the roar of the aircraft circling above us, and I got on my knees behind a concrete wall in the corridor, closed my eyes and waited.

There was the telltale WHOOOOSH! of an incoming missile, then a blinding flash. The blast wave was more horrific even than the suicide vehicle had been, and I found myself back on the floor with my head swimming and my ears screaming. There was a terrible roar around me, and I could see nothing but darkness. I was being struck by lumps of masonry and concrete. 'Christ!' Our building was coming down around me! I squeezed my eyes shut, curled up in a ball and protected my head with my arms. Gradually, the roaring subsided, but I couldn't breathe. With a good deal of effort, I got back onto my knees, which sent the rubble that covered my body falling to the ground. Everything was now white all around me. I couldn't even see my own hand in front of my face. I tried again to take a breath and doubled up choking. The air was a foul mixture of smoke and concrete dust. My lungs convulsed in my chest, and I instinctively gasped for more air, but that only sent more toxic smoke back into my lungs. I got to my feet, walked a few paces, staggered and then fell. I was dying. 'I. Can't. Breathe!' I gasped. Was there even anyone there to hear me or were they all dead? I had to escape, but there seemed nowhere to go. I was trapped in a concrete box full of toxic smoke. I had to try to get out. It was better to risk the ISIS snipers outside than stay inside and suffocate.

I struggled to my feet and stumbled with one hand over my mouth and the other reaching blindly in front of me. I found the door to the front room, tripped on some rubble and fell again. The visibility had improved slightly, and I looked around at a scene of devastation. The entire room was wrecked. If any man or beast had been in the road, on the veranda or in the front room, then they would have died instantly. Everywhere, there were great lumps of concrete that had blown into the room with such force that they had crushed everything in their path. The window shutters, the chair in the corner of the room and the door leading to the corridor were all smashed to pieces. The cloudy air was tinged with gold, where the bright Middle Eastern sun couldn't penetrate the foul smoke and dust that hung around us. I got to my feet again and stumbled out onto the veranda. I could see ruined rooms around me, but the fabric of the buildings and sky above were obscured by a swirling mass of golden dust. I coughed violently and covered my mouth with my scarf. I suddenly had an idea of where I needed to be. I whirled around and hurried quickly back into the corridor.

The door to the back room was half-open and hanging off its hinges. I pushed it and came up against resistance. I could hear the rubble on the other side of the door grinding against the floor. I forced it open and staggered blindly into the room, then tripped on something and, with horror, realised it was Demhat's body. Stepping over him and ignoring the terrible pain in my chest, I reached the shutters at the back of the room, ripped them open, and, for a blissful moment, I was bathed in light. A second later, the smoke in the room rushed for the open window and poured outside. It was like oil and water. You could see the pure white smoke against the clean air. The first breath of fresh oxygen had me coughing until I could taste blood. The next was like heaven on earth. I called out to the others and they rushed to the window. I went back to guide the stragglers and make sure everyone was all right. When we were together at the window, I looked around and was shocked by our appearance. We were covered in dust, our hair and eyebrows were white and even our skin was grey. One of the hevals had a bleeding nose, and the bright red of his blood against the white of his face was a grisly sight. I closed my eyes and took a moment to reflect. We had got away with it! You couldn't get any closer to an air strike and live, I reckoned. It was only the thick concrete walls of our house that had saved us. I didn't know whether to be grateful to the Americans or curse them, but our ordeal was not over.

Hours passed and I was on the verge of collapse. We had endured twelve hours of shot and shell. Our minds and bodies were being tortured and the lack of water was crippling. I spent fifteen minutes spitting a mixture of blood and dust after the most recent air strike. It felt like there was no moisture left in my body. I took off my body armour and carried on with yet more guard duty. There was only one coherent thought in my mind: 'Protect the front door.' I looked down at my watch, willing the time to pass and for our replacements to arrive, but the minutes dragged. At least it seemed the air strike had neutralised the ISIS attacks. For now.

Around me, my comrades looked like ghosts in a haunted house, drifting from one dust-covered room to another. No one really talked, except for the occasional vain request for water. The daylight hours crawled by, but darkness, once it started to fall, was quick to engulf us. I looked at my watch again and realised it was 7 p.m. – 5 p.m. at home – on Friday night. My brothers would be finishing work and getting ready for a boozy evening and a relaxing weekend. More hours passed before things started to happen.

The commander wanted to clear the area around us before the arrival of our relief. He ordered me and Shaheen to sit tight and continue holding the bottom floor while he sent out a team of guys – led by Abjar – to flush out any ISIS fighters who might have survived the air strikes. The night air was soon full of the sound of exploding grenades being thrown through windows and doorways, as the hevals cleared the buildings around us. It was soon clear we had control of the street outside, though every ten minutes I would patrol the now heavily damaged wall in front of our building. I watched YPG fighters coming and going through our gate, darting to different buildings on both sides of the road. I was gutted when three of the lads came back carrying Öcalan's body. There was a confusing disconnect between the laughing, bright-eyed young man I had known the day before and the broken, lifeless body now in front of me. I couldn't bear to look at his face. I only wanted to remember him as he had been when he was alive. They wrapped Öcalan up and placed him next to Demhat. Soon afterwards, a bulldozer arrived and pushed all the rubble off the street.

Another hour passed and a Humvee arrived full of YPG fighters. They unloaded their gear and ran into our increasingly packed house. The two şehîds – Demhat and Öcalan – were then brought out and gently laid out on the back seats of the vehicle. I felt another twinge of sadness watching them go. We had successfully severed the link between the ISIS strongholds at the stadium and hospital, but at what cost? This operation had taken the lives of two brave young men; two Kurdish lads from Afrin who had gone all the way to Raqqa to liberate a city that wasn't even Kurdish.

I managed to beg a bottle of water and some food from the new guys, and the first beautiful glug of life-giving water sent strength coursing through my body, but before I could open the plastic container of rice, we were ordered to move. I leapt to my feet, stuffed the precious food into my pocket and threw my body armour over my head. I checked my rifle, straightened out my gear and joined a small crowd of hevals in the front room. There wasn't going to be any cosy Humvee ride out for us. If we wanted to leave, then it would have to be on foot. I checked my watch again and saw that it was midnight. More than twenty-four hours had passed since the mission had started. There was still a huge threat of ISIS fighters loitering in the rubble, so we made no attempt to patrol out. With 5-metre gaps between us, we jogged back down the road and towards the safety of the YPG forward operating base.

# Fighting Fear

Soon enough, we were safely back at the house we had left twenty-four long hours before. The building was crammed with Kurds and other fighters waiting to move off into different positions, and amid the confusion I could hear Sofian call out to me. He looked pleased to see me. I was certainly pleased to see my good friend and I pushed through the crowd to give him a hug. My heart was still thumping, and I was just desperately grateful to have escaped the nightmare we had endured. Sofian wanted to hear all about it but I could barely talk. 'Tomorrow,' I told him. 'I need to sleep. Got to sleep,' I said, struggling to stay upright. He found me a corner of a room not filled with fighters, watched me lie down and began to talk, but I didn't even hear what he said before I was asleep. I was shaken awake maybe three hours later. It was still dark and someone said, 'You've got to go. There's a car,' and I jumped up and Sofian was there and he opened the door to the street. 'Are you coming?' I said, still slightly confused. He smiled. 'No, I have to stay, but you need rest.' He turned to usher Jake outside with me, and we both got in the back of a waiting Humvee and were driven back to the American base, where I fell into a soft bed for the first time in a week.

★

I woke the next day about noon, when the sun was too hot for me to sleep any longer, but I was so exhausted that I felt drugged. Jake and I stumbled outside, still caked in dust. There was dried blood on my hands and over my uniform, which was lined with salt stains where I had been sweating under my body armour, and my face was filthy. After some food, Matay appeared. 'I have a surprise for you,' he said, and he ushered us to his car. He drove us out of Raqqa and eventually pulled off the road, across a couple of fields. There before us, in an oasis of green, was the large, fast-flowing expanse of the Euphrates. It was a pure joy to take off my boots, to tread barefoot on the grass and then to feel the mud at the edge of the river ooze between my toes as I walked into the water in my uniform, up to my chest, and felt the weight of the current pressing against me, carrying away the dirt and the dust and the blood. I ducked my head under the cold water and felt the trauma of the previous forty-eight hours wash out of my body and hair. I felt elated, as if the weight of the world had been lifted from my shoulders, and I laughed and joked with Jake – until a sudden thought struck me. The aid worker David Haines and journalist Steven Sotloff had apparently been able to hear the flow of the Euphrates from where they had been held captive in Raqqa, but it had never been within their reach. Instead, they had been forced through all sorts of degradations by Jihadi John and his fellow ISIS thugs before they were beheaded. As I stood there, soaking wet, with deep bags under my eyes and the shadow of a beard on my face, I was even more grateful for the feeling of release the river had granted me, and even more convinced of why we were here in Raqqa.

I felt like a new person as we arrived back at the base for a few more days of rest. And then it hit me. I was sitting down with the others for some food when the magnitude of Öcalan's death, and the death of Demhat in my arms, suddenly burst into my consciousness. It started with a simple thought – 'What could I have done differently?' – and then it began to nag at me, growing steadily worse until I had to physically shake my head to try to get rid of the black thoughts that were crowding my brain. Images of Öcalan and of Demhat threatened to overwhelm me with emotion as I thought about Demhat's family at home and about the trust and the faith he had put in me in his last moments and how I had failed him. In my head, I was back in that dusty hellhole, reliving those last moments when I felt Demhat's heart stop beating. At the time, I had not been able to feel much emotion: I had too much else to think about. Now I was back at base, out of danger, clean and fresh, but they were still dead, and their images would not leave my mind. 'Stop it! Just stop!' I shook my head again and told myself to stop thinking about it, because there was nothing I could change. Raqqa was still ongoing and there would be more death and more suffering before it was over.

I had just about managed to put the thoughts out of my head and was sitting in the sunshine when Matay ran up to me and said, 'The radios are saying someone has been hit. You've got to get your medical bag,' and I was instantly alert. We jumped into a truck to head back into the city, but we were already too late. Even before we had left the base, we were passed on the road by a vehicle going the other way. In the front I could see Kane, and lying in the back was Sofian. Our vehicle span around and followed the other truck to the medical facility next to our base, and Sofian was rushed inside. All I could do was wait nervously outside until someone came out to update us. 'He's dead. There was nothing we could do,' said the voice, and my heart sank. 'Why Sofian? Why is it always the best people?' I muttered through gritted teeth, and every last ounce of elation I had felt to be off the front line instantly drained from me. It seemed that Sofian had been on daytime guard duty when he heard some rustling out on the road. He leant out of the window long enough to be hit by a sniper, whose bullet went straight through his chest. He would have died very quickly. It was a huge shock to me and an even bigger blow to the Syriacs, who had now lost two killed and one badly injured in a week. Sofian had been a real pillar of their front-line units, and I had huge respect for him. He had taught me so much about the minority Christian community and how horribly persecuted they are, not just in Syria but across the Middle East; how they face annihilation in the very cradle of Christianity.

It was probably just as well that Jake and I got sent back to the front at 11 p.m. that night. I no longer wanted to be in comfort when my friends were still in danger. Even so, my heart sank as we were driven in the dark and deposited at the house on the other side of the road from the nightmare position where Demhat had died. We were in the very building from which ISIS had been firing at us, but it was now under YPG control. To be there to hold the position just reinforced what a game-changing achievement it had been to sever the link between the two ISIS strongholds.

We slept there that night, and in the morning I dashed across the road and joined five Syriacs who were moving in to the 'nightmare building'. It felt haunting to step back into the now empty house, to clear it again and to set up a nocta on the second floor. We had no senior commander with our small unit, but the guy in charge of the radios at the nocta eventually beckoned me to join him searching the ground floor. It struck me as bizarre that in all the time we had spent there, under siege, we had not explored the whole floor, but as my Syriac comrade went to investigate a kitchen at the back of the building and I began to follow, I was distracted by the urge to look again at the front living room where Demhat had died. I stared in disbelief at the extent of the bomb damage from the US air strike and wondered again how we had managed to survive it. I began to pile up heavy bits of rubble against the doors and the windows, to stop any ISIS fighters getting in to the ground floor. As I did so, there was an almighty BANG! at the back of the house. 'Fuck!' I knew from the sound that it was an IED, as I span around and ran into the corridor that was already filling with noxious fumes. I was expecting to find the unit commander dead, but, just as I got to the kitchen, he came out of the smoke, gasping. To my surprise and relief, he seemed only lightly injured, but I grabbed him and helped him up the stairs, stopping him from collapsing there and then. 'No, no, no,' I told him. 'My medical bag is upstairs.'

By the time we got upstairs he was hyperventilating and clearly going into shock. He was bleeding from his shoulder, and from shrapnel wounds to his legs, but it was a wound to his upper stomach that concerned me. I stopped the bleeding on his legs with pressure bandages, but I couldn't tell if the shrapnel wound to his stomach had penetrated to his intestines. 'We've got to get you out of here,' I said, and I put him on my shoulder to carry him through the buildings, because the risk of sniper fire was still too great in the street outside. It was tough work to manoeuvre him through various windows and holes in walls, until I finally got him to a building a couple of houses away, where Jake and some more Syriacs had set up their own nocta, and they helped me to get the guy into a Humvee.

I was now temporarily in charge of my small nocta, but with my limited understanding of Kurdish, they would need to send someone else to take charge of the radios, so we bedded down for the night and another day passed before Bennie came to take charge. After the hell of a few days before, it felt odd that the worst we had to endure for the next few days were the swarms of flies and the barely edible food. It was still very much an active front line, with constant gunfire from the ISIS positions, but I got to visit the nearby nocta, where Jake and Kane were. Both of them were struggling with their demons. I had done what I could over recent weeks to help Kane with some media work, for which he was grateful. Even better, his mother had seen him on the news as a result and had reached out to talk to him, and his ex-girlfriend got in touch for the first time in three years. Knowing his insecurities, I told him to take it gently, to play it cool, but he was impulsive and things didn't pan out. It broke my heart, knowing his vulnerabilities, to see him lifted onto cloud nine by the media spotlight then dumped back down again. Jake was not faring much better. He was already wound up like a spring after the desperate fight for survival he had endured, fending off ISIS Rambo-style, and now Kane's deterioration seemed to have him in a spiral too. Neither of them was sleeping and their nerves were shredded. They had a young

Syriac fighter with learning difficulties in their nocta, and every time he did guard duty, he would hear noises and rouse Jake and Kane and tell them, 'Daesh coming! Daesh here!' and the three of them would spook one another until they were throwing grenades and firing down the stairwell at shadows.

I had been visiting one of the Kurdish commanders at a different nocta one evening, about 6 p.m., when there was a loud explosion and the commander rolled his eyes and said, 'The Syriacs!' and I knew he meant Jake and Kane. I arrived at their building a day later to find the elevator shaft and the winding staircase to their nocta on the third floor was a mass of twisted metal and broken concrete, pockmarked with machine-gun bullet holes and the signs of grenade explosions. I told them, 'Dudes, you guys are losing your shit! You've got to try to hold it together.' That's not to say there weren't real dangers everywhere and there was no let-up in the attacks from ISIS who, cornered in their strongholds, were still fighting desperately. There were regular casualties, and as I moved around the warren of buildings, there were frantic activities, and trails of fresh blood as evidence that another fighter had recently been evacuated, dead or seriously wounded. Nor was there any suggestion that the guys weren't continuing to operate well as soldiers in spite of their deteriorating mental state.

A day or two later, Kane had to leave his nocta to get food supplies from a pick-up point across the street, and he took one of the young Syriacs with him. Kane dashed across first and was quickly into cover on the other side of the road. The young Syriac went next, and there was a burst of dushka fire from ISIS positions and then a

50-cal shell shattered his leg below the knee. I heard the blast and the scream from my position fifty metres away, but the lad was just sitting in the road, looking in shock at his mutilated leg, the bone virtually gone and his foot hanging by a strip of flesh. In a second, Kane was back in the road, in spite of the threat, and grabbed the kid by the collar and dragged him into cover. He then quickly applied a tourniquet and called in a Humvee to evacuate the casualty. The lad might not have survived were it not for Kane's professionalism, but a day afterwards, Kane was still wild-eyed when I visited him and Jake. He told me, 'I can't cope any more. I've got to go back to rest,' and he was soon on his way back to Tell Tamer to join Paul.

I should have recognised the fear in Jake's own eyes, but I mistook it for the stress we had all been under and the toxic influence Jake and Kane had had on each other. At least the absence of Kane seemed to help Jake's mental state, but by now I was worried about my own, for a completely different reason. I was losing my fear. ISIS snipers remained a constant threat. You were never safe in the daylight, and you dared not even have a torch on in the buildings at night, but I had begun to embrace it. For weeks and weeks there was no sleep at night, and I was in a state of constant alertness, but I was also doing a fair amount of sniping myself, and darkness was becoming my friend. When there were shots or explosions in the dark at night, most people became fearful, but I began to feel more and more comfortable, so much so that everything became mechanical and I actually began to enjoy the night. I began to memorise my surroundings in daytime, calculating distances along hallways and the positions of doors and furniture and other obstacles in rooms. I explored entire buildings, learning entry routes and possible exit routes, so that if we needed to attack or defend in the night, I could find my way around easily, even in the pitch black, while others were stumbling around scared.

Demhat's death, and my acceptance of it, had seemed to leave me immune to the sights of death all around me. When I was out sniping at night, I would see dead bodies everywhere – Syrians killed in their homes or ISIS fighters hit by air strikes or shot in the street, lying amid the rubble, rotting. On one occasion, I went into the neighbouring building, and the bodies of a Syrian couple were on the bottom floor, a girl lying on her back with her hands up in the air, as if pushing something off her. Her head was thrown back and her face had been eaten off by the cats that constantly plagued us. Her body looked intact, and her mass of black hair was all in place, but all that was left of her face was the white bone of her skull. I had begun to absolutely hate cats – cats and flies, both feeding on the shit and waste pouring into the streets and buildings from ruptured sewers; on the decomposing bodies; and on the huge amount of food waste thrown into the streets by thousands of ISIS and SDF fighters alike. Raqqa was just a ruined, dangerous, noisy, stinking cesspool of a place, and it worried me that I had become comfortable there. As time went on, I began to recognise in myself the 'couldn't-give-a-fuck' fearlessness I had seen in Jake and Jordan in Manbij. At that time, I had been full of admiration for them, but now, seeing Jake's signs of post-traumatic stress, I was afraid about what came next, and I was glad that Raqqa was coming to an end, because losing your fear in a place like Raqqa is not a healthy thing to do.

# Surrender

From my over-watch position on the roof of the nocta, I could see thirty or forty YPG fighters gathering in the darkness below me, lined up behind a home-made bulldozer. I waited with baited breath for the roar of the diesel engine and the crunch and scrape of metal against rubble that would signal the advance. We had been just a few weeks in a new nocta, in the building next door, but on our last night there, we had been told to prepare to give covering fire for a YPG attack on the main hospital. I had run up the stairs with a PKM and a large belt of heavy ammunition around my shoulder, and set up on the window sill on the top floor. My heart was still thumping, and not just from the exertion of climbing to the top floor. For about 100 metres, the tabur inched forwards, as I watched along the iron sights of my weapon for any movement in the hospital windows, hearing only the thrum of the bulldozer, feeling the weight of the ammo belt feeding into the PKM. Suddenly, there was a WHOOSH! BANG! as an RPG hit the bulldozer blade and all hell let loose.

The fighters behind the digger hit the floor, and I went to town with the PKM, shooting at the hospital building while other Syriac positions were also firing. The percussion of the first few rounds was shocking in its violence, and the sudden explosive noise after the silence set my ears screaming. I paused for a moment, then pulled the trigger again, and it didn't seem so bad. In the pitch black, on my own on the roof, I was acutely aware that my gun muzzle, spitting fire, might attract the attention of snipers, so I moved position frequently, struggling under the weight of the heavy weapon as I stumbled over the loose rocks and rubble to heave it onto a new firing position. Each time the weapon jammed, I had to clear the stoppage and start again, and all the time my ears were still ringing with the noise of the PKM in the confined space. Then, almost as quickly as it had started, it was over. The futility of the operation became clear and the tabur retreated. What I hadn't realised was that around twenty ISIS fighters had used the cover of the firefight to try to launch a counter-attack, but the YPG had been ready for them. Most of the jihadists had retreated back to the hospital, but the rest I saw later. As we moved to a new nocta next to the wrecked Modern Medicine Hospital, and just 100 metres from the ISIS-held main hospital, I could just about make out the bodies, covered in the grey dust from the constant air strikes and bomb blasts, almost indistinguishable from the other debris of war.

It was the last days of September and siege of the hospital and stadium had created a hostage situation for weeks. Jake and I would regularly head up to the roof at night and hammer the ISIS positions with the PKM, trying to encourage their snipers to reveal themselves to us. Moving frequently so they couldn't anticipate where we would be, we would have an RPG launcher prepped and ready, and, if we got shot at, we would pick it up and fire it at wherever the shot had come from. We would also shoot out the powerful spotlights ISIS used to illuminate the area in front of the hospital, and which made it a killing ground for any SDF forces who tried to get close, but they were quickly replaced.

On a short visit back behind the lines to visit the commanders, Johan updated us on the battle situation. Both the stadium and the hospital were now surrounded. There were huge numbers of civilians trapped with the ISIS fighters. The modern hospital was now just a giant bunker. They had a huge generator in the basement which supplied them with electricity, and they had access to the internet, too, but the conditions inside must have been appalling, with shortages of food and water. ISIS fighters would regularly trade fire with us, and on at least one occasion, a baby was hung out of a hospital window to stop Kurdish rocket attacks on them. We began to see a steady trickle of refugees – civilians emerging from their hiding places in other parts of the city now that ISIS was cornered – and inside the ISIS-held hospital we would hear the occasional sounds of shouting and screaming as the ISIS fighters argued among themselves. There was talk every day of negotiations, and I understood that, though local fighters wanted to do a deal with the SDF, a lot of the foreign fighters wanted to fight to the death. There was even a fear that guns would be drawn inside the hospital and that ISIS would begin to fight with one another, with the hostages caught in the crossfire. Every now and then, one or two civilians would leave the hospital. Whether they had been allowed to leave by ISIS or had somehow sneaked out, I didn't know. Some of them were clearly ISIS supporters from the way they glared at us, but our job was not to stop them. They were forced to keep walking, down the centre of the road, until they were out of sight of the hospital, and then they were checked for weapons, given water, put into vehicles and driven back behind the lines for others to deal with. We were ever watchful because we had been warned of escaping ISIS fighters dressing in YPG uniforms. Indeed, Jac and the 223 tabur had been attacked in that way but had survived.

Jake and I were still spending every night on guard duty, but the six or so hours between eating some lunch and me trying to get to sleep as it fell dark at 6 p.m. left plenty of time for talking. Jake seemed so remorseful as he told me of his fractured relationship with his wife. 'I don't think she will ever forgive me now,' he told me one time. It seemed like he had pushed and pushed and pushed until things had reached a breaking point at home. He was that kind of self-destructive character. I had seen that part of his nature even when I first met him in Manbij. He still had the 'don't give a shit' attitude but there was more of an air of resignation now, like he was tired. He chain-smoked – between forty and sixty cigarettes every day – and was coughing constantly. With his terrible weight gain, too, he seemed like an unwell man. If we could just get to the end of the battle for Raqqa, I thought, maybe he could start to put his life back together. Jake talked with such pride about his two young kids and about how smart his wife was and how they had been childhood sweethearts. I think he said she was a teacher, from quite a well-off family. He had had a great job in the oil industry, he said, but he had lost it because he had started drinking on his return from Syria and that had just made him drink more. It was heartbreaking to hear my friend talk of having let his family down, and I worried again for his mental state, but then he brightened up. 'Fuck it!' he said. 'I'm moving on.' He had met a girl on the internet, he revealed, and, with a grin, he added, 'I'm getting some nudes from a girl online. Maybe when this is all done I'll go and see her,' and he puffed away on his cigarette. 'Listen, man,' I said, 'we all get stuck in a rut sometimes, but you've just got to fight your way out of it. You'll be all right when you get back to the States.' Jake smiled again and slipped me a laminated piece of paper. 'What's this?' I said. 'Take a look,' he said. It was a patch featuring a grinning monkey in a bandana. 'You are now my official Suffer Monkey,' he said. 'That sounds like a sexual perversion,' I joked but he looked serious and said, 'No, it's a position of honour.' I knew he meant it and I felt honoured.

There were much lighter times when Jake and I would visit the nearby Syriac position where Abjar and Bennie were. The two of them had disappeared for a couple of days; when they returned, we found out they had been scavenging. In the midst of all the destruction and rubble, they had turned the living area of their nocta into a most luxurious room, fitted with furniture, rugs and ornaments. They had cleaned it up until it was sparkling. There were soft cushions and statues and vases with fake flowers, and it was bizarre to walk in from the shit and the dirt outside, covered in dust and stinking from days on end of not washing, to find Bennie sitting in his luxurious parlour with his boots and socks off, his legs crossed, on a sofa, puffing away on a hookah and offering us snacks and tea.

After a couple of weeks, Jake and I moved over to Abjar's nocta, and the three of us would keep a keen eye out for any ISIS activity, or sometimes I would go walkabout on my own, in the darkness. It might be 1 a.m. in the morning, and I wasn't due on guard duty until 3 a.m., yet I would seek out whoever was on guard and have a whispered conversation or take them a cup of tea, or I would go up onto the roof and feel the cold wind against my face. The noise of the fighting had died down considerably since it had become a siege situation. There might be the odd clatter of AK fire in the distance, but nothing like it had been before, and I felt fearless. All I wanted was to fight ISIS, and I had never felt more comfortable in a battlefield environment.

Jake was still too wired to rest, even when it was not his guard duty, but I had been sound asleep when I was first roused by shouting, then brought abruptly awake by the deafening clatter of Jake's PKM at around 2 a.m. one night. I desperately tried to get my boots on as Bennie yelled: 'They are breaking out! Daesh are trying to get out!' Jake was hanging out of the upper window, blasting away with his heavy machine gun at the road between us and the hospital, the noise filling the close confines of the nocta. There was no room for me to join him at the window, so I stumbled down the corridor, tripping over rubble in the dark as I rushed to the back of the building to cover the open ground between the ISIS stronghold and the smaller Modern Medicine Hospital with my AK. I was just shooting at shadows, but for Jake and others it was a turkey shoot, and they were enjoying themselves. The noise of Jake's PKM all but drowned out the clatter of my own rifle and the tinkling of my spent cartridges hitting the concrete floor. In no time at all, we were ordered to stop firing. The YPG were satisfied the last of the ISIS fighters had been beaten back or were dead in the dust, and I was left with the dilemma of whether to stay awake or fight the adrenaline and try to get back to sleep. The big ISIS break out had failed, just as the YPG attack on the hospital had failed. It was stalemate.

I was still treating casualties. There were occasional bullet wounds to legs and minor shrapnel injuries, and it would often mean me having to run across open roads, risking sniper fire, to reach them. There were a few scary nights, too, when we heard movement in the buildings around us and began throwing bombs and shooting at the building opposite, but no one ever fought back. A few days later, I snuck over the road and I found that the basement was filled to the rafters with water and cola bottles, all stacked up in the living area and kitchen, and it seemed that ISIS fighters had been crawling out of the hospital at night, making their way to this building and taking back as much water as they could carry. Things were clearly getting bad in the besieged hospital and the end was surely in sight.

I turned to Jake one day and said, 'You know, I gave up a really good career to be here and I have fucked myself financially. I wouldn't change it for the world, but I kinda wish I had the same money that I had before to contribute something to the families of the şehîds. Some of them have kids they have left behind, and I would love to be able to contribute to their college fees and help towards their futures.' Jake listened quietly to my ramblings and then he said, 'Would you help my kids? If I died here?' and I burst out laughing. 'Of course I would, you stupid bastard, but you're not going to die here.'

My own fear of dying in Raqqa had all but disappeared, and my heartbeat rarely rose now. There was an element of being grateful not to be ripped apart by the kind of fear

I had felt in my first year, but now I had to tell myself all the time to remain cautious, because there were still many dangers. We continued to snipe at ISIS positions, but once you had fired you had to change positions quickly because the ISIS snipers would return fire. A couple of Kurds had been killed that way, not changing positions fast enough. At least the drone threat had mostly gone. We had not been targeted by any for a month or so, and there was talk that the Americans had brought in new technology that had neutralised ISIS's ability to fly them. However, one day, around the middle of October, we heard the noise of a drone in the sky, launched from the hospital. I watched it carefully, and one of the young Kurds on the roof of the building next to us stood up to shoot at it. I saw him out of the corner of my eye, and then I looked at the drone again, and it was at that moment that a shot rang out. I didn't see the young fighter fall, but I heard his friends cry out and I saw the hevals rush to him and carry his body downstairs.

On guard duty, Jake and I would talk in whispers about life and women, about our hopes and fears, and try to make each other smile in the darkness, and then suddenly Jake would hear something and his mood would change in an instant. My hearing was so good I could distinguish a cat jumping in an alleyway from a fighter's footstep, and if I heard a shot or a shout I could quickly identify how far away it was and in what direction, but Jake's hearing was fucked from the grenade that had injured him in Manbij, and he would suddenly tell me, 'Shut the fuck up!' and that had started to irritate me. I would be halfway through a conversation, there would be the slightest tinkle outside and he would interrupt me with, 'Shut the fuck up!' I'd tell him, 'Look, mate, relax. It's nothing,' but it suddenly struck me after a couple of days why he was doing it. He was afraid. When he moved to investigate noises and the moonlight caught him, it would reveal a face contorted with fear – eyes wide and manic, like a cornered animal. This was not the man I had known in Manbij. Perhaps I should not have been surprised, but I was shocked and forgave him his outbursts.

We continued to harass the hospital with sniper fire and the odd RPG launched from the roof, until one day we were told, 'Don't shoot at the hospital.' The order lasted for a day before we were allowed to fire again, but as I sat doing guard duty the following day, Abjar came running into the hallway by the stairs, from where I was watching the hospital through a hole. 'I don't believe it! Oh my God, this is crazy!' he said. Abjar had his radio in his hand and there were voices jabbering away. 'What is it, mate?' I asked, but instead of answering, Abjar spun on his heels and went running up the stair at full pelt. 'Shit! Where are you going?' I asked, in alarm. I ran after him and demanded, 'Abjar, what's going on? Where are you going? It's dangerous up there,' but he continued running up the stairs and my heart was in my mouth. I hoped he was just going to the floor above to look out of the window, but he kept going all the way to the roof and ran full pelt onto the top of the building and stood there in broad daylight. Now I was really afraid for my friend. It was 2 p.m., and this was suicidal. I stopped in the stairwell just short of the roof, on my knees, and pleaded, 'Abjar, please. Come back. What are you doing?' I expected at any moment the sound of the shot that would kill my friend, but Abjar turned to me and said, 'Macer. Look! Look!'

and I crawled up the staircase on my belly, got onto the roof and slowly raised my head above the parapet to look out at the hospital. In the middle of one of the fourth-floor windows, just as exposed as Abjar, there was an ISIS fighter, his feet up in the window frame, gazing over the city. He was in uniform, with long hair, and even at that distance, I could see he was very young. He was sitting looking forlornly across the ruins of what ISIS had once called the capital of its self-proclaimed caliphate. I stood up and looked at him, and other people came from downstairs onto the roof, Syriacs and Kurds and Arabs, and we were all standing on the roof and there were instructions blaring from the radios, 'Don't shoot! Don't shoot! They are surrendering. We are sending buses for them. We are going to clear the roads and they are going to get on the buses and leave the city!'

I stood and I watched as ISIS fighters limped out of the hospital, climbing on to the buses. There were wounded fighters and women with prams and people hobbling on crutches. To begin with, we jeered them and called out to them, and one turned, looked right at me, then shouted 'Kafir' ('Infidel!') and hurled a stone pathetically in my direction. I just laughed and everyone around me laughed. All around the city, I could see other people on roofs, watching, and a YPG flag was raised on the building next to us. Above the stadium we could see the start of a plume of smoke that would last for a few days as ISIS burned all of their records and all the weapons they couldn't take with them on the buses. I hugged Abjar, then I hugged Jake and told him, 'We did it, dude. We made it. ISIS has gone!'

Still I stood on the roof, watching, hardly daring to believe that the evil caliphate I had come to Syria to fight had been defeated. I thought of the three years of my life I had spent and the good friends who had been killed. After a while, as the glorious afternoon sun began to set, bathing the ruined city in a golden light, I was suddenly aware of how quiet it was. The explosions, the gunfire, the sound of jets that I had grown so used to was no more, and for the first time in Raqqa I could hear the birds singing.

# Afterword

Within twenty-four hours I had been pulled off the front line, as YPG convoys toured the city with loudspeakers telling surviving occupants that the battle for Raqqa was over. The feeling of triumph was almost immediately tempered by the reaction of the outside world. Amid the messages of congratulations for the SDF and its allies was the widespread condemnation from the naysayers who said the destruction of Raqqa and the loss of civilian lives had been too high a price to pay for the defeat of ISIS. Then, bizarrely from the same quarter, came the question: 'Why did you let them escape?' The BBC, I remember, ran a headline, 'The Dodgy Deal'. Armchair generals the world over were bleating about ISIS fighters being allowed to walk away, though these sofa warriors didn't give a thought to the hundreds of deaths of SDF fighters and civilian hostages that would have been incurred by trying to storm the hospital and the stadium. It was not they who would have been taking the bullets, like Sofian, Demhat, Öcalan and so many others had done, and it genuinely pissed me off. All that ISIS was given was the time to run off, without their weapons, into the desert, where they could more easily be chased later. The beating heart of the so–called caliphate had still been ripped out, depriving ISIS of the right to claim to be a state, and a further bloodbath in Raqqa had been avoided.

Back at Tell Tamer, Jake and I bought a quarter-bottle of whisky to celebrate. The old cattle sheds had been the scene of some of my fondest memories as well as some of my darkest days in Syria, but now we were laughing and joking and raising a toast to victory. I took a sip of the whisky and passed it to Jake, and I went on my phone to message home with a happy news update. We had won and we had survived. When I next looked up, the bottle was empty. People react to conflict in different ways. Some are broken and scarred by it – and I have a much better understanding now of how that is the case, and a lot more sympathy and compassion for people who return home from war as changed people. Regardless of who you are and how well you are trained, anyone who goes away and sees conflict with their own eyes comes back changed, for good or for bad. In hindsight, I can see how Jordan and Jake were chewed up and spat out by the fighting in Manbij, even before Jordan, and William Savage, too, were killed near the end of that terrible battle. I had reached a similar point in Raqqa, I think, but it was my good fortune that Raqqa was over before I paid the price. I certainly look at life with fresh eyes now.

I was skiing with my mother the winter after my return from Syria when I suddenly looked around at the mountains, at the beautiful blue sky, the clouds between the peaks and the people laughing and smiling as they skied. I thought about my father and my brothers at home, and I suddenly realised how thankful I was to be alive. I thought again about all the other people who had gone with me to Syria, who had fought and who had died in Rojava. I had come so close to death myself, and I can't help thinking now that every day I live is a bonus.

It is often difficult and upsetting to look back and think about how things went down in certain areas, but I also know that I can't change them and I have moved on. I am genuinely lucky to be alive and fortunate that I am not crippled by PTSD, and that I don't hear the sounds of bombs in my dreams, or shake in the night, because the toll on the international volunteers who went was brutal. Not all of the 300 to 400 foreigners who went out to Rojava actually fought at any one time, of course, but in certain battles, like Manbij, something like 50 per cent of the foreigners who fought on the front line in operations would die or be wounded. That's around fifty foreigners who died over the three years of fighting. I have to remind myself that not many international volunteers survived to fight for three years, as I did, and people like Kosta, who so impressed and inspired me, sadly never did.

I look back to that first year and only Jac Holmes who was with me then would see it through to the end. That young lad, whose bleary-eyed face appeared from under the bed covers, and who I reckoned would not stick around, had proved me so wrong. He shrugged off wounds, learned Kurdish, helped the YPG to fight ISIS to the death and inspired thousands around the world, on social media, to believe in the Kurds. That directionless young lad from Bournemouth quickly became a man, and was the commander of the 223 sniper unit by the time of victory in Raqqa. The greatest tragedy was that he never made it back. Four days after victory was declared in Raqqa, four days after his fight against ISIS was won, he was killed by an IED. He was just twenty-four. Anna Campbell, who had so impressed me with her determination and commitment, would be killed five months later by a Turkish bombardment while fighting ISIS alongside her YPJ colleagues in Afrin. She was just twenty-six.

In the meantime, Jake reached out to me a few times online after I left Syria. The last time we spoke I was in a Dunkin' Donuts shop in London and sent him a picture of the doughnuts and said, 'Here you go, fatty! Guess where I am?' I told him I was drinking coffee and eating doughnuts when I should have been in the gym working out, and we had a good laugh. Jake was still fighting in Syria at the end of 2017 and heading for Afrin, but then he disappeared. His last Facebook post on Boxing Day 2017 read:

> 'I see the road home. Know how to get there. Who to appeal to. I also see the other road. Road Jake. Where I won't leave this place till I've shed more blood for it. Maybe my last drop. Preferably somebody else's, but who's keeping score? Blood for blood. I don't know how to get back on this road. I'm in limbo like some blind wino in an escalator. I guess I have to pay the piper. If there's such a thing as hell, it's run by bureaucrats. I'll never go there tho. Lost my note on the ride.'

It was a while before the YPG admitted he had killed himself, and it was me who had to tell his family that Jake was gone. I comforted myself that at least the Suffer Monkey would suffer no more.

He had been the epitome of so many of the international volunteers, desperately searching for something and not always knowing what. Kane was similar, always searching for the love and affection and belonging that he had missed as a child; never able to find the fulfilling relationship he was searching for. He shared Jake's last post on his own Facebook page, then posted his own message: 'I was a

Legionnaire. I was A Marine. I was a Rebel Commander in Syria. I gave It up for a woman And She didn't Love Me. It seemed like A good Idea at the time,' he wrote. Then Kane went up into the mountains near his home and shot himself.

It's such a frustration to me still that, along with the hundreds of international volunteers who genuinely went to Syria to fight for what was right, there was a small minority who were there for the wrong reasons. The ones who fought were the ones who were most trusted by the Kurds, and too often they gave their lives, sometimes in circumstances that in the West would have earned them medals. There was not a single international volunteer who died in Syria, or after, who was not a really sound man or woman.

There were a lot of politicians and journalists in the West who chose to ignore the international brigade for fear they would inspire and encourage others, but I think history will judge us well. When the story of the so-called Islamic State is written, I am sure there will be an entire chapter on the 20,000 to 30,000 fighters who came from all around the world to join ISIS and to persecute the Syrian and Iraqi people and to destroy their countries, but I also hope and believe there will be a paragraph or two about the international volunteers who fought against ISIS; who went in the spirit of solidarity to help the Syrian people and who fought and died. Just like the earlier generation of young men and women who fought against fascism in Spain, they stood up to be counted when there was a failure of leadership in the West over what was happening in Syria and Iraq. It was international volunteers who went and who fought against the Islamic State, and that, I believe, is a proud legacy.

George Orwell, in *Homage to Catalonia*, said that when asked why he joined the militia, 'I should have answered: "To fight against fascism," and if you had asked me what I was fighting for, I should have answered: "Common Decency."' I felt, and still feel, the same way. The self-styled Islamic State is a fascist organisation and little more than a death cult that wants to erode and annihilate any trace of civilisation, decency, goodness and history in the Middle East. It wants an apocalyptic future, wiping out the communities of the world to create one dark, terrible state of totalitarian dictatorship. I saw the dignity and decency of the Yazidi people completely destroyed by the Islamic State, and I could not stand by and do nothing. The evil jihadists stole thousands of young girls, some as young as three, and sold them into sexual slavery in market places in Raqqa, to be pawed over by laughing, jeering men, checking their teeth and their ages. These sick fanatics put the highest price on the youngest girls and bought them like cattle, or indoctrinated young boys in special schools to train them to be their suicide bombers.

My hatred of ISIS and my fury at everything they ever stood for is as strong now as it ever was. It has never wavered and was my guiding force throughout my time in Syria, pushing me forward, giving me courage and determination and a reason to keep coming back. Right from the start I had a burning desire to get involved in the conflict; to fight back; to resist this evil, and I invested so much of myself into it. In three years I fought in so many places, made so many friends, lost so many friends and went through such emotional turmoil. I put my family through hell – though they were, and always have been, nothing but supportive – and that played heavily on my mind.

For some ordinary guy who worked in a job in the City of London, to go out and fight ISIS was the least I could do to show my solidarity with the people in Rojava. The most I could do was to use my privilege as a British man, as someone who is articulate and who understands how the media and how the West works, to create a platform for myself and to stand up and tell the world about the Kurdish cause, and that is what I did.

When I first flew to Iraq and got in that car and went into the safe house, I really put my life in the hands of the YPG and the YPJ, because if I could not give them all my faith, and trust them with my very life, then I had no business being in Rojava. For the next three years, I not only fought on the front line but also worked tirelessly to promote the Kurdish cause in Britain and America and around the world, because I believe in them and I feel every injustice against them deeply. I hope that anyone reading my book will have learned something about the Kurdish people; learned about their tenacity and their bravery; learned about their secular values and their belief in equality in society and between the sexes. These people have been wronged. They have been wronged by history, by imperialism and nationalism that have carved up their country and persecuted their people. It is my sincere hope that one day they will achieve their freedom; an independent Kurdish nation; a place they can call home, where they can live, dream and govern themselves in peace. I hope readers will have come on a journey with me to realise that many of the problems in the Middle East can be solved through working with local people, because when the West was looking for an answer to the Islamic State and people were worrying whether we would have to send troops and create new institutions; when the politicians were worrying whether they might have a new Iraq or Afghanistan on their hands, the answer was in Syria the whole time. The answer was local people – Kurds, Syriac Christians, Arabs and Yazidis – who believe in democracy, secular values and freedom and equality, and who were prepared to stand up and fight against the Islamic State.

For myself, I am 100 per cent changed as a person by the years I was in the YPG and MFS. I am more reflect-ive, calmer, more thoughtful, and determined to focus on making the right decisions and moving forward with my life. That contrasts a lot with the young twenty-seven-year-old who quit his job to go and fight in a war zone.

Three years can change a man anyway, but I do think I learned a lot about the world and about myself. I have seen the horrors the world can offer, but, at the same time, I have seen a huge amount of good in people. I have been inspired by people like Kosta, who was totally committed to the Kurds, and I have learned from more complicated people like Jake and other restless souls. Perhaps that is why I am less restless myself. I have learned the hard way to be less self-absorbed. Jake, Mario and Kane were friends of mine who had been talking to me for months, and yet I never foresaw them taking their own lives because I was too wrapped up in myself. So now I hope I am more reflective in terms of my relationships with the people around me; more caring about how they are feeling. I have learned to see that my actions impact the people around me, like my family, and that I have got to be a hell of a lot more careful not to damage those friendships and relationships.

Maybe an element of self-absorption was common to a lot of the international volunteers. Regardless of whether we were fools and idiots, or angels and heroes, the one thing that united us all was a restlessness and a sense of adventure, wanting to get out and do something. I have had people come up to me and shake my hand and tell me I am a hero, and I have had people tell me, particularly when I have been on radio shows, that I am a terrorist and a violent person. The truth is always somewhere in the middle, and I would urge anyone not to think of the international volunteers as all good or all bad.

For my own part, my journey started when I saw the hatred of the so-called Islamic State and the goodness of the people of Rojava, and I was determined to fight against the evil and to support decency. I believe I achieved in Rojava exactly what I set out to achieve. And I survived, which was a victory in itself.

# Acknowledgements

I cannot finish my book without thanking from the bottom of my heart – Martin Phillips, Anna Valentine, Shyam Kumar and indeed all the team at Orion. They turned a rough manuscript and more than 130,000 words into a gem of a book and I am ever thankful.

I would also like to thank my agent – Piers Blofeld at Sheil Land Associates. His advice and support has made the challenge of writing a book a great deal easier!

It was also a privilege to have the remarkable Andy McNab write the foreword to this book. It feels like yesterday that I was a 13-year-old boy reading Bravo Two Zero for the first time. If someone had told that young lad that nearly 20 years later Andy would contribute to his book, I'm sure he wouldn't have believed you!

I feel like a weight has come off my shoulders. The people above have shared the load and supported me through the process, but more importantly, they got my story out into the world. Which, in the end, is all I wanted to do.